Cyber Crisis Management

Holger Kaschner

Cyber Crisis Management

The Practical Handbook on Crisis
Management and Crisis Communication

 Springer

Holger Kaschner
Berlin, Germany

ISBN 978-3-658-35488-6   ISBN 978-3-658-35489-3   (eBook)
https://doi.org/10.1007/978-3-658-35489-3

This book is a translation of the original German edition „Cyber Crisis Management" by Kaschner, Holger, published by Springer Fachmedien Wiesbaden GmbH in 2020. The translation was done with the help of artificial intelligence (machine translation by the service DeepL.com). A subsequent human revision was done primarily in terms of content, so that the book will read stylistically differently from a conventional translation. Springer Nature works continuously to further the development of tools for the production of books and on the related technologies to support the authors.

This Springer imprint is published by the registered company Springer Fachmedien Wiesbaden GmbH, part of Springer Nature.
The registered company address is: Abraham-Lincoln-Str. 46, 65189 Wiesbaden, Germany

Who This Book Is Aimed at, What It Covers, and How It Is Structured

Target Group

This book is intended for crisis team members who are experts and/or leaders in their field but are only peripherally familiar with crisis management and cyber risk. It is also intended for CISOs who want to better integrate their responsibilities with organization-wide emergency and crisis management.

Crisis Management Team, Emergency Organization, and IT Specialist Level

While the IT specialist level (or a service provider to whom IT is outsourced) carries out technical troubleshooting in the event of a cyber crisis, the crisis management team (CMT) must keep the big picture in mind, i.e., the objectives and the key stakeholders of the organization as well as their expectations of the organization. The bridge between the CMT at the strategic level and the operational IT specialist level is formed by the emergency organization at the tactical level, which ensures the emergency operation of the critical (business) processes. The interaction of the three levels is an essential success factor for professional and successful crisis management.

What Actually Is a Crisis?

According to BS 11200, we understand a crisis to be an "abnormal and unstable situation that threatens the strategic objectives, reputation, or viability of an organization." If we follow the ancient Greek root word, we get the characteristic of a "turning point" on top of that.

Crisis management

- Serves the protection of (im-)material goods (first and foremost people)
- Cannot be planned in detail

- Must take place at different levels
- Must also include topics such as stakeholder and issue management, business continuity, and incident response.

In doing so, we follow the standards BS 11200 and BfV/BSI/ASW 2000-3.

... and a Cyber Crisis?

A cyber crisis is therefore a crisis in which IT systems and the data processed on them play a central role. This involves the classic protection goals of information security: confidentiality, integrity, and availability of the data as well as authenticity of the communication participants and contents of the communication (technically as well as organizationally).

We are therefore dealing with a cyber crisis whenever a breach of the protection goals (can) result in real dangers to the life and limb of people or to the strategic goals, reputation, or survivability of our organization.

By the way, the management of crises of all kinds and thus also of cyber crises is part of the risk provisioning, to which executive boards (§§ 91, 93 AktG) and managing directors (§ 43 para. 1 GmbHG) are obliged (according to German law).

Psychology

No matter what kind of crisis it is, for those involved and affected, it is an exceptional situation that takes them out of their comfort zone and puts them under pressure of time and expectations. In other words, crises mean stress, and stress often causes people to react differently than they normally would. Therefore, the book contains background information on the behaviors that people display under stress—and, of course, tips on how to deal with stressful situations.

We deal with this in Chap. 2.

Coping with (Cyber) Crises

In order to be able to deliver in a cyber crisis

- CMT's work
- Crisis communication
- Emergency management (IT and process side)
- Technical countermeasures

from a single source, not only the CMT members need to understand how cyber crises can

- Arise
- Typically develop
- Be tackled

But in order for the management to be successful, regardless of the person involved, the crisis management must also be initiated quickly and take place using a structured process. All members of an emergency and crisis organization must be able to do this in their sleep.

Practical crisis management can be as good as it is—without effective accompanying communication, it loses much of its impact. Often, especially in the early hours of a crisis, no progress can be seen. It is precisely then (but not only then) that crisis communication takes on central importance.

In crisis management, we have to consider different levels. While most crisis management books only deal with the strategic level, we also focus on the tactical-operational elements—without these, all strategic approaches are just smoke and mirrors.

Crisis management—operational and communicative, strategic and tactical-operational—is dealt with in Chap. 3.

Preparation for (Cyber) Crises

In order for the various levels and elements of crisis management to be fully effective, we must take precautions. This includes, in particular, establishing a powerful emergency and crisis organization and providing it with the necessary tools to deal with (cyber) crises. We present these and other measures in Chap. 4.

Prevention of (Cyber) Crises

But not only that, because, with a little luck (and especially the right preventive measures), organizations can certainly prevent a cyber incident from turning into a full-blown crisis.

The following management disciplines and systems are particularly helpful in this respect:

- Asset management
- Business continuity management (BCM)
- Cybersecurity management
- ICT readiness for business continuity (IRBC) or IT service continuity management (ITSCM)
- (Cybersecurity) Incident management
- Information risk management (IRM)
- Information security management (ISM)
- Stakeholder and issue management
  We will look at this in more detail in Chap. 5.

Cleaning Up After (Cyber) Crises

After the crisis is before the crisis (and vice versa). When the dust has settled and the situation returns to normal, there is important follow-up work to be done. Most often, a crisis damages an organization's relationships with its stakeholders. Those relationships need to be repaired. In the case of cyber crises, there is often a technical-organizational dimension as well. In all of this, we need to look both inside our organization and outside. Such aspects are the subject of Chap. 6.

Disclaimer: Governance Systems and (ISO) Standards

Those who have already dealt with governance systems and (ISO) standards will recognize many elements in this book, especially from the standards ISO 22301, ISO 27001, ISO 27005, ISO 27031, ISO 27032, ISO 27035, ISO 31000, as well as BSI 200-x and ITIL®v3 and v4.

However, the elements are not strictly sorted according to the respective governance systems or (ISO) standards. Instead, they are distributed throughout the book so that it is clear what concrete contribution they can make to the management of cyber crises. The same applies to references from the crisis management standards BS 11200 and BfV/BSI/ASW 2000-3.

Structure of the Book

This book explains all that (and a bit more) and gives tips on how to put each element into practice. To do this, however, we do not have to read one chapter after the other, and certainly not the whole book. Rather, the book is structured so that each chapter can be read in isolation. Where appropriate, there are references to chapters that are closely related in content. In this way, each reader can focus specifically on the content that is of interest to him or her.

However, this flexibility comes at a price. It is not possible without minor redundancies; otherwise, the book would consist of nothing but reciprocal cross-references. Should the ratio of redundancies to references not be a balanced one, the author alone bears the responsibility for this.

Contents

Textbook Cyber Crises

1

1.1 Cyber Crisis Re-invented: Sony Pictures Entertainment

Why SPE of All Things?

The 2014 attack on Sony Pictures Entertainment (SPE) is a prime example of why professional cyber crisis management must be a key competency for any organization in the twenty-first century. Every organization has data that is confidential and must always be available. Similarly, the integrity of data is important—not just for accounting, but also for manufacturing processes, transactional and control systems. And who likes the idea of entrusting information to a complete stranger just because we don't notice?

At the same time, the case fulfils other criteria that make it virtually predestined for our purpose:

- The dramaturgy of the course of the crisis is prototypical—from an incorrect situation assessment to inadequate crisis communication, insider activities, precedents within the company to embarrassing public reactions and culpability that has not been conclusively clarified.
- Numerous details are publicly known, i.e., there is no suspicion of acting contrary to customer interests.

What if . . .?

Let's imagine we received an email threatening to take over our IT systems, publish salaries, internal emails, or customer data, in short, a massive attack on both our tangible and intangible assets. Would we know what to do in the event of blackmail, a cyber attack or if confidential information is threatened with leakage? What if we had made disparaging remarks about regulators, journalists, or cooperation partners via our company email account and now the whole Internet can read along? That may have sounded unrealistic and exaggerated. The management of SPE had to experience how quickly such a scenario can become reality.

Out of Nowhere

24 November 2014 begins like any Monday for the employees of SPE, a U.S. subsidiary of Sony. The employees chat at the coffee machine about the sports results and experiences of the weekend. But then suddenly everything is different. A message on their workstations announces that the Guardians of Peace (GOP) have hijacked the machines. While on the one hand this meant that employees had to resort to pen and paper for days, on the other hand it was the prelude to a complex crisis for the company's management and executives.

But first things first. On 21 November 2014, a Friday, SPE received an email demanding a certain amount of money. Three days later, hackers attacked the IT systems. They stole several terabytes of data and published them later on the Internet, among others via Wikileaks:

- Movies
- 47,000 social security numbers
- Payroll
- Health information
- internal mail
- Passwords
- A list of aliases of famous actors
  On top of that, the attackers hijacked several SPE Twitter accounts.

And SPE does...?

After this shock, SPE called in experts and investigative authorities, but still claims not to have noticed until 12/1—a week after the attack—that personnel data had also been affected. On that day, SPE began informing employees.

Sony also asked the media to stop reporting on the hack and threatened legal action. The company also threatened Twitter if it did not deactivate accounts that were used to spread stolen information. Reddit deleted the subpage about the hack ("SonyGOP").

Finally, on 12/15 (!), SPE published information for those affected on the home page of its homepage in a black banner reminiscent of a funeral pennant.

By the way: For a long time, a press release about the events was searched for in vain on the company's homepage.

Insider and Historical Drama

Former employees publicly stated that SPE knowingly neglected information security and filed suit against the company.

Not enough: Almost simultaneously, another hacker group claimed to have hacked Sony's video game division in order to point out security gaps. Tenor: Sony should actually have the financial means to guarantee the security of its networks.

The Nightmare

As access to the accounting systems had not yet been fully restored even at the end of January 2015, SPE had to apply for an extension of the deadline for the quarterly report. For companies listed on the US stock exchange, this is anything but a desirable situation. In the first quarter of 2015 alone, SPE invested approximately US$15 million in cyber crisis management. Against the backdrop of the attack and its aftermath, Amy Pascal resigned as Co-Chairman of SPE in May 2015.

Groping in the Dark

At least to public knowledge, it has not been conclusively clarified how long the attack lasted from the intrusion into the IT systems to the publication of the data and who is actually responsible for it. The predominant assumption is that it lasted at least 2 months and, against the background of the SPE film The Interview, that North Korea was involved in some way. If this is true, there is an asymmetrical conflict situation: on the one side a private-sector company, on the other a state actor.

1.2   Dramaturgy of Inadequately Managed Cyber Crises

Phases

Regardless of whether we slip into a cyber crisis due to a cyber attack, classic technical problems or an outage caused by force majeure (elementary events, etc.): We can identify prototypical phases and recurring events within them.

Everything Seems Calm

At first, everything seems quiet, business as usual. The public and all our stakeholders are only interested in us insofar as they have a specific concern for us. Otherwise, they are not interested in us and, as a rule, do not want to be bothered by us.

It is in this phase that we make the first, fundamental mistakes: We

- Fail to create the technical or organizational conditions that ideally prevent an outflow or failure of IT resources (systems, data) or, alternatively, at least restore them as quickly as possible;
- Fail to systematically identify or address vulnerabilities and associated risks—often in defiance of explicit warnings from staff or service providers that the vulnerabilities may be technical, organizational or human;
- Have no regulated process by which we continuously develop our security architecture;
- Fail to establish business continuity plans for critical processes that describe how to compensate for the loss of key IT resources;
- Are blind to host- or network-based attacks, as we do not use IDS or IPS, nor SIEM solutions, nor do we operate a SOC in 24/7;

- Fail to gain a good understanding of our information architecture—thus we lack elementary knowledge for well-founded decisions in the event of a crisis;
- Cultivate a negative feedback and error culture, which is not exactly conducive to securing the loyalty of (former) employees;
- Have taken no or only rudimentary organizational measures to be able to carry out effective crisis management, including crisis communication, if necessary;
- Accept or deliberately minimize risks in an IT system migration project due to the costs and timelines involved.

It Begins

Trigger
- Something goes seriously wrong during the final migration of IT systems. However, we don't notice it immediately, but only after some delay. Until then, we celebrate ourselves and post pictures of the celebration on social media platforms (ok, admittedly, the postings are not typical, but unfortunately have happened before).
- A blackmail letter is received but may be lost or not taken seriously.
- Rumors that data files that belong to us are circulating on the Internet are surfacing. Or the data itself.

Operational level
- IDS/IPS and SIEM strike.
- The large number of alerts can hardly be handled by the Cybersecurity Operation Center (CSOC), especially since it suffers from too many false positives anyway or is tasked with additional duties or is not operated 24/7.

Escalation
- There is uncertainty at all levels as to whether, and if so, who should be alerted and how.
- Emergency team members are difficult to reach because the situation occurs outside of normal working hours.

Tactical level
- The descriptions in the emergency plans are inadequate.
- The start of the emergency operation was hampered by the fact that not all critical business processes had been correctly identified.

Strategic level
- The crisis unit and/or the highest management level is alerted with a delay at best.
- There is disagreement on how to assess the situation.
- There is uncertainty about the extent to which measures are necessary.
- The crisis unit finds it difficult to decide whether a crisis has occurred and to take over the management of the crisis.

Stakeholder
- Dissatisfaction is spreading among customers and partners: We are incompetent and not even reachable. And if we are reachable, our answers are meaningless.
- Customers are sending us more and more enquiries, which we can only answer inadequately.
- The first inquiries from the media are trickling in. We are not ready to talk.

In the Crisis

Operational level
- Network segments are shut down, systems are shut down.
- Containment and elimination of the cause of the incident is progressing on a technical level.

Tactical level
- At first, there is a hitch in the start-up of emergency operations, but after some time the critical processes are available again, at least to a certain extent.
- The output that can be produced in emergency mode is not sufficient.
- The recovery of IT systems and databases is progressing.

Strategic level
- The crisis team is lost in discussion.
- It takes far too long to give an official signal that we are aware of the problem.

Stakeholder
- Customers are up in arms.
- Employees complain that they are not informed or that they are informed inadequately.
- "Snipers"emerge: former employees, service providers or other insiders declare that such an incident was to be expected. (Alleged) deficits had long been known internally but had been ignored.
- Data protection, regulating authorities, and pressure groups: All demand clarification.

Crisis Seems to Have Been Overcome

Operational level
- The further forensic investigation begins.

Tactical level
- The essential IT systems and data have been restored.
- We are returning to normal operations with our critical (business) processes.

Strategic level
- The crisis unit shall lift the crisis alert.

Stakeholder
- Our business operations are returning to normal.
- Trust in our organization is damaged, but with a little luck not yet irreparable.
- If promises from previous phases are not kept: Expressions of displeasure via social media, if necessary also via traditional media.
- Overall: Public interest is waning as other topics are newer and more exciting.

Crisis Reloaded

Operational level
- Forensic investigation uncovers parts of a root kit.

Tactical level
- We are trying to work through the backlog that has built up due to the restrictions of the last few days.

Strategic level
- All indications are that data has been leaked or manipulated over a much longer period than previously thought.
- A new situation analysis and assessment is necessary.

Stakeholder
- Information about dormant time bombs is leaking out.
- If promises from previous phases are not kept: Expressions of displeasure via social media, if necessary also via traditional media.
- A real shitstorm breaks loose, against which everything from the previous phases was a lukewarm breeze.
- Accusations are repeated and ever louder: we are still incompetent or even unwilling and, above all, ignorant and resistant to learning.
- Our regulating authority announces a special audit.
- Data protectors threaten with fines, pressure groups with warnings.
- Partners and competitors publicly distance themselves.
- Actors from politics (local, state, federal) give in to temptation and position themselves against us.
- Shareholders demand clarification.

After the Crisis

Operational level
- IT systems are rebuilt from the ground up.

Tactical level
- IT operations and business processes return to normal.
- Additional capacity (e.g., from external sources) is needed to deal with the backlog that has built up.

Strategic level
- The management of our organization is under pressure: shareholders, regulators and customers alike are angry.
- The lessons learned show that far-reaching changes are needed in the governance of our organization.
- Considerable costs are expected—for customer loyalty and acquisition measures, for penalties, but also for technical and organizational changes.
- Personnel consequences—also at management level—are unavoidable.

Stakeholder
- If promises from previous phases are not kept: Expressions of displeasure via social media, if necessary also in the classical media.
- Customers expect redress.

And What Do We Do with These Findings?
Now that we know the prototypical process, we can target the issues that cause us the most headaches. How are we positioned in terms of preventive measures, i.e., what are our chances of preventing at least some types of cyber crisis? How prepared are we organizationally for Day X? Are we able to handle different types of cyber crises in the short term? Do we trust ourselves with professional crisis communication? How do we approach stakeholder management? What do we need to consider in post-crisis care?

First Things First: The Human Factor in the Management of (Cyber) Crises

2

2.1 Decisions or the Essence of Crisis Management

Crisis Management Means Managing People

Even cyber crises are not about people, on the contrary. It is not only not without them, but explicitly about them. Why is that? Well, crises are not created by any events, but only by the valuations we all give to these events. A data leak or data encrypted by an attacker and thus withdrawn from our access are initially a technical problem—but only initially, because the technical problem quickly becomes a real problem: a data leak can result in exposure and a technical problem can, for example, lead to missing, delayed, or incorrect transfers, etc. These are precisely the consequences that we have to deal with. It is precisely these consequences that we evaluate according to our specific (and often quite subjective) standards. But we don't stop there: depending on the outcome of the evaluation, we may expect an action. And this is the crucial point. If we are able to influence our fellow human beings, we can influence their attitude towards the event and thus their reaction. Unfortunately, we have little time to do this. Decisions want to be made, always and constantly—especially in crisis management, when everyone involved is under great tension (vulgo: stress).

Decision-Making Constraints at All Levels

In managing cyber crises, we are constantly confronted with questions at both the strategic and tactical-operational levels. We need little imagination to picture some prototypical questions: Should we

- to convene the crisis management team (CMT)?
- to the public that we had a data leak?

© Springer Fachmedien Wiesbaden GmbH, part of Springer Nature 2021
H. Kaschner, *Cyber Crisis Management*,
https://doi.org/10.1007/978-3-658-35489-3_2

- disconnect certain IT systems from the network and thus prevent the spread of a virus, but at the same time paralyze important business processes at least temporarily and thus provoke a situation which obliges us to notify authorities?
- backup or take the risk of creating data inconsistencies?
- ...

We can continue this list at will. But no matter which questions we add—they have one thing in common: our decision will usually have far-reaching consequences.

Challenges

The challenges are manifold in view of these permanent decision-making constraints:

- We do not have anything even close to a complete picture of the situation.
- The robustness of the available information is often unclear.
- The interest of key stakeholders (press, shareholders, customers, regulators, etc.) significantly reduces the scope for error.
- The crisis itself creates stress, makes us tired, and drains us—especially in the case of prolonged crises.
- ...

All of this influences our decision-making behavior.

Requirements for Crisis Management Decisions

Our decisions must meet (at least) two requirements:

- Speed
- Expediency

To avoid misunderstandings: speed does not mean actionism, on the contrary. Rather, speed means indicating as promptly as possible that we are aware of the situation and, at the same time, it is an expression of the fact that the "wait and see" strategy (i.e. playing dead and hoping for new insights), which is popular in day-to-day business, especially among middle managers, is rarely an option when it comes to crisis management. A slow response is interpreted as inaction or weakness. Both characteristics do not exactly have positive connotations and are thus not very conducive to our overriding goal in crisis management: maintaining trust in our organization.

Expediency does not mean that we should always prefer the safest option for us personally. Such defensive decision-making may be appropriate, but it does not have to be. Rather, expediency means that our decisions must be both appropriate and adequate to protect confidence in our organization, directly or indirectly, given the specific crisis situation. Mind you, this applies to the timing and context from which we make the decision. We will always be smarter in hindsight, so we would be well advised to record the context and timing of every significant decision in writing.

Consequences of the Challenges

If we now contrast the challenges with the requirements that our crisis management decisions must meet, one thing becomes clear: we need to act. To do this, we can start at different points at the same time or one after the other. For example, it helps us if we take measures to

- Reduce the probability of occurrence and impact of crises (Chap. 5). The reason is simple: where there is no crisis, there is no need for crisis management decisions as well as
- to lose no time in the event of a crisis, to be able to use automatic mechanisms and to have the right tools at hand (Chaps. 3 and 4).

  But that is only half the battle. Above all, it is essential that we understand why people assess and react to situations in the way they do (see Sect. 2.2).

2.2   Assessments, Behavioral Patterns and Stress

2.2.1   How People Perceive and Assess Situations

Perception Is Subjective

How our stakeholders perceive a situation is highly individual and depends on a whole range of factors that we as an organization cannot always influence. These factors include, among others:

- Affected

  Is the person directly or indirectly affected?
- Near

  How great is the spatial and emotional distance of the stakeholder to the risk?
- Voluntariness

  Did he or did he not voluntarily take the risk that our crisis created? Did he or did he not voluntarily get involved with us?
- Controllability

  Is or was the situation subjectively controllable for the individual or not?
- Immediacy

  Is the stakeholder affected immediately or only with a delay?
- Socialization

  What does the person's personal environment think about it?
- Public

  How is the issue covered in the media?
- Cultural filters

  Different countries, different customs—but which cultural background shapes the stakeholder?

- Purpose

  Does the risk trigger promise fundamentally positive things?
- Threat level

  What is threatened? Life and limb? Property? One's own existence?

This list is not exhaustive, but it does not have to be. Even in this form, it helps us to assess whether or to what extent a stakeholder (the crisis team members and employees are also stakeholders!) feels affected.

Assessment Based on Experience

From the sum of these factors, an overall picture is finally formed, which the human brain automatically compares with empirical values that we have made with (potentially) comparable situations. We will take a closer look at this process in Sect. 2.2.3.

The result of the evaluation in turn leads to reactions. We now turn to their prototypical variants (Sect. 2.2.2).

2.2.2   Behavioral Patterns and How They Manifest Themselves

It Is in Our Genes

In the face of a threat, evolution has planted three behavioral patterns in our genes:

- Attack
- Escape
- Playing dead

We can also see these prototypical response options in cyber crises (but not only there) among our stakeholders.

How Do the Behavioral Patterns Manifest Themselves in Practice?

Let's imagine the following case: We run a dating platform and have customers (of any gender) who are looking for new (or additional) happiness with us, although they may currently be in a happy relationship from the point of view of their respective partners. Using the basic search parameters (woman looking for man, man looking for man, man looking for woman, woman looking for woman, gladly supplemented by variants that include the third sex), basic sexual preferences can be derived (i.e., special types of personal data). Now our beautiful portal is confronted with the unpleasant circumstance that user and credit card data are offered on the Darknet. The media is reporting and many of our customers are facing a problem. What should, indeed what can they do?

- Attack: unleash a shitstorm against us or sue us
- Escape: log out of the portal
- Playing dead: doing nothing and hoping that your partner does not find out.

One of our quite numerous problems in this situation is: A decision is not always based on a sober, analytical process—but rather on a quick, emotionally driven reaction, which in turn creates additional stress for everyone involved and further intensifies the stress that is already there.

2.2.3 Stress and How It Arises

Eustress and Distress

Even if it may sound strange after this derivation: stress is good. At least to a certain extent. Numerous studies prove that humans need a certain level of arousal in order to perform optimally. We often perceive this kind of stress as positive (eustress). It is different with stress, with which we react to a (supposed) excessive demand. This distress is the main focus here.

Stress

But how does stress actually arise from a systemic perspective? Changes in the environment (stressors) lead to adaptation reactions of the human organism. The stronger the change, the sharper the adaptation reaction (stress). To make matters worse, our individual personality makes the reaction sometimes more violent, sometimes less so (personal stress amplifiers). We also experience this mechanism during a cyber attack.

Stressors

From a systemic perspective, a cyber attack is a stressor, i.e., an anomaly, a complex situation with numerous uncertainties that we do not anticipate in our everyday routines and to which we react to a greater or lesser degree.

Stress research divides stressors into four categories:

- physical stressors (noise, light, ambient temperature, wetness, etc.)
- physical stressors (pain, wounds, hunger, etc.)
- Performance stressors (time pressure, quality and quantity targets, error culture, exams, etc.)
- social stressors (interpersonal conflicts, competition, separation/loss, etc.)

Knowing these categories is a good thing—it enables us to systematically mitigate or even eliminate the stressors. But more of that later.

From Practice: Shitstorm as a Stressor

Shitstorms are on everyone's lips. By this we mean a wave of indignation that sweeps through the social media and usually bundles more or less qualified opinions via Twitter or Instagram under a keyword (= hashtag; "#"). A shitstorm can sometimes last for days and is an extraordinary strain for the people affected. This is especially true because the communication participants can use anonymity to hurl insults and (death) threats against the victim (or their relatives) and create a feeling of defenselessness in the addressee. Unfortunately, such verbal lapses are anything but uncommon. Shitstorms usually hit the members of an organization who are visible to the outside world: Senior management and/or the communications department. If the worst comes to the worst, we are well advised to consider this and offer (psychological) help to those affected.

If you want to learn more about shitstorms and their effects, read Sascha Lobo's "Realitätsschock" (see the appendix "For further reading").

Personal Stress Amplifiers

In addition to stressors, there are personal stressors:

- Perfectionism
- Impatience
- Do-it-all-at-once
- Striving for control
- Self-overload
- Fear of failure
- Fear of loss
- Shame
- …

While we can at least partially point to our environment when it comes to stressors, we must look to our own personal stressors—our motives, attitudes, and evaluations.

Stress Response

The combination of stressors and personal stress amplifiers leads to the notorious stress reaction. Who hasn't experienced it: hands begin to sweat, blood pressure rises, the heart races. Muscles tense, blood retreats from the extremities to the inside of the body, and we find it difficult to think. We may become nervous, feel overwhelmed or paralyzed, unable to solve problems in a structured way and black out. Perhaps we react irritably or withdraw into a shell. In very extreme situations, we may even wet our pants in fear.

Let's try stress research again for a systematization. We show reactions in different ways:

- Mental
- Emotional
- Physically
- Behavioral

All of this is human. And all of this should be known by every member of an incident response, emergency and crisis organization—because we all react in this way and such symptoms can (not to say will) occur not only in ourselves but also in our colleagues. Only if we recognize the symptoms and interpret them correctly can we respond appropriately.

Evolution

But how does that happen? What was evolution (which is otherwise quite clever) thinking when it programmed us in this way?

To put it simply: so that we could escape the saber-toothed tiger—and since we are now in the twenty-first century and are dealing with cybersecurity, while the saber-toothed tiger is only an exhibit in prehistoric museums, the principle of the stress reaction seems to have been (not entirely) bad. It's just stupid that we still function today in the same way as Homo habilis did in prehistoric times, and that the typical stress reaction is more of a hindrance than a help when it comes to complex tasks.

2.2.4   Stress and What We Can Do About It

Course of a Stress Reaction

Stress arises—and, with the appropriate opportunities for regeneration, is also reduced again quite quickly, so that we do not easily enter the realm of stimulus overload.

Many Small Pinpricks

Put simply, our stress level increases whenever we are confronted with something that takes us out of our comfort zone. This does not have to be a single, strong stimulus, but can also happen thanks to a chain of stimuli that follow each other so closely that we don't even get to a recovery phase. This is a particular problem in prolonged crisis situations, especially if the people involved are not only dealing with the cyberattack, but also have to maintain their everyday operations "on the side".

In this way, a stress response is predictable to insiders but often surprising to outsiders.

The pattern shown in the illustration below is—by the way—at least as dangerous for health in the long run as a single, particular stressful experience. A persistent stress response not only weakens the immune system but can also lead to mental illness and exhaustion reactions. And an employee who is out with burnout is usually out for more than just 14 days. Colleagues have to compensate for his absence—often by working extra hours, which leads to an increase in the stimulus density and a shortening of the regeneration phases. We can see where this is going, can't we?

Goals of Stress Management

In order to prevent the slide into the area of stimulus overload, we can start at different points: at the

- External causes (stressors);
- Internal causes (personal stress amplifiers);
- Stress reactions themselves.

It should come as no surprise that a combination would yield the best results.

For those who would like to learn more about structured stress management, I would particularly recommend "Stress Management. Training Manual for Psychological Health Promotion" by Gerd Kaluza, which has proven to be extremely valuable for this chapter and real crisis situations alike.

Instrumental Stress Management as a Task for Managers

As a manager, we can make various adjustments if we want to reduce stress for our employees (and ourselves). Above all, we can address the stressors. For example, continuous professional training helps to prepare employees for new, challenging tasks and situations (such as dealing with cyberattacks; for those of us who work in the banking environment: MaRisk AT 7.1 sends its regards). Realistic quality and time targets, clear priorities, responsibilities, tasks, and procedures (processes!) reduce uncertainties and thus the need to regulate and decide ad hoc again and again. In this way, we can prevent decision fatigue, which is becoming increasingly well researched, especially in the Anglo-Saxon world. A constructive feedback and error culture as well as sufficient freedom to get involved in (informal) networks (and to receive support from them) also help. All in all, the goal must be to increase expectations, to reduce the fear of making mistakes and to offer support. Stress research classifies such measures as instrumental stress management.

Basic Attitude, Experience, Training

Whether an event stresses us depends on various factors, including our basic attitude, training and experience. However, when we broaden our horizons through professional qualification, this also affects our attitude towards critical events. The event is the same, however, it is now within the scope where we can manage the unexpected without great stress reactions. Admittedly, the illustrations are quite schematic, but they illustrate the underlying idea.

Mental Stress Management

We must be clear that, unlike stressors, we cannot really influence the personal stress amplifiers of the members of the incident response, emergency, and crisis organization. Attitudes and evaluations always depend on the individual perception of a situation and can only be changed intrinsically. Therefore, at this point, the motivation of each individual person is required (mental stress management) to work on the personal stress amplifiers. As a manager, however, we can do one thing: offer training measures that take colleagues by the hand in this process.

Regenerative Stress Management

To mitigate the stress response, we can make use of regenerative stress management. Similar to the personal stress amplifiers, the possibilities for influence on the part of managers are rather limited here at first glance. In the short term—stress research refers to this as palliative stress management—there are various options (psychotropic drugs, distraction through parties, films and series, physical abreaction, short meditation, etc.), but these are largely beyond the influence of an organization. Largely because there is actually a useful starting point: Peer conversations, where additionally trained colleagues provide a channel for the sufferer to vent freely and bluntly—without fear of it coming right back to the manager's ears. Long-term, regenerative stress management also usually takes place outside the organization: cultivating hobbies and friendships, doing regular sport or relaxation exercises (autogenic training, meditation, progressive muscle relaxation, etc.). Whereby—offers for company sports, massages, yoga, etc. can also be booked under company health management, can't they?

How to Start Stress Management?

A good start to structured stress management is to systematically examine our processes and workflows for stressors. A good format for this is workshops. Once we have identified stressors, we can try to eliminate them, for example by adapting our processes and procedures, adjusting responsibilities, or bringing about personnel changes (yes, this can also be part of it). If, on top of that, we cultivate a constructive feedback and error culture, we are prepared for crises of all kinds.

In the immediate event of an incident, it helps if we make our workplace "crisis-proof" in the short term. This includes clearing the desk of all documents that have nothing to do with the crisis, putting the phone on silent if necessary, and closing messenger and mail programs. The latter, of course, provided that we remain reachable on the communication channels defined for the crisis organization. But do not worry: just clearing your desk helps to clear your head and switch to crisis mode.

2.3   Requirements for the Members of the Emergency and Crisis Management Organization

Task Determines Requirements

The crisis management team (CMT) is in the eye of the storm in every (cyber) crisis. Its members are the main people responsible for crisis management. Their core task is to make decisions. To do this, they must have the (overall) overview—which can only succeed if they are free from (almost) all other tasks.

But what makes a good crisis CMT leader or CMT member?

Characteristics of CMT Leaders (and CMT Members)

The CMT leader is the rock in the storm. He does not necessarily have to have the greatest technical depth, because the variety of possible crises is so great that she or he would otherwise have to be a universal genius. And to keep appointing different people as CMT leader depending on the type of crisis is not very practicable, as each CMT leader must be prepared for his or her associated tasks. Deep, technical issues are therefore the responsibility of the CMT members and their subordinate units. Instead, the CMT leader must be able to radiate calm even in confusing and hectic situations and create an atmosphere in which the individual crisis unit members can perform their tasks to the best of their ability. Where necessary, he must act in a balancing manner or also in a firm manner. Ideally, he or she will be able to create a consensus in the crisis team on how to proceed, and if not, he or she must have the strength to make, explain and enforce decisions, even in the face of resistance. Strong communication skills and composure are therefore the most important characteristics of a crisis team leader.

The members of the CMT in turn advise the CMT leader, prepare decisions and must not only rely on subordinate areas for the implementation of the decisions, but above all also control them. Therefore, specialist knowledge, solution orientation, a little creativity, the ability to deal with conflict and communication skills are central characteristics of all CMT members.

General Properties

Intelligence, resilience, and decisiveness are other qualities that all members of our emergency and crisis organization should have.

Oh yes, they should also have another non-trivial quality. In particular, (senior) managers should be able to establish a positive error culture in their area of responsibility. A culture in which employees can also express critical and dissenting opinions and admit mistakes—without fear of sanctions. However, an error culture can only develop if it is desired and exemplified throughout the organization. Even if all the committees of the emergency and crisis management organization are not grassroots democratic debating clubs, there is one thing they certainly must not be: authoritarian assemblies consisting of ducking mice.

Cyber Crisis Response 3

3.1 Alerting, Escalation, and Notification

3.1.1 Principles and Success Factors

Automatisms Instead of Brooding
When we are driving and other road users once again interpret traffic rules as non-binding suggestions (we never do this ourselves), we must act instinctively. Braking, swerving, accelerating—all of these can be right for a given situation. There is no time to think about which reaction is the right one. The reaction in the brain must therefore not run via the neocortex but must come from the spinal cord.

The extent of our (evasive) reaction depends on its success, i.e., there is a continuous feedback between our brain and our extremities (hands, feet), by means of which we communicate our will to the car (steering, acceleration, or braking maneuvers).

The two key aspects in any potentially dangerous situation in (road) traffic are

- fast reaction and
- continuous feedback.

But not only in (road) traffic. Rapid response and continuous feedback are also at the core of any alerting and escalation procedure.

Tempo, Tempo, Tempo
Just as with evasive action, the same applies to crisis management: if we react too late, the consequences are often unnecessarily bad. In crisis management, we thus forfeit the opportunity to combat a potential problem as it arises or, if the problem is already acute, to quickly mitigate the damage—in practical terms and, above all, regarding our relationships with our most important stakeholders.

© Springer Fachmedien Wiesbaden GmbH, part of Springer Nature 2021
H. Kaschner, *Cyber Crisis Management*,
https://doi.org/10.1007/978-3-658-35489-3_3

Better Safe than Sorry

This results in the principle: It is better to alert once too often than once too little. In case of doubt—keyword: feedback—we can cancel the alert, or the crisis management team determines that the situation does not (yet) represent a crisis. In such a case, we have not lost too much, on the contrary. Every successful alert increases both the certainty of action and the confidence in the underlying processes or technology used.

A duty to escalate is helpful in this regard. Whoever believes to have discovered a potentially dangerous situation for their own organization MUST pass on their observation along the alerting and escalation path. How does one say in the public administration? Reporting liberates (and burdens the superior).

Incident, Emergency, and Crisis

We have already learned about the term escalation. But what exactly does it mean in our context? It means that events can be divided into different categories. For each category, there are usually certain framework conditions that are available to manage the event.

Category[a]	Responsibility
(Cybersecurity) incident or malfunction	Line organization
Emergency	Emergency organization (according to BCM and ITSCM)
Crisis	Emergency organization
(disaster)	Emergency organization

[a]Sample definitions can be found in the appendix "Abbreviations and Glossary"

From Practice: Standard Categories

In principle, we can define these categories as appropriate for our organization. But beware: this freedom has its pitfalls, for example with regard to compatibility in the customer and supplier network and vis-à-vis authorities.

Sometimes organizations have, out of their history, reversed the meaning of the categories emergency and crisis, i.e. the emergency is worse than the crisis:

- Incident < Crisis < Emergency

instead of

- Incident < Emergency < Crisis.

For the long-established employees of the organization itself, the modified order is perfectly normal—but not for specialists and managers who come into the company from outside or for customers or suppliers and authorities with whom emergency concepts must be coordinated.

Need for Escalation

As soon as it becomes apparent (or perhaps even already determined) that we can no longer manage the event at a certain level, we have to upscale the event and hand it over to a higher level, i.e., escalate it.

The alerting and escalation procedure in turn must reflect these levels and responsibilities.

What Causes Alarms to Fail in Practice (I)

In everyday life, there are many reasons why the crisis management team (CMT) is not alerted or not alerted in time:

- The alerting and escalation channels are not defined, not documented, not known or do not work.
- Those who must be involved in alerting and escalation are not reachable (lack of accessibility regulation or on-call service, outdated contact data).
- The technical solution used for alerting does not work.
- Potentially threatening situations are not recognized as such in time or are (systematically) underestimated.
- There is a poor error culture in the organization that prevents employees from daring to report potentially threatening situations (the messenger being beheaded...).
- To avoid further questions from external auditors (supervisory authorities, auditors, etc.) and regulatory constraints on action, organizations are reluctant to formally declare an emergency or even a crisis.
- Fear of wear and tear: If you are alerted 99 times for nothing at all, you won't answer the phone the hundredth time—just when you really need to.

The following example shows that these cases, in reality, are somewhat blurred.

What Causes Alarms to Fail in Practice (II)

Let's say a hard-working accounting staff member is working a night shift on the evening of Maundy Thursday to make important payments to various suppliers. Recently, there have been delays in invoice processing, so timely instructions are extremely important for the organization's reputation—there must be no suspicion of liquidity shortages.

Irritated, the colleague discovers that she can no longer access some data records, and shortly afterwards the entire accounting system.

Hand on heart, how would this all play out in our organization?

- Would the employee realize that a cryptolocker might be to blame for her IT problems?
- Would the employee know,
  - what she would have to do immediately in such a case?
  - who she could reach late at night given the long weekend and what channels would waste the least time—phone, mail, SMS, WhatsApp, etc.?

- Would anyone in IT still be available to initiate technical countermeasures?
- Would the employee and IT be aware of the far-reaching consequences this initially purely technical problem could have for the external image of our organization?
- Would the next alerting and escalating authority dare to alert the CMT?
- Would the CMT be reachable if the problem could not be contained on the IT side?

Success Factors

We can reduce all these hurdles to a few success factors:

- Awareness
- Clear responsibilities and practiced procedures
- On-call or reachability arrangement
- Practical tools and up-to-date contact details
- Rigid escalation criteria vs. responsibility and error culture

We'll take a closer look at these factors in a moment.

Principle: Robustness Above All

Before we do that, however, we need to keep in mind what is perhaps the most crucial principle: No matter what we make of the individual factors in practice, we must make it robust. So robust that an outsider immediately says: "The whole thing works". If we receive this testimony, we have already done a great deal right.

3.1.2 Responsibilities and Processes

Objective: Create Structures

Our employees must know what to do if they think they are confronted with a potential crisis trigger. That means we must not be forced to improvise first when the alarm is raised. (Don't worry, there's still plenty of time for improvisation in crisis management. But in alerting, we should do without it if possible).

Unsurprisingly, we can avoid the need for improvisation by defining in advance, and as generally as possible, how an alert should proceed and who should be involved.

Notifier, Filters, and Distributors

In alerting and escalation procedures, we can in principle distinguish three different categories of roles:

- Notifier
- Filter
- Distributors

All three are equally important and can sometimes be gathered in the same role/function.

The notifiers detect a potential crisis trigger and (hopefully) inform a filter that cross-checks the notifiers' assessment. If he shares the assessment, the escalation of the incident continues, possibly in different directions. This brings us to the distribution list. Depending on the size of our organization, there may be multiple filters and flow heaters built in. But beware: the more filters, the thicker the layer of clay and the less likely that the CMT will become aware of the development in time.

But who are the notifiers, filters, and distributors?

From Practice: Notifier

First, let's look at the notifiers. These are all employees without exception, as anyone can notice something that could be a potential crisis trigger. The notifiers' observations can come from their own work with IT systems, production facilities, etc., but also from contact with external stakeholders. If something is wrong, ideally, we notice it before the outside world gets wind of it. As I said, ideally. But the world is not ideal, so that all those who deal with customers, partners, service providers, authorities and other external stakeholders have a special responsibility. From the sum of feedback and external contacts, they sometimes get a picture that may not be known elsewhere in our organization. If many customers complain within a short period of time that they cannot access their data in the customer portal (outside of maintenance work) or that the data is incorrect, this is valuable information that we should transport in the direction of a filter as quickly as possible.

From Practice: Notifiers, Filters, and Distributors

In addition to the individual employees, there are three functions that are predestined to be the detectors of emerging cyber crises:

- IT Help Desk
  (first level support and thus first point of contact for IT problems of all kinds)
- IT management/IT operations/system control
  (monitors the smooth functioning of IT systems, often in 24/7 operation)
- Cybersecurity Operation Center (CSOC)
  (monitors IT systems and networks for anomalies that may indicate security-relevant events; usually in 24/7 operation)

By definition, these functions are specialized in troubleshooting and act as filters and distributors themselves.

From Practice: Filters and Distributors

Back to our little example. Assuming that the colleague (notifier!) immediately understands what is at stake—who has to take care now? Well, she could contact (depending on the time of day and availability) the IT helpdesk or, in a pinch, the IT control center/IT operations/system control. However, the best addressee would be the Cybersecurity Operation Center

(CSOC), as it specializes in just such cases. There's just one catch. Although the threat of cyber risks has been growing continuously for years, CSOCs are still hardly widespread, especially in medium-sized businesses.

All these functions, in turn, can approach further filters and distributors. This is often the Manager on Duty (MoD), who is usually the person to whom major IT disruptions are escalated 24/7. The MoD must then decide whether the disruption can be managed with the existing line organization or whether further escalation towards emergency and crisis committees is necessary or which stakeholders must be informed.

These can be:

- The emergency manager, who, among other things, ensures that we activate business continuation plans drawn up in advance for critical business processes in good time (see Sect. 4.6.1);
- The IT emergency management team and the Cybersecurity Operation Center, which can initiate countermeasures at the technical level, for example to contain the event, restart IT systems, or recover lost/corrupted data (see Sect. 4.6.2);
- The CMT, which examines the existence of a crisis and, if necessary, initiates organization-wide measures for crisis management (see Sect. 3.2.1).

From Practice: Alerting and Escalation Procedures
No matter which roles and functions we want to include in our alerting and escalation process—success or failure in an emergency is determined, among other things,

- whether we have documented the procedure in a comprehensible manner and made it known to those who have to implement it;
- that those involved, even under the psychological pressure of a serious incident
  - know what to do;
  - master the tools to be used for alerting;
- that the tools to be used for alerting function properly.

Therefore, the sensitivity of the reporters to potential crisis triggers and their consequences, even in conjunction with an accessibility or standby regulation, is not sufficient on its own. Above all, we need to practise the process of contacting those who can specifically help or arrange for help. And, of course, we cannot avoid regularly testing the technical solutions provided for this purpose to ensure that they function properly.

More on this in the sections

- Sect. 4.5,
- Sect. 5.2,
- Sect. 5.8,
- Sect. 4.7.

From Practice: Avoiding Flow Heaters in the Alerting and Escalation Process
When we come up with a structure to ensure the responsiveness of our crisis organization, it is essential to avoid pass-throughs. Loop heaters are roles and people that do not add qualitative value, e.g. through relevant assessment or distribution of information, but at the same time represent an additional link in the alerting chain. Additional links increase the complexity and the time required from the notifier's noticing of the problem to its ultimate addressee, the CMT. Without question, in every organization there are people who (want to) feel important and therefore insist on being on board when the CMT is alerted or when an incident escalates. Depending on the situation, tact, putting your foot down or some other clever tactic may be required.

In short, we need to keep the process lean and robust—the best way to do that is to eliminate (technical, organizational, and human) confounding variables.

3.1.3   Availability or Stand-by Arrangements

Objective: Ensure Capacity to Act
However, defining and staffing the various roles and committees for our alerting and escalation process is only half the battle. The other half of the rent is to ensure that the individual committees are actually capable of acting—365 days a year and around the clock, depending on the risk profile of our organization. The means to this end are accessibility or standby arrangements.

Availability and On-call Arrangements
As the name implies, a reachability provision requires being reachable (mind you, reachable and basically able to provide information, but not at a specific location). No more, no less. The obligation to be ready for work within a certain reaction time (if necessary, at a certain location) only exists in the case of an on-call regulation.

For those who are involved in an accessibility or even a standby arrangement, this is associated in practice with quite unpleasant restrictions. Cinema, opera, church, travelling by train or plane are difficult to impossible, as we either have the mobile phone (hopefully) muted, flight mode activated or simply no reception. Even the after-work beer shouldn't taste quite as good to us when we're on call (to put it mildly).

From Practice: Little Desire for Formal Regulations
Employee representatives are often reluctant to see on-call and reachability arrangements and have their agreement (if any) bought at a high price. This leads (unfortunately!) to many organizations refraining from formal accessibility or on-call arrangements and instead

- implicitly expect members of the emergency and crisis organization (especially the managers) to be available at all times and all the time in spite of this;
- accept the risk that outside regular business hours an alarm may only work haltingly, and the CMT may only be able to act after a delay.

3.1.4   Information Channels or: Alerting tools Vs. Telephone Cascades

Objective: Harden and Accelerate Alerting and Escalation Procedures
The question now is: through which channels do we reach those we need in the context of alerting, escalation and, above all, crisis management? And not at some point, but ideally immediately?

At this point, it is important that we once again remind ourselves of the central principle: The whole thing must be absolutely robust.

Single Point of Failures
For our process to be robust, we must avoid single points of failures.

This means that the success of the alert must not fail because we cannot reach a certain person. Similarly, our procedure must not depend on a particular technical solution or infrastructure. Both would mean that our procedure is not robust—and a lack of robustness is a knock-out criterion in crisis management.

Therefore, we should neither rely on single persons nor on a single information channel (Voice-over-IP; VoIP!) but think about redundancies from the beginning.

Tip: We should test regularly how robust our procedure really is. More on this in Sects. 4.7 and 5.8.

Information Channels
In order to inform the parties involved, various channels come into question, all of which we also encounter regularly in practice. These include:

- Landline phone
- Mobile phone
- Email
- SMS
- Short message services (WhatsApp, Signal, Threema, Telegram, WeChat, etc.)
- Hybrid systems (Skype etc.)
- Personal contact
- . . .

(Telephone) Cascade
The functional principle of a telephone cascade (often called a call tree) is comparatively simple (see Fig. 3.1): Level 1 calls level 2, level 2 calls level 3, and so on.

Pros
- Cheap
- Hardly any implementation effort

Fig. 3.1 Telephone cascade

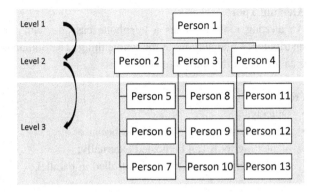

Contra

- Redundancies (mail, messenger) must be set up and triggered separately
- Calling several addressees costs valuable time
- Inaccessibility of a single addressee increases time expenditure
- Private contact details (for alerts outside normal business hours) can only be given out voluntarily.

Predefined Mail and Messenger Distribution Lists

Pre-made mail and messenger distribution lists are an important addition to the telephone cascade. Those who have turned off the sound of their phone or cannot speak freely can still read a message if necessary.

Pros

- Cost-effective.
- Hardly any implementation effort.
- Any number of addressees can be contacted simultaneously
- Text modules for alert messages can be prepared and thus used for different types of crises.
- Different groups of addressees (distribution lists) for different types of crises can be prepared.

Contra

- Redundancies (telephone) must be set up and triggered separately.
- Release of private contact information (for alerts outside normal business hours) can only be voluntary.
- Radio holes in rural areas set limits to the procedure.
- Individual messenger services have a limit on the number of addressees for forwarding messages.
- Depending on the functioning of the data connection.

Alerting Tool

An alerting tool combines a telephone cascade with ready-made mail and messenger distributors—and automates the whole thing. The human only has to maintain the contact data and press the start button.

Pros
- Quickly.
- More robust, among other things because
  - alerting tools can be hosted externally;
  - different channels can be controlled in parallel.

Contra
- Implementation efforts.
- Cost.

For more information, see Sect. 4.2.

From Practice: Contact Data as a Stumbling Block

Even if it sounds trivial, one phenomenon causes problems again and again: the up-to-dateness of the data stock on which our alerting procedures are based. The most stable technology, the fastest procedure and the most willing employees can do nothing if the contact data is outdated, and the alerting is therefore dead. In this respect, a multi-channel alerting (i.e., the combination of telephone cascade and mail/messenger messages or an automated solution by means of an alerting tool) makes double sense—because if the telephone number has changed, the mail address may still be correct (and vice versa).

From Practice: Risk Factor VoIP Technology

The inability to communicate either exacerbates existing crises or can itself be the trigger for a crisis.

With the almost nationwide switch to voice-over-IP telephony (VoIP), we have bought into a significant risk factor. The moment we experience a major power outage, the failure of our telephony provider or the WAN connection, mobile phones or e-mails usually fail as well. This leaves us without perhaps the most central element to managing crises in general and cyber crises in particular. And this despite the fact that in such a situation we are more dependent than ever on being able to communicate with all our stakeholders.

This leaves only (expensive) satellite phones and (functionally limited) (traffic) radios as a backup solution. But this is of little or no use if our stakeholders are not equipped with them themselves.

3.1.5   Escalation Criteria Vs. Responsibility and Error Culture

Objective: Smooth Alerting and Escalation Procedures
An alerting and escalation procedure is only as good as it is permeable to an appropriate extent. If the filters interpret their task too strictly or too loosely, there is a risk of extremes: Either no event makes it to the CMT, or all events are simply routed through. The means to avoid such extremes are escalation criteria, which the filters can use to decide if

- the alert should be continued,
- the event is tackled with the instruments available at the time (regular or emergency organization) or
- the alert should be cancelled.

Escalation Criteria
We should align the criteria with our definitions for each event category:

- incident
- emergency
- crisis

With regard to the definition of the individual event categories, the following applies: As soon as the essential characteristics of the next higher event category are fulfilled, our filter must escalate the event further and continue alerting.

From Practice: Granting Discretionary Powers
In most organizations, unfortunately, there is an almost submissive attitude towards the (not always expediently) established criteria that justify escalation. "Justify", however, is the crucial point. The criteria are allowed to be a guide, that is, to dictate when escalation MUST occur. But the procedure and escalation criteria should in no way prevent an event from being escalated BEFORE the situation goes to hell in a handbasket. In practice, this means that we should certainly give the filters discretionary powers for early escalation.

In case of doubt, early escalation saves valuable time and thereby protects financial resources, the reputation of our organization, and saves it from legal or contractual violations, too. Not to forget, depending on the situation, may even save lives.

From Practice: Consultation Phase
It is not unusual for us to alert the CMT in a situation where we cannot yet say for sure whether there is actually a crisis. In this case, the CMT may first meet for consultation. This can take place by telephone, video conference or in person. During this consultation phase, the CMT members can discuss whether they want to pull the event and declare a crisis or leave it (for now) at one of the lower event categories. The advantage of this procedure is

that we give the CMT all the cards in good time: If it identifies the crisis event and initializes the crisis team (see Sect. 3.2.1), good. If it does not, that is also good—the CMT members are already in the picture if the situation should worsen.

3.2 Response at Strategic Level

3.2.1 Setting the Course: Initializing the Work of the Crisis Management Team

Why Initialization?
Before we fall into operational hectic, we need to understand what is going on in the first place and what matters now. This sounds simple and logical at first, but in practice it is quite treacherous. Deeply anchored in us is the impulse to react and act immediately when we are under pressure. This immediate reaction relieves us by taking away the feeling of helplessness and passivity. Unfortunately, we often rush in blindly, without a real understanding of what is important and urgent from a strategic point of view. Thus, we run the risk—figuratively speaking—of running incredibly fast, perhaps even very, very far. But unfortunately, away from our strategic goals instead of towards them.

We refer to the alignment of crisis management with strategic goals as the "initialization" of crisis management. The time factor plays a major role here. An organization that seems to sleep through a crisis puts itself on the defensive even more through its own fault than the situation as such necessarily requires—and completely unnecessarily. Therefore, it is important that we set the first, rough course as soon as possible. Rough decisions, mind you. The CMT is the wrong body for tactical and operational details and, moreover, the facts will still be so confused at the beginning that the course can only be set in a rough direction anyway.

From Chaos to Order
In principle, there is only one thing at stake here: to peel a minimum of order out of the supposedly completely confusing chaos. We may interpret order a little more freely here, namely as fields of action or—somewhat more vividly—problems. Because working on fields of action (or solving problems, if we prefer the honest form of expression) is exactly what we do in our day-to-day business. Sure, there are a few differences in objectives and methods, but at the core the principle is comparable. Let's take a look at the main differences between day-to-day business and crisis management.

Rule of Thumb
The rule of thumb is: speed before completeness. This credo applies above all to crisis communication in the first phase. It is important that we signal that we have understood that we have a problem—and that we care. A quick response builds trust (or at least slows the erosion of trust) and reduces the vacuum of speculation that otherwise occurs. Those of us who are followers of the Pareto Principle (80/20 rule) can probably relate to the idea.

Perfectionists often have a problem with this, as the rule of thumb means accepting residual risks that we may not even be aware of. More on this in a moment. Nevertheless, it is better to be quick and roughly right than to come up with a 99.9999 percent solution at some point.

Steps During Initialization
In order to begin the CMT's work.

1. Do an initial situation assessment to understand what's going on in the first place;
2. Identify the stakeholders who are affected or involved to understand who we need to empathize with;
3. Try to anticipate the worst case with a view to what has happened and the expectations of the stakeholders, as this gives us a further, decisive orientation;
4. Finally, we must distil the objectives from this mixture of factors, towards which we have to direct our measures.

In Order
If we conclude that there is indeed a crisis, we must formally establish it. Now we can move on to identifying options for action, implementing them, and monitoring their effect, in short, to go through the crisis management process. This is not witchcraft, but simple craftsmanship.

From Practice: Really Strictly in Order?
A large number of real crisis cases and training situations show: The order of the steps is not that important and can vary. Even though in 99 percent of cases the first step begins with the W-questions (we will talk about this in a moment), each CMT usually finds its own sequence for the remaining steps. One CMT gets used to a fixed order, while another varies the sequence of steps from case to case. Both—as experience shows—are equally expedient. The only important thing is to go through all the steps, otherwise there is a risk of overlooking the crucial problem. In this respect, we may think of initialization less as a purely sequential process and more as a mosaic (see Fig. 3.2).

What Helps Us Initialize: Principles
There are a few principles we should keep in mind when initializing crisis management:

- Speed before completeness (Pareto!)
- Separate facts from assumptions
- Process discipline
- Do not lose sight of time

We'll take a closer look at what's behind each of these principles in the individual initialization steps.

Fig. 3.2 Initialization of crisis
management

What Helps Us with the Initialization: Tools
Numerous (interim) results from a wide variety of governance processes make it much
easier for us to initialize crisis management, these include:

- Checklist with W-questions
- Listing of all time-critical processes incl. emergency-relevant IT applications as well as
  availability requirements
- Stakeholder map with issues/expectations
- Overview of reporting obligations
- Overview of information categories, their protection needs and the IT systems by means
  of which they are processed
- prepared cards with stakeholders
- prepared cards with overall goals/priorities
- Crisis log (template)
- . . .

In addition to those mentioned here, there are many other tools that we can provide to
the emergency and crisis organization. For more information, see Sect. 4.2.

We will see exactly what role all these tools play in the individual initialization steps.

3.2.1.1 Before We Go into Action: The Get-Out-of-Jail-Free Card. . .
Crisis Log

To put it bluntly: (Cyber) Crisis Management means making decisions. It is inevitable that
there will be decisions that turn out to be wrong in retrospect. Therefore, we must be able to

show, for our own relief, on what level of knowledge we made the respective decision. The tool for this is the so-called crisis log (often also called crisis log).

This protocol

- we should, from the first consultation of the crisis management team and
- we must, at the latest from the time of the formal determination of the crisis situation

lead.

Minimum Requirements

The minutes of the crisis management team shall state clearly, inter alia,

- where it's fact and where it's conjecture;
- who has delivered information or been assigned a task;
- when this (see above) took place;
- whether a task has already been completed or is still in progress.

It is also essential to protect the log against subsequent manipulation of the entries.

Documentation Software

Such a template can be created in different software solutions. Important for the choice of the software solution are

- their availability in an IT emergency (offline and remote capability);
- simple manageability;
- Acceptance by all who have to work with it in a crisis.

Usual Suspects

The usual suspects for this are Word, Excel and, more recently, Sharepoint. Word is usually considered the most convenient tool for the actual creation of minutes, but offers little support for tracking open items, for example. Excel offers great options for tracking open items via its filtering features and shortcuts for date and time entries but is rather uncommon for logging. The same is true for Sharepoint, which has an automated change history and can play to its strengths especially in decentralized organizations but is at best only conditionally suitable for offline use (while Word and Excel also work offline on almost every notebook).

In this respect, it always comes down to a compromise—which compromise each CMT must decide for itself.

From Practice: All-Purpose Solution

Regardless of the industry or organization, the following approach to logging has proven successful:

- Excel
  Excel can also be used offline and is known to almost every user. If the logger fails, an invaluable advantage.
- Real-time logging
  Logging in real time has the advantage that one does not have to laboriously reconstruct the concrete information that was available at time X in retrospect.
- Visualization via beamer
  When all CMT members see the minutes, you keep track of them and can give guidance to the minute takers.
- Protocolists specially trained for the crisis management team
  The efficient use of the template (abbreviations, filters, content correlations in the Excel template) under the conditions of a crisis (including simultaneously incoming information, ambiguity about facts vs. assumptions, etc.) is anything but trivial.
- Tracking of open points based on the template
  No recapitulating open points off the top of your head—that's what the log with its filter functions is for.
- Distinguishing between information and decisions as well as facts and assumptions
  In tracking, it helps if we can filter by incoming information (I) and decisions made (E). But also if we want to systematically distinguish conjectures from facts. Then the following applies: A piece of information remains a conjecture until it is provided with a confirmation time. Only then should we assume it to be a fact.
- Printout + signature
  If we end the crisis or the shift, that may be relevant from a liability perspective. And we want to get out of prison, after all.

One way to implement this is shown in Fig. 3.3.

Guiding Questions for the CMT
When starting the crisis log, the CMT can be guided by the following questions:

- Have we noted in the minutes that we have formally established the crisis situation or set a flag for ourselves to do so in due course?
- Have we noted the date and time of the first meeting/consultation of the CMT?
- Have we recorded the people involved and their CMT roles?
- ...

What's Next?
The first step in terms of content is the initial analysis of the situation. With this we answer the question: What is going on at all?

No.	What	Type (I/E)	Receipt/ Initiation (Time)	Acknowledge-ment/discharge (Time)	Who	Notes
1	Data access not possible → cryptolocker or ransomware?	I	09:40	10:15	Meier	
2	Blackmail letter	I	10:15		Hoffmann	Receipt via info@... Inquiry at BSI?
3	Determination: crisis case	E	10:17	10:17	Kernkrisenstab	
4	Isolate affected network segments	E	10:20		Meier	
5	Design communication strategy	E	10:20		Müller	
6	Initiate emergency operation of critical processes	E	10:20		Schulze	
7						
8						

Fig. 3.3 Crisis log

3.2.1.2 Initial Analysis of the Situation or: What's Going On?

What's Going On, Anyway?

The prelude to any crisis management must be that we get an overview of what is going on in the first place. It is important that we first simply collect and structure information about this. The assessment comes later—now it would only cloud our view and possibly steer us in the wrong direction.

W-questions

When collecting and structuring information, the W-questions we know from the first aid course give us good orientation. With minor adjustments (better: additions) we can ask:

- What happened?
- Which IT systems are affected and what kind of information/data are processed with them?
- Which protection goals are at risk—confidentiality, integrity, availability, authenticity?
- What measures have we already taken?
- When did it happen?
- Who is affected by this?
- Who is already involved?

The (Almost) All-Important "Which"

Whether we are actually facing a real cyber crisis depends very much on what information (= data) is affected. To do this, we need to understand which IT systems process which data—because data itself cannot be attacked, but the IT systems that process it can.

This information is (hopefully) provided by our → Information Risk Management (IRM) or our → Asset Management, two of the central building blocks for the prevention of cyber crises. Conversely, from potentially stolen or otherwise leaked information, we can draw conclusions about affected systems as well as fundamental potential internal perpetrators. Our Identity and Access Management (IAM), which controls the authorizations for IT systems, helps with the latter.

Answers to the question "which" therefore provide us with starting points for further research that we can initiate as a CMT. It is at least as important, however, that we can draw conclusions from the data concerned about the stakeholders who will play a decisive role in crisis management.

And the "How" and "Why"?
The attentive observer may have noticed that (at least) two W-questions are missing from our list: those about how and why, or why and why. There is a very simple reason for this. In the vast majority of cases (in strategic crisis management!), asking these questions does not really help us in our initial stocktaking. Why is that? Well, on the one hand there is the problem of the information situation. To conduct qualified root cause research, we need considerably more reliable (!) information than is usually available in the initial phase of a crisis. And since it does us no good to spend our precious time on speculation (which can be dangerously misleading to boot), we should leave it alone at this stage. On the other hand, we are concerned with containing the impact of an event, so its causes, while not insignificant from this perspective either, are rarely critical in initializing crisis management team's working procedure. The question of how and why is important later. But then very much so. If we understand why and how something happened, we can work toward preventing the event from happening again. This is an essential step in → crisis aftercare.

Excursus: Tactical-Operational Level
As said before, this applies to the strategic level of crisis management. On the tactical-operational level, on the other hand, the question "How could this happen?" is quite central. Only when the causal chain is sufficiently clear can we respond expediently on the IT side and contain the event. We must

- prevent the leakage of confidential information (if the confidentiality protection goal is violated);
- start with the elimination of inconsistencies in data sets (if the protection goal integrity is violated);
- trigger the recovery of data sets (if the protection goal Availability is violated);
- isolated/deactivated network components and segments or communication subscribers, IP addresses, and certificate holders can be reconnected or reactivated (if the authenticity protection goal is violated).

Therefore, at the tactical-operational level (as opposed to the strategic level), we should have answers to the question of why.

Facts vs. Conjecture

Former US Secretary of Defense Donald Rumsfeld (whether we like him or not is irrelevant here) has variously worked with the following categories of information:

- The known known → Facts we can work with.
- The known unknown → Information that we can specifically review/research.
- The unknown known → Treasures of data and knowledge that would be helpful to tap into (and that we often don't even know we have).
- The unknown unknown → the famous unknown unknown, which is both a danger and an opportunity.

When we get an initial overview in this way, we must be scrupulously careful to separate facts from assumptions. Since we will rarely have all the information we think we need to make a robust decision, we will have to work with assumptions anyway. And to make good decisions, we need to understand what we really know—and what we don't.

Guiding Questions for the CMT

During the initial situation assessment, the CMT can be guided by the following questions:

- Have we worked through the W-questions?
- Have we been careful to separate fact from conjecture?
- Did we keep a clean record of this?
- . . .

Where Do We Go from Here?

The next step is to identify the stakeholders. This clarifies the questions: Who wants something from us—and what?

3.2.1.3 Affected Stakeholders or: Who Should We Expect?

Why Stakeholders When It Comes to Data?

Focusing on the stakeholders of the crisis may seem a little odd, especially in a cyber event, but it is critical, nonetheless. If we understand who is affected by the event, we can try to minimize the impact on them. However, (objective) affectedness is not the only relevant circumstance: Mere interest in the situation is often enough for people and organizations to feel affected and to have expectations of the organization confronted with the event.

Trust

Trust is the sum of promises kept, the basis for the reputation of any company, in short: the trust of our stakeholders is our most important asset. Winning it takes years, squandering it only hours. Regaining lost trust is costly and time-consuming at best, often impossible. Our goal must therefore always be to retain the trust of our stakeholders.

Expectations

Especially in crisis situations, trust is a problem, at least to a certain extent. Because every stakeholder has different expectations of our organization, which he or she wants to have confirmed. If we disappoint these expectations, we lose their trust. So we have to do everything we can to meet their expectations in such a way that our other interests do not conflict with them.

Here, the problems just mentioned become evident. On the one hand, we can often only speculate what the exact interest of a stakeholder is. On the other hand, we will simply not manage to take care of all stakeholders and their expectations at the same time or to fully balance mutual conflicts of interest. While for some complete transparency about the background and framework conditions of a cyber crisis is non-negotiable (regulators, media, consumer advocates . . .), others have the highest concerns here (often rightly so) (legal department, security experts . . .), while still others expect a mixture of transparency and discretion (customers!) that is favorable for them.

Expectations play a major role, at the latest, when we deal with the question of what the concrete goals are that we are pursuing in the context of our crisis management. More on this in Sect. 3.2.1.5.

Procedure

Consequently, if we want to protect our reputation, we must put stakeholders at the heart of everything we do. If the stakeholders are doing well, our organization will also do well. Cynically speaking, one could speak of sheer complacency, soberly of pragmatic stakeholder centricity.

First, we need to be clear about which stakeholders are involved—directly or indirectly—in our current incident, how they are affected or involved, and what their expectations of us are. So we need to develop what might be called systemic empathy. A change of perspective helps us to do this. To do this, we put ourselves in the shoes of the respective stakeholder and formulate a concrete set of demands on our organization from his or her perspective.

From Practice: Change of Perspective Made Easy

This change of perspective is nothing unusual. Those of us who use design thinking as part of our innovation projects are probably familiar with it. So are the representatives from the communications department and customer management. In this respect, we are using a proven process here, albeit under different framework conditions.

Moreover, such a change of perspective is often not too difficult, especially in the case of cyber crises. We have probably all been in the situation where an organization to which we have entrusted data or from which we have received services has been the victim of a cyber attack (and if not the organization itself, then at least a provider or at least a competitor). At the latest then we have, at least briefly, dealt with the question of what the whole thing actually means for us and what we actually need now in order to have a good feeling towards said organization.

From Practice: Trust Is Like Toothpaste

Regaining disappointed trust is almost impossible for repeat offenders. When an organization comes under public scrutiny multiple times for similar mishaps or offenses, the image tips and so do expectations. Stakeholders now expect negative news, not positive. Each of us immediately thinks of companies from the banking industry, the automotive industry, the transport industry, or other sectors that have worked hard to earn their now bad reputation through consistently below grade (crisis) management over many years and have thus lost the trust of their customers.

External Stakeholders

Back to stakeholders. Usually, we first look at the external stakeholders and automatically stumble upon the following categories, depending on the industry:

- Pressure groups
- Media (TV, radio, online media, print)
- Influencer
- Customers, users, patients
- Competitor
- Vendors and partners
- Trade unions
- Shareholders
- Regulating authority
- Police forces (local, regional, federal)
- Investigating authorities, public prosecution
- Politics (local, regional, federal)
- Testimonials
- Former employees or applicants
- Uninvolved but interested third parties
- . . .

What Does This Mean for the CMT?

Quite a range of players to deal with if the worst comes to the worst. The good thing is: Not everyone is ill-disposed towards us from the outset or wants to make money or gain profile with our problem. But these are precisely the players we need to identify in order to take the wind out of their sails as best we can. Conversely, this means that we must take special care of those actors who are well-disposed towards us. But it must also be clear: We will not succeed in getting every stakeholder on our side. We therefore need to understand where commitment and dedication are worthwhile and where it is better to skimp.

Crisis Management Maxims

For those of us who want the principle of effort and resource control a little more general, "The Art of War" by Sunzi will help us. Chapter XII, nicely titled "The Attack with Fire," states:

> The enlightened ruler considers it.
>   The efficient commander directs it.
>   No advantage, no movement,
>   no perspective, no action,
>   no need, no fight.

It should be clear that this maxim naturally applies not only to crisis management, but also to day-to-day business.

From Practice: What Customers, Users and Patients Expect

To avoid misunderstandings: In this initial phase of crisis management, we do not have the time for the tried and tested marketing instrument of the customer survey (keyword: concretizing expectations). However, if a member of the CMT has any insights from a reasonably up-to-date survey, please let us know.

For starters, from countless cyber crises, we can note the lowest common denominator: Customers, users, and patients

1. entrust us with their lives (depending on the industry in which we operate). They expect us to do everything in our power to protect their lives and health.
2. have entrusted us with their data, such as telephone numbers and other contact details, birthday, medical conditions, sexual preferences, account details, biometric information and much more. The least they expect is that we handle it carefully. This includes taking appropriate measures to protect the confidentiality, integrity, and availability of the information, as well as performing authenticity checks on all communication participants (technical solutions, people, organizations).

   As soon as it becomes apparent that we are no longer able to meet these expectations, they become even greater. Customers, users and patients now expect additionally,
3. to be informed as quickly as possible in order to be able to decide for themselves, as responsible citizens, how they want to deal with the situation. Disappointment and loss of control are the dominant feelings we will be confronted with, especially in crisis communication.
4. that we consistently put our own interests behind and do everything we can to restore the original state (which often only partially works, especially when confidential information has already become public).

Expectations of the BSI
When we speak of supervisory authorities in Germany, we are referring in particular to the Federal Office for Information Security (Bundesamt für Sicherheit in der Informationstechnik, BSI), to which all operators of critical infrastructures have a tightly timed reporting obligation for IT disruptions and information security incidents. The exact reporting obligations are regulated by the BSI Act (specifically § 8b (4) BSIG). It becomes clear that we do not even necessarily have to deal with an IT security incident in order to have to submit a report. However, the BSI's expectations are much more far-reaching. In simple terms, it expects (as an extended arm of the legislator) according to § 8a BSIG that operators of critical infrastructures take appropriate organizational and technical precautions to prevent the risk of an IT security incident.

Expectations of Other German Supervisory and Regulatory Authorities
In addition to the BSI, there are of course other, sector-specific supervisory authorities to which companies regulated by them are accountable. These include (in alphabetical order)

- BaFin and EBA (German Federal Financial Supervisory Authority (Bundesanstalt für Finanzdienstleistungsaufsicht) and European Banking Authority (Europäische Bankenaufsichtsbehörde); reporting obligation for payment transactions in accordance with PSD II and MaSi, among others)
- BfArM (Federal Institute for Drugs and Medical Devices (Bundesinstitut für Arzneimittel und Medizinprodukte); obligation to report, among other things, incidents involving a risk to patients in accordance with the Medical Devices Safety Plan Ordinance (Medizinprodukte-Sicherheitsplanverordnung) [MPSV])
- BNetzA (Federal Network Agency (Bundesnetzagentur; notification obligation); obligation to report, inter alia, pursuant to § 109a TKG in the event of a breach of the protection of personal data)
- Data protection officers of the federal states as well as the federal government (obligation to report according to EU-DSGVO, if personal data are or can be affected)
- LBA (German Federal Aviation Authority (Luftfahrtbundesamt), i.a. for incident reports according to the 18 (!) different incident types from Art. 4 of Regulation (EU) No. 376/2014)
- and much more.

Not meeting their expectations is neither regulatory compliant nor makes strategic sense. Serving them does not create any immediate added value for us, as this alone does not keep a single customer happy or earn us an additional cent, but what we do achieve is the following: We retain the trust of a stakeholder who, depending on the background, can also impose fines and make life quite difficult for us in the medium and long term.

Note: The reporting obligations mentioned here do not necessarily refer directly to cyber incidents. Mostly, they refer to the consequences that a cyber incident can entail. And that is the reason why in cyber crisis management we should not only focus on the BSI as the addressee of reports.

From Practice: Information About Expectations

A source of information for our stakeholders and their expectations that is unfortunately rarely considered in practice is Business Continuity Management. Via the recovery requirements established in the Business Impact Analysis (BIA), we get the expectations regarding response times, and via the business continuity plans of the critical processes, we even get the stakeholders who want to be informed.

From Practice: Reporting Obligations

Across sectors and organizations, it has proved useful to include a checklist of reporting obligations in the crisis manual, which shows, among other things, the following for each report:

- Recipient incl. contact details
- Requirements/conditions
- Deadlines
- Intra-organizational responsibility
- If applicable, registration form (if available)

Indirectness and Immediacy

An important criterion that determines how intensively we need to address a stakeholder is the degree to which it is affected. We are concerned here with the degree to which they are affected at the present time and also with the degree to which they are likely to be affected in the near future. It is sometimes problematic that stakeholders can feel directly affected without being so at first glance.

Multipliers and Influencers

Another, equally important criterion, is the potential of a stakeholder to influence the attitudes and behavior of others.

In B2B relationships, these are the classic multipliers, which include associations as well as conventional media (whether online, TV, etc.) and politicians as well as (regulatory) authorities. In the B2C business, we also need to have the relevant influencers on the screen, i.e. people or profiles on Instagram, Facebook, Twitter and other portals with particularly many followers from our actual target group. Having them on our own side is an essential aspect if we want to have the authority to interpret our crisis management.

From Practice: Preliminary Work Pays Off

Let's be clear: we don't have time to look for multipliers and influencers during the initialization of the CMT's work or to build them up yet. We have (hopefully) already done that as part of our crisis prevention, for example through stakeholder and issue management. If we have not carried out separate → stakeholder and issue management, there is still the chance that we will find something in our communications department or that our colleagues from marketing will use influencers for their purposes.

Internal Stakeholders
Now let's move on to those we (hopefully) don't have to convince of our good intentions and even better work. Let's move on to the internal stakeholders:

- Supervisory Board,
- Board of Directors,
- Management,
- Employees,
- Works Council,
- Directly value-adding areas,
- Support functions, governance functions
- etc.

all belong to the category of internal stakeholders, but that does not prevent them from having different expectations of our organization and, in the event of a crisis, of the CMT. Some just want to be informed, others want and need to help with crisis management.

Principle
This general, industry-independent list of stakeholders already shows us that we cannot lump together all the stakeholder groups that are gathered around and within our organization. Some can contribute more to crisis management than others, and some see us simply as the perpetrators (or culprits, causers, whatever), while others are capable of a more nuanced view.

Divide and Rule
Even if the maxim of divide and rule is a little skewed here, it does put us on a not insignificant track. Whether internal or external stakeholders—a more precise subdivision is often useful. This target group-specific segmentation (again, a well-known and proven method!) can even mean that we differentiate between individuals in individual cases.

From Practice: Segmentation
Such a distinction within a stakeholder often helps us when informing supervisory boards. Employee and shareholder representatives have interests and thus expectations that are sometimes not congruent. This is even more true for the media. Here we can distinguish between (individual) trade and general media. Or between online media, radio, print, TV and social media. Or between individual journalists or influencers. Or . . . well, the idea should be clear.

From Practice: Preparations

In every (cyber) crisis, it is not very useful for us to think about which stakeholders there are in our orbit and who of them has what attitude towards us or how powerful they are. Instead, we can prepare stakeholder cards that already show influence and attitude. These cards remain in the CMT's operations room and are thus ready for use at any time. Best of all, we have also created a good way of visualizing this part of the initialization process. Keyword: stakeholder map. This is also a useful tool for crisis communication, see Sect. 3.2.3.

Guiding Questions for the CMT

In identifying and analyzing stakeholders, the CMT can be guided by the following questions:

- Do we have a sense of which internal and external stakeholders we are and will be dealing with (and why)?
- Do we know which stakeholders are particularly influential?
- Have we sufficiently understood the expectations of our stakeholders?
- …

Where Do We Go from Here?

The next step is to identify the worst-case scenarios. In this way, we answer the question: What can happen in the worst case and what must come together for it to happen?

3.2.1.4 Thinking Negatively for a Change: What If?

Worst-Case Scenario

While we are well advised in normal business life to always see the positive, we now have to think negatively for once. It is the hour of all those who always look for the fly in the ointment, only see problems and prefer to take on the role of the advocatus diaboli.

However, we often find it difficult to do this, especially when we are otherwise always solution-oriented and have been taught to avoid even the word "problem" and to speak of "challenges" instead.

Why Think in Terms of Worst-Case Scenarios?

If we understand what must not happen under any circumstances, we can work to avoid that very eventuality. Every ending has a history from which it has emerged. And we can intervene in that history. So our goal is to write an alternative ending for our story—preferably a happy ending.

Put more soberly, we can modify the image a little: Every event, every effect has certain triggering factors. We have to find out what these triggers are and work around them. This is how we reduce the risk of a worst-case scenario. Either we reduce its probability of occurrence (trigger 1) or its impact (trigger 2).

Maxime

Let us not misunderstand each other: Of course, we can and must always hope for the best. But not preparing for the things that could break our necks would be grossly negligent in business terms. That is why the following principle applies to crisis management: Hope for the best and prepare for the worst.

Change of Perspective: Stakeholders

The stakeholders we identified in the previous step help us to work out the worst-case scenario. We don't have to look at all the stakeholders individually—we can limit ourselves to the four or five that have the greatest influence on the reputation of our organization. We now look at their expectations and ask ourselves two questions:

1. What headline do we definitely not want to read?
2. What accusations do we definitely not want to have to listen to?

In this way, not only the unpleasant end of our history becomes clearer, but also, and above all, the way to it. The way in which we must intervene.

From Practice: The Bad Word "Too"

If we look at any number of poorly managed (cyber) crises, we quickly see a pattern in the stakeholders' statements. The pattern is based on just two letters: the Z and the U.

The usual accusations that testify to the loss of trust in organizations in crisis are:

- Informed too late
- Underinformed
- Too little was done to prevent the event from occurring
- Too little was done to limit the impact on [here we can insert the name of any stakeholder].
- reacted too late to limit the effect on [here we can insert the name of any stakeholder].
- to . . .

From Practice: Know-It-Alls and "Snipers"

Admittedly, there is another, similarly unattractive accusation that is often made by supposed experts, critics, former employees who have left our organization in disarray, or other "snipers". Their argumentation revolves around the opposing poles of "always" and "never".

Let's imagine that there has already been some kind of cyber incident in our organization in the past. For the sake of simplicity, let's take the case that access to SAP databases was not given as part of a test switch to the data center, resulting in inconsistencies in the database. In the event of—and this is important—almost any cyber incident, we can expect the above-mentioned "snipers" to make statements that sound something like this: "I ALWAYS said back then that the organization did not have a sensible data backup concept.

I also pointed out numerous other deficiencies in IT security. But they NEVER listened to me, but rather treated me as a troublemaker."

PESTLE Scheme

Alternatively, we can try to approach the worst case using the PESTLE scheme. The acronym stands for

- political,
- economical,
- social,
- technological,
- legal, and
- environmental

    and describes in the classic analysis model various influencing factors that play a role for our industry, our organization and thus also our current problem. Above all, however, we can ask ourselves how our situation is affected in this respect. How can the current situation affect the

- relations of our organization with politics?
- economic situation of our organization, including relations with customers, applicants, partners, service providers and competitors?
- embedding in the social environment (neighborhood, media)?
- technical infrastructures of our organization (machines, equipment, databases, IT systems)?
- legally relevant aspects (legal-regulatory requirements, contracts, etc.)?
- environment?

    Again, we can sum up the bottom line with the question, "What headline do we definitely not want to read in the media?"

From Practice (I): Pre-mortem Analysis

If we have difficulty with the shift in perspective in favor of individual stakeholders or the somewhat cruder PESTLE model, a pre-mortem analysis can help.

    Among other things, I had the pleasure of training the CMT leaders of a large German energy supplier in this approach to initializing the crisis management team's working procedure. The individual steps instantly made sense to the participants, and they immediately felt comfortable in the process thanks to the flexible sequence of steps. During the feedback session, we revisited the point of the worst-case scenario. It turned out that a similar approach had already been an integral part of major projects in the company for some time. In the past, a project with a considerable investment volume had run into difficulties, so the energy supplier introduced the so-called pre-mortem analysis as an additional risk management tool. In the pre-mortem analysis, we mentally jump 5 years into the future and assume that the current project has failed miserably. Then we ask ourselves what could have caused it to fail. By doing this, we identify the pitfalls we need to avoid. We can also use this approach in a cyber crisis and ask ourselves the question: If our organization no longer exists in 5 years—what role did the current event play in that and what might we have underestimated?

From Practice: Worst-Case, or a Disaster Seldom Comes Alone

Let's imagine that we are being blackmailed with a stolen data set. What it contains is not important here. What does matter are the implications. If someone had access to our IT systems to the point where they could steal confidential data, we can and must assume that they have

(a) also steal further data (beyond those mentioned in the data set) AND
(b) could also manipulate our data.

From there, it is only a small step to assume that the perpetrator was able to plant a cryptolocker on us. This means that we are not only dealing with a breach of the confidentiality protection goal, but possibly also with one of the integrity and availability protection goals. In short, if one protection goal is violated, it is not too far-fetched to assume a worst-case violation of the remaining protection goals.

Worst Case Scenarios: Note on Semantics

For the sake of good order, a semantic clarification: Worst case means "worst case". "Worst" is a superlative, i.e., an absolutization that expresses uniqueness and knows no further increase. Strictly speaking, there can only be one worst-case scenario—and not several worst-case scenarios. In practice, however, the term worst-case scenarios has become established, even if an expression such as "really bad cases" or "really bad scenarios" would be linguistically more appropriate.

Guiding Questions for the CMT

In identifying the worst-case scenario, the CMT can be guided by the following questions:

• Which stakeholder should we definitely not get on the wrong side of?
• On which product or service is our dependence the greatest?
• Which precedents from
• of one's own history,
• of its own industry,
• other industries can serve as a reminder to us?
• …

Where Do We Go from Here?

The next step is the definition of the goal. With this we answer the question: What do we want to achieve concretely?

3.2.1.5 From Identification to Assessment: Objective, Objective, and Objective Again

What Is the Specific Objective?

As banal or academic as it may sound, it is crucial to remember that we cannot manage a crisis sensibly without a clearly defined goal that is accepted by all parties involved.

We must therefore agree on one or more objectives when we initialize the crisis management team's working procedure. That, too, is easier said than done. Sure, we all want the situation to calm down as quickly as possible and we can get back to day-to-day business. But in which direction do we have to steer our ship, which is in heavy seas, to achieve this?

From Practice: Hierarchy of Objectives

In order to define the concrete objective or objectives, we can start from a generally accepted hierarchy of objectives.

Regardless of the type of crisis, we can work with the following hierarchy:

1. Protection of life and limb.
2. Objectives derived from the worst case scenario and its triggers.
3. Meeting the expectations of key stakeholders.
4. Strategy and mission statement of the organization.

But how can we distil these more or less universal goals into concrete ones that are useful for our crisis management? Let us now take a closer look at the individual priorities.

Prio 1: Protection of Life and Limb

Protecting the life and limb of all involved must always be the top priority. Must. Always. This is not negotiable. It's not just a matter of ethics, it's a matter of common sense. As soon as it comes out that some other goal was the top priority, it's a meal ticket for all the critics. It does not even matter whether anyone was actually harmed. The mere fact that such harm was implicitly accepted is usually enough to erode trust in our organization. And erosion for these reasons can hardly be stopped, let alone repaired. That is why the protection of life and limb always has top priority—even in cyber crises. This may surprise us at first, but it is particularly explosive.

Protection of Life and Limb: Example Control Systems

Let's take a look at any control systems. We find them in production plants, power stations, signal boxes, trains, airplanes, etc. Even in the car, the German's favorite child, "intelligent" "assistance systems" are becoming more and more important.

The moment the control systems are compromised, the plant to be controlled no longer does what it is supposed to do. This can result in danger to life and limb.

Protection of Life and Limb: Example Health Care

The link between cyber security and immediate threats to life and limb in the healthcare sector is becoming even clearer, especially on the part of healthcare providers and their supply chain. Hospitals and general practitioners, laboratories, pharmacies, pharmaceutical companies, medical technology—all are affected. Incorrect (product) specifications or specifications that are not available at the decisive moment endanger the lives of patients, regardless of whether the error or unavailability was deliberately created or not. This applies equally to patient data as well as to drugs and medical technology products. It does not stop there. If confidential information about patients becomes public, this is not only an issue regarding the EU-GDPR, but also and above all a potential trigger for irrational actions of all kinds on the part of the patients concerned. How does a person who, for whatever reason, has kept a diagnosed illness secret from his social environment react when this information suddenly becomes public, threatens to become public or is even blackmailed?

Protection of Life and Limb: Example Banking

But even in the banking sector, risks to life and limb can arise under certain circumstances in the context of cyber crises. A large part of the cash supply in Germany is provided by ATMs. Let's assume that—for whatever reason—the ATMs are not operational throughout the country. In that case, savings banks and other credit institutions with their branch networks, which have thinned out considerably in the meantime, would have to ramp up their cash capacities. But would this be possible to such an extent that long queues and chaos around the branches could be avoided? Panic could break out—which in turn could result in danger to life and limb. Now let's imagine a 78-year-old lady, already a little frail, who gets caught up in such a commotion, falls and suffers a femoral neck fracture. Perhaps there is also a camera crew on site to report on the chaos. Then it is good if the credit institution in front of which she fell has at least tried to provide some kind of order service.

Prio 2: Avoidance of the Worst-Case

As a reminder, our worst-case scenarios don't just fall out of the sky. They are the result of different events that precede the worst case in time and effect. We call these events triggers. So if we want to prevent the worst case, we need to identify the triggers and make preventing them our goal. This is our task if we want to derive goals from the worst case scenarios. Mind you, at this stage we are only concerned with WHAT we want or need to achieve. We answer the question of HOW when we start developing options and planning measures.

Prio 3: Stakeholder Expectations

Now our stakeholder and expectation collection comes into play again. Not every disappointed stakeholder expectation immediately brings us the worst case. Rather, there are always other stakeholders and expectations that we have to take into account in a crisis. Which stakeholder's expectations are worst-case-worthy and which are not always depends on the individual case of the cyber crisis, one's own organization, the point in time, the history, etc.

Prio 4: Own Specifications

We must not completely disregard our internal strategy documents (corporate strategy, IT strategy, information security strategy, etc.). These also provide us with orientation when formulating our objectives. So far, so good. But self-commitments such as mission statement, mission statement, code of conduct, homepage, press releases, marketing and advertising measures, annual report etc. also contain statements about values, priorities, objectives and intentions. And this is where it gets problematic because these sources are available to the public. And this means nothing other than that we must also be measured against them in the event of a crisis.

From Practice: Values as a Compass

By the way, our mission statement helps us to resolve conflicts of interest of all kinds. In case of doubt, our reputation protects what corresponds to the values and convictions that we publicly proclaim.

Classic Conflicts of Objectives

Unfortunately, conflicting goals are inevitable, especially in cyber attacks. Let's take a typical case. We discover for ourselves that we are under attack. This could be ransomware (a cryptolocker that encrypts our data so that we can no longer read it), for example, or an uncontrolled leak of information, including presumably confidential customer data. No one outside our organization knows about this yet (ok, except for the attacker and his eventual client). Let's further assume that we are pursuing these goals, among others:

(a) Cut one's losses
(b) Secure evidence and traces (how exactly the attack is structured, which data has already been leaked, etc.)
(c) Protect the reputation of our organization
(d) Not endanger the basis of trust with the customer
(e) Live the corporate values of openness and transparency

And here we are in the middle of a conflict of objectives.

Objectives (a) and (b) are in many cases mutually exclusive for technical reasons. To limit the damage, we must immediately stop the spread of the cryptolocker or the leakage of confidential information. This requires disconnecting the network connections of the affected systems and, for safety, turning them off. However, if we turn off the systems, we will lose the information stored in the cache of the systems.

In turn, the scope for (c), (d) and (e) depends on our decision on (a) or (b). What is the effect on our customers' trust if we let the attack continue? How if we approach customers on our own initiative and inform them (after all, the problem is not yet public)? Does demonstrating openness and transparency protect reputation and build trust? The CMT must make these trade-offs. This is a strategic decision that must not be made at a downstream level (for example, in the CSOC or an emergency management team).

Strategic Definition of Objectives vs. Tactical-Operational Implementation

Quite incidentally, we have become acquainted here with a crucial form of interplay between the strategic and tactical-operational levels. And also, a conflict of interests. While from a tactical-operational and here also from a technical point of view letting the attack go on for the purpose of securing evidence and traces (goal b) is the obvious goal, from a strategic point of view this often brings the higher risk and the lower benefit compared to stopping the attack immediately. That is, from a strategic perspective, the prioritization of (a) and (b) is exactly the opposite than from a tactical-operational perspective.

Caution: Strategic objectives should take precedence over tactical-operational considerations. Not that the tail ends up wagging the dog.

From Practice: Wrong Objectives

In addition to conflicting objectives, we encounter an all-too-human desire in practice: to pursue and apprehend the attacker. This impulse is perfectly understandable—but not very effective. There are several reasons for this: technical, legal, and practical.

If the attacker is only halfway clever, he will disguise where he actually is located geographically, and who he is. To do this, he can, for example, not carry out his attack directly from his own computer, but hijack several other computers and interpose them, so to speak. When our organization is attacked, the trail first leads us to the computer that is furthest away from the attacker's (in his chain of computers).

In order to find the attacker, we have to trace the entire computer chain, i.e., search each individual computer for the traces that lead us to the next computer. Although this is technically possible in principle, it is not trivial, but time-consuming and, above all, highly illegal. Such an investigation requires a court order—for every single computer. It goes without saying that it is not our right to carry out the searches, but rather the task of the investigating authorities. Now let's imagine that the attacker himself is not based in Germany, but in any third country, and that the computers in our beautiful chain are distributed across different countries. For the investigating authorities, this makes the work many times more cumbersome, as national borders and different legal systems can be time-consuming obstacles (at best) or even showstoppers. Anyway, let's assume for the fun of it that we don't follow the law and find the attacker or his computer with considerable investment. What then? It would hardly be possible to retrieve stolen information because the attacker could (and would) have taken it to safety from us long ago (safe from his point of view, of course).

In short, wanting to pursue and confront the attacker is human, but not an appropriate goal.

From Practice: Visualization Strongly Recommended

Again and again, it proves its worth if we visualize the goals clearly visible for all CMT members their operations room. Whether on a meta plan wall, a whiteboard, a flip chart, as catchwords or as sketch notes is irrelevant. What matters is that we visualize them. This ensures that we literally NEVER lose sight of our objectives.

Guiding Questions for the CMT

In identifying the worst-case scenario, the CMT can be guided by the following questions:

- Have we set a time limit to define our objectives?
- Have we defined the protection of life and limb as Prio 1?
- What triggers trigger our worst-case scenarios?
- What stakeholder expectations serve as our point of direction?
- What commitments can we be measured against?
- ...

Completion of the Initialization Phase

If we have

- facts gathered,
- stakeholders identified,
- worst case scenarios described and
- objectives defined,

we have also completed the initialization phase.

Where Do We Go from Here?

The next step is the situation assessment. This is already part of the cyclical management process as a variant of the crisis management process (Sect. 3.2.2.1). With the situation assessment we answer the question: How bad is our situation?

This is how we enter the crisis management process. But don't worry, we will regularly come across the points from the initialization phase again.

3.2.1.6 The Formal Establishment of the Crisis Case: Houston, We Have a Problem

Formal Authorization Act

Even though the formal determination is not a complicated act, it is so crucial that it deserves its own (short) chapter. The declaration of a crisis is so crucial because it gives the CMT the right to intervene in the normal processes of our organization through its decisions. The fact that it can empower itself to do so underlines that we should not use this power lightly.

From Practice: Focus on Documentation and Information
When we discuss in the CMT whether there is a crisis, we must at some point bring ourselves to say yes or no or perhaps later. Whatever the decision, we have to record it and our picture of the situation on the basis of which we make the decision in the CMT's minutes. And as soon as the decision is "yes, there is a crisis", it is essential that we inform the areas whose work will be affected by the CMT's decisions and who must contribute to their implementation. Otherwise, they will rightly wonder why a body that is not particularly present in everyday life suddenly throws everything out of kilter—contrary to any customary practice.

From Practice: Criteria for Emergencies and Crises
Similar to the process of identifying a crisis, organizations often struggle to declare an emergency. The reasons are the same. However, the threshold for declaring an emergency is lower than for declaring a crisis (or at least it should be). The following criteria are encountered again and again in our daily work and therefore seem to be practicable for many organizations:

- Danger to life and limb.
- Significant breach of confidentiality, integrity, availability or authenticity of information and communication link.
- Interruption of central (business) processes and services.
- Threat to the reputation of our organization or its key representatives (members of management).

As a rule, it does not matter whether the event has already occurred or whether its occurrence is merely imminent.

By the way, we can apply the same criteria to an emergency as we do to a crisis. All we have to do is define a lower threshold that an event must reach or exceed.

3.2.2 Managing Cyber Crises in a Structured Way: Crisis Management Process

Aim and Purpose of the Crisis Management Process
A structured crisis management process helps us, regardless of the type of crisis, to identify and deal with the relevant problems from the supposed chaos. The adjective "structured" is important at this point in several respects. In situations where nothing is clear, people need and seek orientation. This is also true for CMT members. Above all, however, a structured process enables us to work with roles that we can prepare the acting persons (CMT members!) to perform.

Leadership Process vs. FOR-DEC

What can such a crisis management process look like? As is so often the case, there is no right or wrong answer to this question, but at best one that is appropriate or inappropriate. What is expedient (or not), however, depends heavily on the preferences of the CMT or its members—they are the ones who have to implement the process. At least in the German-speaking world, we repeatedly encounter two variants of the crisis management process. Mostly it is the so-called leadership process, much less often the FOR-DEC scheme. Therefore, we will go into the leadership process in more detail here and present FOR-DEC merely for the sake of good order.

What Helps Us Cope with Crises: Principles

There are a few principles we should keep in mind when dealing with crises:

- Process discipline
- Do not lose sight of your goals
- Regular control meetings so that everyone has the same level of information

We will take a closer look at what is hidden behind the individual principles in the individual initialization steps.

What Helps Us Cope with Crises: Tools

There are a few tools that make crisis management much easier for us. These include:

- Crisis log
- Visualization of the objectives
- . . .

The exact role of these tools is described in the individual initialization steps and in Sect. 4.2.

Interfaces

- Business Continuity Management (Business Impact Analysis, affected business processes)
- IT Service Continuity Management (RTO vs. RTA, RPO vs. RPA)
- Information Risk Management (risks resulting from a breach of confidentiality, integrity, availability and authenticity of an information asset)
- Information Security Management (protection goals per affected information class)
- Stakeholder Management and Issue Management
- Documentation and results of the "Decision and implementation" process step
- Documentation and results of the initialization of the crisis management

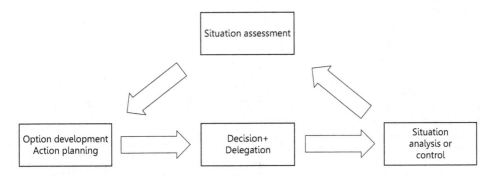

Fig. 3.4 Cyclical leadership process

3.2.2.1 Variant A: Leadership Process
Process Phases
The classic leadership process consists of four steps:

- Situation analysis/Situation review
- Situation assessment
- Options and action planning
- Decision and delegation

We must go through these steps as often as necessary until our assessment of the situation shows that we have the essential fields of action of a crisis under control to such an extent that we can formally end the crisis case (see Fig. 3.4).

Strengths of the Leadership Process
In Germany, the leadership process is set in blue-light organizations and many authorities. Whether disaster control, THW or fire brigade, whether police or Bundeswehr (German Armed Forces)—their staffs have been working for decades, in the case of the (German) military even for about 200 years, exclusively and usually highly professionally according to this scheme, whose visual representations there, however, are usually structured somewhat differently. This should be an indicator of how robust and universally applicable this approach is.

CMT members are often already familiar with it—either because they are involved in voluntary fire brigades, rescue services, THW and disaster control in their private lives or because they were previously soldiers or police officers. This means that the leadership process is also fully compatible with the procedures of many important partners in a crisis. This becomes apparent at the latest when our CMT exchanges personnel with the blue-light organizations involved in order to improve coordination among themselves (the good old liaison officer); an aspect that should not be underestimated, especially for CRITIS operators.

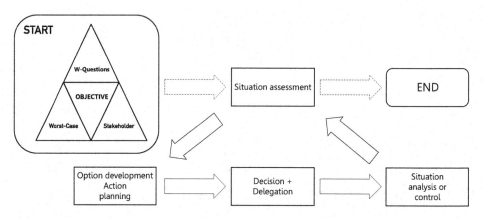

Fig. 3.5 Leadership process (overall view)

On top of that, the management process is absolutely robust. Not only can we use it to manage all types of crises (after all, there are not only cyber crises), but we can also use it wonderfully in day-to-day business. It goes without saying that it is fully compatible with the initialization process (see Fig. 3.5).

Weaknesses of the Leadership Process
Unfortunately, the original terminology (blue-light organizations have their very own jargon) in private-sector organizations is sometimes a bit hard to digest, as it is everything but typical business-speak (e.g., "giving orders", "intention of superior leadership", etc.). We also encounter recurring reservations about anything to do with government agencies and, in particular, the Bundeswehr (German Armed Forces). While the latter is an ideological issue that we can rarely deal with using factual arguments, the terminology can be smoothed out or adapted linguistically with a little background knowledge and experience. In this book, we present a linguistically smoothed variant of the leadership process.

End = Beginning
While we collect the facts at the beginning of the CMT's work as part of the initialization process and use this as the basis for the situation assessment step, the implementation and impact review and thus the updating of the facts simultaneously form the end and starting point of all further runs of the management process.

3.2.2.1.1 Situation Assessment: Where Is the Shoe Pinching Most?
Aim and Purpose of the Step Situation Assessment
There are two issues at stake in the situation assessment:

1. Where do we stand with regard to
   • objectives?

- worst-case scenario?
- stakeholder?

2. Where do we have the greatest need for action?

Procedure

To do this, we systematically and sequentially relate our situation to our goals, the worst-case scenario and the stakeholders (first the directly affected and influencers, then the indirectly affected, and finally the interested third parties). We can vary the order according to need (and personal gusto).

From this, our fields of action become visible. As in everyday life, we can rank the topics according to the criteria of importance and urgency to get a feeling for the priorities. The urgency describes how quickly something has to happen, thus expresses a temporal component. Importance, on the other hand, describes the consequences that result from something—in other words, a qualitative component.

Discussions Welcome!

Setting these priorities is a task that all CMT members must tackle together. This usually cannot be done without discussion, because each CMT member brings in his or her own perspective and therefore perhaps weights one goal or stakeholder higher than the CMT members sitting to the left and right of him or her. From the discussion, we get a prioritization of action items that is (hopefully!) supported by all CMT members. However, this approach is not without its dangers. As CMT leaders, we must be careful to end the discussion at some point. Mere discussion has never solved problems.

Guiding Questions for the CMT

In assessing the situation, the crisis management team may be guided by the following questions:

- What are the most urgent fields of action in view of the defined goals of our CMT's work?
- Which stakeholders do we need to pay particular attention to?

3.2.2.1.2 Options and Action Planning: What to Do, Said Zeus?
Aim and Purpose of the Step Options and Action Planning

The situation assessment has provided us with the fields of action and priorities. Now we have to get creative and see what we must and can do in the individual areas. Mind you, can, not will. This means that we ideally provide ourselves with several options for each field of action, from which we then select the most appropriate one.

Procedure

When planning measures, we strictly adhere to the prioritization of the fields of action from the situation assessment step. This means that we start with the field of action that has the highest priority and end with the field of action that has been given the lowest priority.

We can proceed in two ways to achieve this. Either we jointly develop solutions for the individual fields of action in the CMT or CMT leader delegates a corresponding task to individual CMT members, who in turn (can) make use of the knowledge from the specialist departments and who must then also implement the planning.

Options

Regardless of who takes on the task of planning measures, working out different options for each field of action is a good thing. On the one hand, there is often no right or wrong in crisis management, but rather an expedient or inexpedient. On the other hand, the individual options will inevitably have their advantages and disadvantages or will also depend on other decisions made by the CMT (or on developments beyond its control). In this respect, it is good if the CMT can choose from various paths that all lead to the same goal.

From Practice: Delegation in the Case of Dependencies

Which option we choose depends to some extent on how detailed the planning should be. Detailed planning usually requires subject-related expert knowledge, which not all crisis team members may possess.

When we delegate action planning, we must be unequivocal about two elements:

1. What is the objective towards which the measures for this field of action must be directed?
2. Who is responsible for the planning and by when must it be implemented?

In defining the goals for the individual fields of action, we are guided by the goals that we defined during the initialization of the CMT's working procedure. We now need to concretise these in terms of specific fields of action.

In order to be able to go through the management process properly, the timelines must be coordinated as to when the planning must be available to the CMT (see Sect. 3.2.2.1.3).

Guiding Questions for the CMT

In developing options and planning actions, the CMT can be guided by the following questions:

- For which fields of action do we need more than one option?
- How detailed must the planning be so that the CMT can decide on implementation?
- For which areas of action do we implement the point directly in the CMT and for which do we delegate the task to experts outside the CMT?
- How much time can/will we take to plan?

3.2.2.1.3 Decision and Delegation: Don't Talk, Act!

Aim and Purpose of the Step Decision and Delegation

After the previous step has provided us with at least one option for each field of action, we now have to select the most appropriate option(s)—again for each field of action. However, selection alone is not enough. The mere decision is one thing, the delegation is another. It, too, is the subject of this last step in our management process.

Procedure

To do this, we take the individual fields of action and their measures in turn, according to their priority. The person who, according to the crisis log, has responsibility for an area of action presents the available options. If we consider it appropriate, we can supplement the presentation of the individual options with an assessment. The assessment should address, among other things, the suitability for achieving the objective and the risks associated with the option. The presentation and, if applicable, the assessment ALWAYS end with a recommendation as to which option(s) should be implemented.

As soon as the CMT has received the recommendations for each field of action, it must examine the recommended measures across all fields of action for interactions and mutual dependencies. It is essential that these are taken into account in the decision and it may even be necessary to repeat the planning phase again (at least in part).

Once the CMT has reviewed the individual recommendations for interdependencies and interactions, it shall

- select,
- prioritize and
- delegate, i.e., instruct to implement,

which it considers most appropriate in order to achieve the objectives of the CMT as defined during the initialisation phase.

From Practice: Fighting Against Time

We must not under any circumstances academicize the presentation and evaluation of the individual options. There is simply no time for that in the management of (cyber) crises. Depending on the complexity of the situation, the examination of interactions and dependencies will sometimes lead to lively discussions. This is absolutely normal and also expedient. But once again, we must not lose sight of the clock. In cyber crises, we are usually working against hard (and documented!) restart or further protection goals, so the CMT leader must manage the discussion and end it at the appropriate time.

Documentation

At a minimum, the recording secretary must document the following information in a comprehensible manner:

- which options will be implemented;
- what they're aiming at;
- who is responsible for implementation;
- when we made the decision for an option;
- what the deadline for transposition is.

Documenting these points helps us as we go through the leadership process again and again (see Sect. 3.2.2.1.4).

Ideally, the minute taker will record other information as well. This includes, among other things:

- Minimum content (see above);
- What other options were up for discussion;
- Why the chosen option was chosen, or the others were not chosen (level of information at the time of the decision!).

This information helps in the follow-up of the crisis, for example in the identification of lessons learned or an "appraisal" by auditors, accountants or investigating authorities. In this way, the protocol becomes what the "get-out-of-jail-free card" is in Monopoly.

Guiding Questions for the CMT
In making decisions and delegations, the CMT may be guided by the following questions:

- Have we examined the individual options and measures for interactions and interdependencies?
- Are at least the subject matter, deadlines, responsibilities, goal and time of the decision documented in the crisis log for each task?
- How do we ensure that the persons responsible for implementing the measures decided upon understand their mandate as the CMT means it, i.e. how do we reduce the risk of misunderstandings in the transmission of the mandate?

3.2.2.1.4   Situation Analysis/Situation Review: Is It Working Yet?
Aim and Purpose of the Step Situation Analysis/Situation Review
The situation analysis/situation review step serves to track changes in the situation. Since the situation is constantly evolving, but not every member of the CMT can be aware of everything (after all, it is important to remain in close contact with one's own substructure), this step in the process also always involves a comparison of information. What has happened? What do we know? What do we suspect? Implementation and impact control are the keywords here.

Situation Report

The start of the leadership process is always the collection of the facts that we are dealing with at that particular moment. This is nothing other than the initialization of the CMT's working procedure that we have already learned about. Similarly, the step serves to ensure that all members of the CMT have the same level of information. This reminds us of school: good teachers make sure that all students are on the same page.

Review

As part of the review, we should rely primarily on our crisis log (see Sect. 4.2). By setting filters in the protocol template, we should systematically look at the following points:

- Confirmed information (= facts)
- Unconfirmed information (= assumptions)
- Completed tasks
- Open tasks

In this way, we gain an overview of the points that have changed since we entered the previous cycle of the leadership process.

Procedure

Once we have completed the protocol entries, the individual CMT members complete the situation picture for their area of responsibility or their fields of action. After all, it may be that not all the information has found its way into the minutes. These contributions are (of course) also recorded in the minutes by the keeper of the minutes.

From Practice: Systematic Contribution

It has proved useful for the CMT leader (or the chief of staff, if the CMT leader is assisted by one) to ask for these contributions in a fixed order, so that each CMT member has to make a statement as to whether they have any relevant additions. This brings structure to the process and prevents relevant information from being lost. In addition, this procedure makes life a little easier for the minute-taker.

Guiding Questions for the CMT

Since we have completed the initial situation assessment as part of the initialization of the CMT's working procedure, we can concentrate here on monitoring our measures, i.e. on updating the situation picture.

To this end, the crisis team—using the crisis log!—can be guided by the following questions:

- How do we ensure that all the key players involved in incident management have a common picture of the situation?
- What information has been confirmed or refuted in the meantime?

- Which orders have been completed in the meantime or are still open?
- Where do we stand in the individual fields of action with regard to the goals we have set ourselves?
- Where are we behind schedule?
- ...

3.2.3   Variant B: FOR-DEC

Origin of FOR-DEC
FOR-DEC is a model for decision making in aviation. The acronym stands for facts (F), options (O), risks and benefits (R), decision (D), execution (E) and check (C).

Process Phases
In the application of FOR-DEC, the crisis management team works through six phases in sequence:

- Collection of Facts
- Development of options for action
- Identification and weighing of the risks of the individual options and the overall situation as well as the benefits of the individual options
- Making and formulating the decision
- Execution of the decision
- Monitoring the impact of measures

Since a crisis is only rarely overcome by working through it once, the CMT must work through these points again and again until the objectives of the initialization phase have been satisfactorily achieved.

Strengths of FOR-DEC
The model is well established in aviation, so that little persuasion is usually needed there to encourage (new) CMT members to use the model. Moreover, it is internally consistent and its structure is quite plausible.

FOR-DEC Has Weaknesses
If we take a closer look at the entry and exit of the FOR-DEC process, the cyclicality of the process is not apparent at first glance. Nevertheless, we have to check the individual points as often as necessary until the crisis is over—otherwise we will be left halfway.

More problematic, however, is that in German blue-light organizations the leadership process is set. These include disaster control, fire brigades, police, rescue services and the Bundeswehr (German Armed Forces). This can make cross-organizational cooperation more difficult.

From Practice (I)
In implementation projects and in training sessions, one of the regular issues is to provide the CMT with a crisis management process with which they feel comfortable. When we introduce FOR-DEC in particularly down-to-earth companies (mind you, introduce it, don't recommend it), we sometimes observe a negative attitude among the CMT members—due to the English terminology of the acronym. The tenor is then often: "We are a German, regionally anchored company with a customer base almost exclusively in Germany. Our corporate language is German. So we don't even start with Anglicisms, especially in the event of a crisis."

From Practice (II)
Since CMT members are often already familiar with the leadership process thanks to voluntary activities (fire brigade, rescue services, etc.) or previous professional stations, FOR-DEC means for them the need to relearn. This is not in itself problematic, certainly not in today's world of volatility, uncertainty, complexity and ambiguity, for which the term VUCA is becoming increasingly common. What is problematic, on the other hand, is the human characteristic of falling back on familiar routines, especially in stressful situations (such as crises). And as a rule, FOR-DEC is not the learned routine.

3.2.4   Crisis Communication

Purpose and Objectives of Crisis Communication
Crisis communication is the second pillar, alongside operational-tactical measures, on which our strategic crisis management rests. Crisis communication is there to explain to stakeholders our efforts to solve the current problem and, conversely, to solicit their expressed opinions as guidance for our own decisions. Our guiding principle must therefore always be to foster stakeholders' trust in our organization and what we are doing as much as possible.

From Practice: Information Is NOT Communication
To clear up a widespread misunderstanding right away: information work is only one part of communication. If we place the responsibility for organizing and setting up the CMT (and everything that belongs to a crisis organization) with one of the various governance functions (usually BCM), then there is a certain risk that information and communication will be understood synonymously. This does all communicators an injustice! For the BCMer, the focus is usually on providing instructions and information to emergency management teams and other staff in the event of an emergency, around the initiation and coordination of emergency operations. In this role, the focus is clearly on GIVING information, and yet it is (incorrectly) referred to as communication, even though the crucial aspect of true communication is not present at all: feedback.

Communication Models

Communication scientists have been working on so-called communication models for generations. Don't worry, we'll spare ourselves a deeper excursion into these realms and concentrate on the core. This is: In contrast to the mere sending of information (= information), communication is necessarily dependent on a content-related feedback. In addition to the sender, there is always at least one other participant in the communication who, after receiving information, can (but does not necessarily have to) become the sender. The transmission of information takes place by means of a communication channel (sometimes also called a medium; for example, e-mail, Twitter, letter, press release, telephone call, personal conversation, etc.).

So if we want to communicate, we need:

- Information
- Transmitter
- Receiver
- Communication channel

3.2.4.1 Rules of Thumb for Crisis Communication
Credibility Comes First

We don't have to say everything we know. But everything we say must be true. True means that it not only matches our own (sometimes richly subjective) reality, but stands up to objective fact-checking by an unbiased third party. As noted elsewhere: trust is the sum of promises kept. Here we can add: He who lies once is not believed.

Internal Communication Is Never Internal

As an aside, we need to clear up another (incomprehensibly still widespread) misconception at this point. The misconception is:

> Internal communication is directed only at the employees of an organization. They are bound to confidentiality by the confidentiality provisions of their employment contract. Ergo, things that we communicate to employees remain confidential if we classify the respective information accordingly.

These kinds of assumptions are dangerous. What is communicated internally inevitably gets out. The question is only when, about whom and to whom. Who among us doesn't tell family or friends about work? On top of that, there is the phenomenon that the more secretly something is presented, the more exciting it becomes. That's why we have to be careful about our choice of words in internal communication as well—and about what information we actually want to reveal.

To put it simply, three people can keep a secret—if two of them are dead.

Do Good and Talk About It
"Do good and talk about it" is a good start. Even better is: Do good and let people talk about it! If we want to follow the principle, this means for us that practical crisis management cannot bear fruit without accompanying crisis communication. Crisis communication without practical progress, however, fizzles out and weakens stakeholder trust even further.

So we need (at least)

- A few aspects that our target group might perceive as positive. And we can only do that if we also do something in practical (and not just communicative) terms that meets our stakeholders' expectations.
- Someone outside our organization who is publicly committed to us even in this turbulent situation, who is seen as credible by our stakeholders and who makes positive statements on our behalf (see Sect. 3.2.4).

Breaking Evolutionary Patterns
If we want to be successful in crisis management, our crisis communication must break through the evolutionary behavioral patterns that are inherent in all of us (see Sect. 2.2.2). To do this, our crisis communication must at the same time be

- quickly,
- in person,
- empathic,
- factual,
- credible and
- reliable

If we would like to go into these points in more depth, we would recommend Höbel/Hofmann: Krisenkommunikation (see Appendix "For further reading").

3.2.4.2 Starting Point: Stakeholder Needs and Distress in Cyber Crises
How Do We Know What Our Stakeholders Think and Want?
If we are to address the needs and wants of our stakeholders in a cyber crisis, we must (again unsurprisingly) have an idea of how they assess situations (see Sect. 2.2.1), but also what drives them in an acute crisis (see Sect. 3.2.1.3).

- In the B2B environment, sales and key account managers should keep in touch as closely as possible, especially now—even if it hurts. But keeping in touch has another indispensable effect in addition to gaining information: In this way, we show that we take responsibility even in difficult times and do not duck away.
- Especially in the B2C environment, social media monitoring is an essential tool. What are people saying on Twitter, Facebook, and Instagram? Keeping an eye on the essential hashtags and forums is key.

Let's take a look at the prototypical needs and wants that our stakeholders are plagued by when we make our cyber crisis theirs.

Confidential Information Becomes Public (B2C)

In the B2C environment, the disclosure of confidential information can destroy livelihoods. Let's just assume that we've been in a committed relationship for what feels like an eternity, and that after all this time, the harbor of our marriage no longer offers an all-too-exciting balance between excitement and routine. But since we don't want to jump overboard completely, we first try to buy a small, maneuverable, and inexpensive dinghy—for the uncomplicated, fun and non-binding tour in between. In short, we sign up for a paid platform for casual dating (which we would never do in reality, of course—it's purely a thought experiment). So on the one hand, we have a middle-class existence with all that entails: partner, kids, house, family, pre-nup, friends, and maybe even a job that requires a certain amount of discretion (or at least a middle-class facade). On the other hand, we have left behind a digital footprint that reveals not only our dissatisfaction with the current course of our relationship, but also and especially our sexual preferences, including a fairly accurate track record of our successes in satisfying those preferences—namely, communication with all the people we have met through the platform and perhaps even met in person in the end.

Prize question: What goes through our minds when we learn that the platform—as was actually the case with Ashley Madison, one such portal, in 2015—has been hacked? We probably change face color a few times and then spend quite a while trying to get our blood pressure back to semi-reasonable levels. We feel exposed, vulnerable, helpless. Because one thing becomes clear to us now at the latest: our search for a dinghy could sink our efficient marriage steamer—capsized by a full-blown tsunami—and thus destroy our bourgeois existence. What do we want from the portal operator in this situation? Well, first and foremost, certainty as to whether we ourselves are affected by the hack and thus exposed—and pronto, please! If we think one step further, we realize that we need to know even more: What happened to the data? Is it for sale on the dark net somewhere, or is it even just available on the internet? What about the accounts of the people we had contact with? Have they been hacked and are we at risk of further danger in a roundabout way, so to speak? What the hell can we do? Is it enough to change our password? How do we do that again?

Admittedly, this example is a drastic one. But in (cyber) crisis management, we are well advised to think about worst-case scenarios. And by the way, the financial dimension remains relevant for all online services where we have deposited payment information.

Other Problem Areas

We can now make comparable worst-case observations for other problem areas in the cybersecurity context:

• Confidential information becomes public (B2B)

For example: payrolls, job reduction plans, design plans, research results, personal misconduct of employees, etc. become public or threaten to become public, which means potential for blackmail attempts, competitive disadvantages, and reputational damage.

- Confidential information is stolen (B2C)

For example: health data, credit card information, account transactions, telecommunication data, video and other image and sound material (all this offers blackmail potential, especially for celebrities or executives from business, public authorities, or politics).

- Integrity of data is no longer given (B2B)

Example: Control systems, e.g. of power plants, are fed with manipulated data, reach critical operating states and endanger people and the environment.

- Integrity of data is no longer given (B2C)

Example: Control systems, e.g., of cars or medical devices, are fed with manipulated data and endanger life and limb.

- Information is not available (B2B)

Example: Payment transactions between financial institutions cannot be processed with massive consequential damage for end customers (private and corporate customers).

- Information is not available (B2C)

Example: Account balance cannot be called up, transfers are not possible.

- Authenticity of communications and transactions is no longer given (B2B and B2C)

Example: An unknown third party successfully impersonates a communication participant known to us and obtains confidential information or even access to our IT systems. This opens a Pandora's box.

In all these cases, our stakeholders will have questions for us that we should definitely answer—and in the short term. So much for the bad news. But there is also good news: the questions are almost always aimed in one and the same direction.

3.2.4.3 W-Questions of Crisis Communication
Questions at Event Occurrence

We are almost always asked the following questions as soon as we become the focus of our stakeholders due to an unpleasant event:

- What happened?
- Why did it happen?
- What are the consequences?
- What are you doing to make sure it doesn't happen again?

We do not have answers to everything at this point—certainly not to the why. Nevertheless, we have to react. Otherwise, we lose the authority to interpret right at the beginning. To (re)gain this is difficult, if not impossible. That is why we are well advised to have a sample statement (see Sect. 4.4) in our (digital) drawer, which we only have to adapt slightly if necessary and which we can publish almost in real time without cumbersome coordination and approval loops.

Answers Required!
Absent or implausible answers suggest:

- Diversionary
- Lack of empathy
- Shirking responsibility
- Inability

All of which are not positive associations and hardly conducive to maintaining the trust placed in us. Rather, our stakeholders will perceive a communication vacuum on our side that any other players will be only too quick to fill. From a communication perspective, this is deadly.

3.2.4.3.1   Who Communicates with Whom?
Initialization of the CMT's Working Procedure
Here it helps us (once again) if we have been disciplined in the initialization of the CMT's working procedure and have identified the stakeholders who are or can become important in our specific situation. If we were sloppy in the initialization, we should now at the latest take care of identifying the stakeholders with whom we want (and need) to communicate.

Organization of Crisis Communication
"We" means either the CMT, a special communications team or, if necessary, other committees of the emergency and crisis organization—including representatives of the regular organization if we want to delegate the communications work to them. Incidentally, the latter makes perfect sense, because many of our stakeholders are used to having fixed contact persons, especially in the B2B environment. Replacing them in a crisis seldom brings advantages, on the contrary. Therefore, we should, if possible, rely on communicators who are already familiar to the respective stakeholder. Often, the distribution looks like this:

- Press spokesperson → Media
- Social Media Team → Members of the Social Media Platforms
- Sales, Account Manager → Customers
- Internal communication → Employees
- Management → Supervisory Board, investors
- Legal/Compliance → Supervisory and investigative authorities
- Specialist departments or provider management → Key service providers

It is essential that our messages to the various stakeholders are consistent, i.e. that the crisis communication is all of a piece.

Algorithms, Trolls, and Troll Farms

We must expect, especially in social media communication, that some communication participants are not interested in serious dialogue, but only in provocation. These include, in particular, agents provocateurs whose sole mission is to make opinions and incite other communication participants. Such individuals are referred to as trolls. Often it is not apparent to us whether the troll is a real person or a disdainful algorithm (social bot)—and certainly not who is behind the profile. Especially in large-scale campaigns in the political environment, trolls are sent into the race via entire troll farms and thus concertedly influence the sovereignty of interpretation on topics. By the way: Since it is unclear who is behind the accounts, trolls and troll farms are the prime example for the question of the protection goal of authenticity of communication links.

3.2.4.3.2 What Do We Communicate?

Objective (I): Satisfy Stakeholders' Information Needs

The stakeholders' need for information is one of the two central aspects of our communication. The need can be a purely subjective one and can extend to a formal objective one including a legal claim.

At the core, we usually must answer the classic W-questions for our stakeholders:

- What happened?
- What are the consequences for me?
- What can/should I do myself to avoid negative consequences?
- What are we doing as an organization to prevent these consequences?
- What's next?
- Where can I get more information?

The recipient therefore determines the message. No matter what we try to convey—we are always dependent on the addressee of our message understanding everything the way we want it. But since we can only influence what happens on our side of the communication (feeling empathy, formulating messages), we have to take responsibility for exactly that. That means we have to

- put ourselves in the recipient's shoes and try to anticipate what information and reactions they expect from us (as best we can, see also Sect. 3.2.4.2);
- formulate our messages in such a way that they offer as little scope as possible for misinterpretation. In a flippant and politically incorrect way, we could formulate the credo: "suitable for housewives and board members". This is easier said than done, and the character limits of some communication channels (Twitter, etc.) make our work even more difficult.

That's the duty.

Objective (II): To Bring Positive Messages to the People

The free skate consists of sending out as many convincing positive messages as possible that portray our organization as professional, caring, competent, etc. and at the same time have both a close connection to the acute crisis and a certain relevance for our stakeholders. This is the second key aspect of our crisis communications. We achieve this by focusing on positive aspects and avoiding signal words that have (potentially) negative connotations (see Sect. 4.4. Admittedly, avoiding these and other terms is not easy and requires some practice as well as preparation).

Responding to Needs and Wants

We should therefore meet every need for information with a positively formulated message. Ideally, we can work with concrete factual information. Where this is not possible—because we simply do not have any—it is advisable to respond to the stakeholder at the relationship level, and to do so as appreciatively and empathetically as possible. In order to systematize our communication options and at the same time visualize them for the CMT, a crisis communication plan is a good idea (see Sect. 4.4). Don't worry, for the CMT it does not have to (rather: must not) be too detailed.

From Practice: Shitstorm

Particularly in the case of stolen user data, the stolen company itself sometimes needs quite a while until it is clear which users are affected and which are not. However, this does not prevent potentially affected users from triggering or intensifying a quasi-prophylactic shitstorm out of—justified or unjustified—concern. Twitter, Instagram, Facebook, etc. make a public reaction (unfortunately) all too easy, which can then (again unfortunately) in turn be seized upon and amplified by rioters of all kinds.

3.2.4.3.3   How Do We (Hopefully) Communicate?
The Nuts and Bolts

In order to counter the evolutionary behavioral patterns (attack, flight, play dead, see Sect. 2.2.2), we must react appropriately—preferably yesterday and above all in word and deed. Being quick is the key. As soon as the flight reflex (or worse, the attack reflex) kicks in, it becomes difficult to bring people back to the issue level. Therefore, the goal must be to prevent these reflexes from occurring. Once the shitstorm spreads, it is usually too late and emotions triumph over (factual) arguments.

But speed alone is not enough—what we do and say plays an almost equally important role. It is important to take into account that every person ticks differently (see Chap. 2)—we can use this. We reach some people on a factual level, others more emotionally.

Relying only on the factual level therefore means ignoring an essential factor. Conversely, it is not enough to serve only emotions—without factual information it is not possible either. And since crises are always associated with emotions, this aspect cannot be emphasized enough.

Factual Level

Facts are the means to keep people on the straight and narrow. They offer answers to the most pressing questions and are intended to enlighten, which is sometimes not so easy: the information situation may still be unclear. This makes it all the more important that we convey our messages in the simplest possible language. We will not only be dealing with academics, but also with people from the other end of the educational spectrum. We also cannot ignore the question of the mother tongue of our addressees. Rule of thumb: We should explain things the way we would explain them to our 12-year-old nephew (if we had one).

Emotional Level

We will encounter emotions above all wherever we are dealing with private individuals. Their emotions will run high the more they feel affected by our cyber crisis. So perhaps the most important thing right here: showing sympathy is not an admission of guilt. Neither morally, nor legally. Showing compassion requires empathizing with those affected and their loved ones. Let's ask ourselves the simple question: what would we expect if we were in the place of the victims and their relatives? This change of perspective gives us a good orientation as to which messages and which measures are appropriate.

Factual or Emotional Level: Rule of Thumb

Which stakeholder we have to pick up and where (on the factual level or rather on the emotional level) depends very much on how "private" the addressee is. The least need for emotional appeal is (unsurprisingly) with public authorities and other government organizations, medium need is at B2B level and in the B2C environment it is often the most important thing of all. Public media, on the other hand, often expect our messages to serve both levels.

Reliability

Regardless of whether we communicate on a factual or emotional level: Our stakeholders rightly expect us to reliably keep our promises. Even if it's just the announcement of when new information will be available or that a link to further information is correct. In theory, this is all self-evident. Under the pressure of an acute crisis, however, it is unfortunately not always easy to manage.

The Stakeholder Determines the Channel
In all of this, we do ourselves a great favor if we make it easy for our stakeholders not only through language, but also through the choice of communication channel. We should not succumb to the temptation to limit ourselves to one channel and one information package and then try to pick up all our stakeholders via this one channel, with this one information package. That will not work.

Reputation Management
We should do everything we can to bring a variety of our own content and messages to the web. Channels are the own blog, social media, press work and video formats. This dilutes the value of the individual (critical) press reports and offers further information to neutral interested parties.

Netiquette
Especially when communicating via social media, we will sometimes experience that not too much of the notorious netiquette remains. This can also happen in analogue interactions, for example in interviews. No matter when, no matter where, no matter why and no matter how we experience such a breach of polite manners: We ourselves remain polite. Certainly, but politely.

3.2.4.3.4 When Do We Communicate?
Speed
Those affected have a right not to hear from the media (be it social or conventional) that something is happening that affects them negatively.

An example from the 00s shows how difficult this is. On 15 January 2009, US Airways Flight 1549 gained notoriety when the pilot was forced to make an emergency landing on the Hudson River. While in the good old days, when social media didn't exist, we would have had a solid 30 minutes to respond with a press release, Twitter pulverized that time frame. For it was through this very channel that a passenger spoke out—while still seated on the wing and before he could be evacuated from the emergency-landed plane.

Without an appropriately quick initial communication, we lose the already difficult battle for the interpretive authority of an event. Once the mood has turned thoroughly against us, it is difficult to turn it around again—and above all, it narrows our scope for action. The tolerance for possible (consequential) mistakes decreases further or possibly disappears completely. And that can be expensive. Rarely has the saying "time is money" been so true.

Regularity

After our initial communicative reaction, we need to communicate regularly, because this is the basis for successful crisis communication. In doing so, it has proven useful to give indications as to when we intend to get back in touch. However, it is essential that we adhere to this timing. The intervals between our announcements may of course be longer in the case of longer-running crises if developments so permit. After all, we are at liberty to give an update in the meantime in the case of important developments.

3.2.4.4 From Bloggers, YouTubers, and Journalists: Limits of German Press Law

Bloggers and YouTubers Are (Not) Journalists

Journalists have various duties. That comes with the job. Among other things, this includes conducting thorough research, i.e., checking information using different, independent sources. It also includes refraining from personal assessments and expressions of opinion (gloss, commentary) in the results of the work when presenting facts (report, reportage). The Press Council's press code is very clear on this. Bloggers, YouTubers and (other) influencers can also be journalists, but do not necessarily have to be. In particular, if they do not see themselves as journalists and do not subscribe to the Press Code, they are free to express their opinions and are not bound by the basic due diligence obligations of journalists. The expression of opinion, on the other hand, is protected by the Basic Law, so that we simply have to put up with corresponding expressions. Taking action against expressions of opinion is not exactly easy from a legal point of view, and in many cases it is also not sympathetic. The approach must therefore be friendly and binding, even if the message is very negative. One option is to build up a relationship by inviting people to a conversation. The atmosphere of the conversation must be open. The publicist receives all the information requested. The pressure cooker principle is undermined by not giving out facts slice by slice, but by lifting the lid completely to avoid an explosion.

Streisand Effect

Taking action against a publication inevitably means drawing the public's focus even more strongly to our dispute with the medium in question. An experience also made by actress Barbara Streisand when she wanted to prevent pictures of her estate from being seen on the internet. Result of the story: the public became even more curious, she was proven right, but the pictures remained discoverable, albeit through other channels. And incidentally, she became the namesake of the Streisand Effect.

Forbearance

We can obtain a cease-and-desist declaration against statements of opinion as well as statements of fact. If we are proven right in court, the medium must undertake to refrain from making such statements in future and pay a contractual penalty in the event of contravention.

Restraining Order

We can also use an injunction to ensure in the short term that, for example, certain claims are not repeated. However, this is only promising to a limited extent because the medium can already nullify our application for an interim injunction by depositing a so-called protective letter. To do this, it merely must deposit the protective letter electronically in a central, cross-border register, the so-called protective letter register.

Correction Claim

If a medium works with inaccurate factual allegations, we are entitled to correction and, if necessary, compensation. Mind you, factual claims. This means that statements made in comments and glosses are excluded from the outset. The correction can either consist of a retraction or a correction. The medium must publish the correction in the same place and in a comparable form as the original contribution in question. It should be noted that the correction must be very specific, line by line, video sequence by video sequence, and must be justified.

Rejoinder

Our legal right to a rebuttal is enshrined in state press laws. A counterstatement is our version of a media's factual assertion. We must request the counterstatement in writing within 14 days, i.e., we must act in close temporal connection with the reporting we are complaining about. This also includes drafting and signing the counterstatement. If we are eventually proved right, the media is obliged to publish the counterstatement in the next issue—in the same place and in comparable presentation as the article we are complaining about (just like a correction). Now come the snags. First, we should briefly describe in the rebuttal what it is against. In doing so, we bring up the issue again, even though it had presumably long since disappeared from the media in the meantime. Secondly, the media is entitled to attach its own statement. This is known as an editorial tail and usually reads as follows: "The state press law obliges us to publish this counterstatement regardless of its truth content. Nonetheless, we stand by our representation." We should therefore think carefully about whether a counterstatement will actually help us. If in doubt, keep your feet still, because today's newspaper will have fish wrapped in it tomorrow. But on the other hand, it's just as true that the web doesn't forget anything.

3.2.5 From Practice: Strategies in Acute Cyber Crises

Basic Questions

Regularly we encounter these questions: Should we

- admit to everything?
- comment on this? If so, on what channel, in what language, by whom?
- publicly dismiss or at least release the guilty parties?

- bring in outside investigators or crisis professionals?
- ...

The answer is, as usual in complex situations: It all depends on what the framework conditions are and what options we have.

Is There THE Most Promising Strategy?
As is almost always the case, there is no one solution that is vastly superior to all others. The only thing that is clear is that, in case of doubt, we are always smarter afterwards.

(Therefore, once again, the advice to always document all facts and assumptions on which our decisions are based in the crisis log and to track them accordingly).

3.2.5.1 Victim Care Above All
Threats to Physique and Psyche
The reassuring thing about cyber crises compared to other crises is the fact that, so far, only in exceptional cases is life and limb at stake. But in cases where life and limb are not at stake, there are also victims, for example of data leaks. We must also take care of such victims. Somewhat exaggerated, we can say that while safety issues threaten the physicality of our stakeholders, data leaks threaten the psyche. Being digitally exposed causes feelings of powerlessness and sometimes shame—negative experiences with which we must not leave our stakeholders alone.

Compassion and Help Are NOT an Admission of Guilt
To all the lawyers among the readers: Offering help and expressing sympathy for the adversity suffered is not an admission of guilt. Instead, it shows that we also consider the emotional side of crisis communication. But be careful: hardly anything can fall more heavily on our toes than promising help and then failing to provide it. When in doubt, the same applies here: underpromise and overdeliver.

When (Cyber) Security Problems Lead to Deaths and Injuries
Let us imagine that we work for a provider of passenger transport services and are shocked to discover that certain components of the electronically controlled safety systems of a particular bus model have now failed to behave as they should on several occasions. This has now resulted in an accident with numerous injuries, perhaps even fatalities. The cause of the malfunctions is currently unclear.

What can promises of help look like in such a case?

Involve Relatives
Let us now put ourselves in the position of those who are most affected: the injured and their relatives. Some want to join the injured in hospital, others want their loved ones with them. This is where we can help, by offering not only to arrange travel and accommodation for the relatives at the place of treatment, but also to pay for it. It is possible that there will

be knock-on effects in the environment of those affected by their absence, for example in childcare or the care of other relatives. If we show ourselves to be sensitive and willing to help in this area as well, this will greatly relieve the burden on those affected.

Ensure Accessibility

The basic prerequisite is that we are accessible for those affected. This does not mean a hotline or info@. . .-address, but personal contact persons. In other words, we are no longer in first level support here, but at least second, if not third level. If we are dealing with a large number of affected people, we need our customer management or less from now on considerable capacities in the first level. The basic options for this can be found in Sect. 4.4.

Visits to Injured Persons and Relatives

Visits to affected persons are in principle a nice gesture. Whether these are actually desired, we should clarify in advance of a possible visit, since we want to appear neither intrusive nor encroaching.

In any case, probing has a positive side effect: if we care intensively and sympathetically for those affected (injured persons as well as relatives), we work on the image they have of us. If we succeed in transforming ourselves from a faceless organization into real, tangible people for those affected, that is a good sign. Because people are quicker to say bad things about a faceless organization than about people who have not avoided unpleasant situations.

Offer Complementary Solutions

We need to return to the scene of the accident for a moment. Prize question: What means of transport do we offer for the onward journey to people who are not injured or only slightly injured?

Continuing the journey by bus could revive or even intensify the misfortune in people's (sub)consciousness. In this respect, we should offer complementary means of transport: Train, plane, car. Of course, the destinations are not always (well) reachable by train or plane and even if they are, not everyone will accept our offer. But that is not the point: it is the gesture that counts.

By the way: Please always upgrade—both in terms of travel and accommodation.

Victim Care as a Permanent Commitment

If we want to appear credible as "responsible caretakers," we are entering into a commitment whose duration can easily exceed the term of standard management and board contracts. For this reason, we should choose this strategy option—as sympathetic as it may make us look in the best case—with caution.

Victim care is not a sprint, but a long-distance race. Seriously injured victims often need therapeutic support in the medium to long term in addition to short- and medium-term medical care. If we later retreat after the acute initial phase, it can come back to haunt us all the harder in public reporting. Who of us has never seen a report in which those affected have said: "In the beginning they cared. But later, when the cameras were gone, they no longer cared about us". So should we ever find ourselves in a situation that is halfway exploitable by journalists in the future, our past will catch up with us.

For the Sake of Good Order (I)
Those of us who have dealt with other types of crises than cyber crises and/or the topic of Victim Care rightly note: Victim Care in cyber crises is no different from that in other crises. Only the trigger is a special one.

For the Sake of Good Order (II)
Even if supposed crisis experts go on at length about delivering death notices—that chalice passes us by. Unless we are active in a few select professions and organizations, we will never deliver death notices to victims' families as representatives of our organization. That is the responsibility of the police, doctors, armed forces, emergency chaplains, etc.

3.2.5.2 We Ourselves Are Also Victims!
Perpetrator or Victim or Both?
Basically, we always have an easier time communicating when our cyber crisis is the result of outside influence—especially when that outside influence is a criminal act. Then we have the opportunity to present ourselves as victims.

Use Cases
We can consider this strategy in principle for:

- DDoS attacks
- Data leaks or data theft
- Fraud cases (cyber and non-cyber related)
- Attacks by ransomware and other cryptolockers
- Data manipulations that have led to the malfunction of machines and systems
- . . .

Condition (I): Homework Is Done
But be careful, this communication strategy has its pitfalls. For example, we should be able to show that we have done our homework and implemented state-of-the-art measures long ago:

- Measures for the management of cybersecurity (for example, according to ISO 27032 or the NIST CSF)
- Information Security Management System (ISMS, for example according to ISO 27001 and preferably certified)
- Business Continuity Management System (BCMS, for example according to ISO 22301 and preferably certified)

- Management system for IT service continuity or ICT readiness for business continuity (ITSCM or IRBC, for example according to ISO 27031)
- (Cybersecurity) Incident Response Teams (CSIRT, for example according to ISO 27035 or best practices of SANS)
- Training and awareness program for systematic empowerment and sensitization of the workforce
- Audit and testing program to check the effectiveness of the individual measures and their interaction

Among other things, we take a closer look at this bundle of measures in Chap. 4.

Condition (II): Supporting Documents
The decisive factor is that we are able to convince a broad public that we have actually taken all these measures (or at least a subset of them). Certifications (see above) are helpful in this regard, as are auditors' attestations (PS951, ISAE 3402). Although the latter are usually confidential information from our organization's point of view, if they contain statements that can exonerate us in a crisis … Well, in such a case we are well advised to critically question the confidentiality classification and to quote relevant passages. But be careful: We absolutely must clarify beforehand to what extent this procedure is legally okay—after all, we have concluded a contract with the auditing company, the terms of which could become a stumbling block here. (By the way, this is a prime example of why a lawyer should be on the core CMT). If our organization is a listed public limited company, we have to submit an annual report anyway. This always contains statements on (operational) risks, so that we have a certain chance of also finding statements on security and related measures.

Key Messages
Our core messages can then read as follows:

- We are victims ourselves.
- Our safety precautions correspond to the state of the art.
- Independent auditors have checked and certified our safety precautions.
- We have invested an average of [amount] euros in the security of our customer data/IT systems/… over the last 3 years.
- Our investment in the security of our customer data/IT systems/… has increased by [number] percent per year over the last 3 years.
- Our investment in the security of our customer data/IT systems/… has been [number] percent higher than what competitors invest in security for years.
- We have created [number] new positions in the area of [information security] or hired employees in the last 3 years.
- …

Risk: Insider!

It is almost certain that insiders who have always known better will emerge. Often, these are former employees who left in a dispute and/or feel they were not sufficiently heard. Service provider employees are also a possibility.

Insiders make themselves available as interview partners and experts or become active themselves via social media. It becomes dangerous when these "snipers" have material to back up their claims (keyword: whistleblowing). Sure, we can take legal action against the publication and hold the insider accountable. But how promising is this attempt? And above all, does it help us to retain the authority to interpret events and the trust of our stakeholders? Or does such an approach not tend to steer the public's focus even further in our direction? With whom do the sympathies lie—with the whistleblower or with the (alleged) wrongdoer and those who are to be held responsible for it?

3.2.5.3 Attack Is the Best Defense
Counterattacks in Word and Deed

In the event of a threat, going on the attack ourselves is an evolutionary behavioral pattern. We can not only experience this with our stakeholders, but also use it ourselves in a targeted manner. On the one hand, by taking concerted action at the communicative level and, on the other hand, through practical measures.

Argumentum ad rem

Correcting misrepresentations in terms of content and in a way that can be objectively verified by independent third parties is indispensable in very many cases. However, corrections entail two not entirely insignificant risks, especially when it comes to formal corrections (counterstatements) as defined by press law. On the one hand, it is questionable whether we will be proven right in court. As is well known, being right and getting right are two different things. On the other hand, a correction (whether through press releases, statements or Twitter messages) always automatically means keeping the topic alive and in the public eye. Especially when the medium we forced to issue a rebuttal comments on it from its point of view in the editorial tail.

Argumentem ad hominem

If we are attacked by individual stakeholders, we can try to attack the stakeholders themselves instead of their arguments.

If we decide to take this step, we can choose the following points of attack:

- Research statements from the past that may point in a completely different direction and confront the person with them in a public way.
- To challenge competence (past failures, formal qualifications, etc.)
- To challenge responsibility

- To challenge motivation
- To point out exposed lies (also from other contexts)
- Personal misconduct, e.g., tax offences
- Stains in private life
- . . .

The aim of such attacks is to shake the credibility of the stakeholder and thus also the trust placed in him by others.

This approach should be taken with considerable caution, as it often makes us look less than sympathetic. Therefore, launching our counterattack via an inherently unsuspicious third party may be an option. But even here, caution is advised. As soon as our connection to this person or organization becomes known, the approach can fire back on us.

Charm Offensive

In practical terms, our counterattack can also be positive. For example, we can launch a charm offensive and offer our customers special conditions or upgrades, in other words, take particularly good care of them. This approach reaches its limits when it comes to questions of profitability and staying power. It cannot be ruled out that this generosity can also be interpreted as an act of desperation.

If you will, the charm offensive is (just) a particular manifestation of the Victim Care approach.

Own Cyber Attacks

Let's be clear right away: Responding to a DDoS attack or ransomware with a digital counterattack is humbug. By the way, this already applies to the attempt to even identify the attacker (see also Sect. 3.2.1.5).

Let's look at one of the examples from the above chapter again. An attacker will not carry out the attack directly from his own computer but will have connected several others between himself and us. Computers that he has taken over quietly and secretly and that can be located anywhere in the world, i.e. in the most diverse legal areas. In order to identify the attacker, we would have to trace the entire chain back to him, i.e., gain access to all these hijacked computers ourselves (only in reverse order). Quite apart from the fact that this is anything but easy, it is also and above all a criminal offence. We are violating e.g., 202c StGB, the so-called hacker paragraph. Depending on the computers involved, a violation of the German Act for the Protection of Trade Secrets (GeschGehG) is also within the realm of possibility. Both also apply to the digital counterattack (whatever it should look like). But let us now come to what is perhaps the crucial point. Regardless of legal and practical hurdles, what good is a counterattack going to do us anyway? If we've had data stolen from us, it's not going to get it back. If we have a cryptolocker in our systems, it won't get rid of it. If we paid a ransom, it's not going to get it back. If . . . We see: Responding with cyber attacks of our own is not an option.

3.2.5.4 Putting the Cards on the Table Vs. Refusing to Communicate

Refusal to Communicate as a Communication Strategy

If we refrain from communicating adequately quickly (or at all—that can also be a strategy!), one thing must be clear to us: The resulting speculative vacuum will be filled by others—and not necessarily those who are well-disposed towards us, on the contrary. Friends and allies who openly declare their support for us in crisis situations will be few and far between. As a result, we forfeit the opportunity to present our perspective on events to a potentially neutral public.

Nestlé proved to us in 2009 that refraining from a public reaction can nevertheless be a good strategy, when the company simply took its Facebook page offline in the midst of a shitstorm. To the horror of all "communication professionals" and to the delight of investors, because along the course of the shitstorm, which lasted several weeks, the share price rose by a double-digit percentage.

But beware: Olympus tried the same strategy in 2011 in the face of disguised losses, whistleblowers and inflated consulting fees—and nearly went under.

We Don't Have to Say Everything

Either way, we are by no means required (possibly even allowed) to say everything we know—but everything we say must be true to the facts. This implies two things in particular:

- Never lie—the truth always comes out at some point -

and

- Don't promise anything we can't deliver in practice.

Ignoring these two principles is a sure way to permanently damage our stakeholders' trust in our organization. This sounds kind of familiar? That's right—this is the very first principle of crisis communication.

Lowest Common Denominator

To put it bluntly: Admitting only as much as can be definitively proven at the time can be expedient from a legal perspective. However, it becomes dangerous when more and more details come to light that can be interpreted to our disadvantage. Therefore, from a communication perspective, the clear recommendation:

Stay away from the infamous salami tactic, i.e., giving out information bit by bit. This only leads to

- continuous news interludes, so that the topic has no chance at all of disappearing from the consciousness of our stakeholders (one or the other DAX company can tell you a thing or two about this);
- blatant and almost irreversible loss in the credibility of our organization and the people who run it (again: one or the other DAX corporation and its executive boards have some experience in this regard).

From Practice: Underpromise and Overdeliver

Instead, it is better to formulate promises and forecasts rather cautiously. In case of doubt, we are already extremely on the defensive, so we cannot gain much by optimistic (or even realistic) forecasts. But we can lose all the more if we don't deliver to the extent we promised. There's no question that in a situation like this, it's extremely difficult for us as CMT or business leaders to follow this advice. The pressure we are under is immense. For this very reason, we are usually well advised to promise less in a crisis situation than we believe in good conscience we can deliver. It is often helpful to explain what our forecast depends on—especially when it concerns external factors that we cannot influence ourselves. Promises of improvement and compensation are also important and should be treated with caution. Our directly affected stakeholders and especially the notorious interested third parties usually have an elephantine memory and act according to the biblical principle: "By their deeds we will judge them".

3.2.5.5 Getting Out of the Line of Fire

Elegantly Solved

Sometimes there are elegant solutions for getting our heads out of the noose in acute crises, for damage limitation or for getting ourselves out of the line of fire. We can get our heads out of the noose with the help of the leniency program, self-disclosure can help to limit the damage and spin-doctoring is a tried and tested means of stealthily disappearing from the line of fire.

Self-Disclosure and Leniency

A leniency program (Section 46 of the Criminal Code) assures leniency or even immunity from prosecution (but only in the legal sense, not in the moral or reputational sense). The underlying idea is this: If in a criminal trial (decisive) evidence can only come from among the suspects, the one who provides the evidence should benefit from it.

Let us imagine the following, of course purely fictitious case: Any industry must comply with certain values for its products. Before the product is approved, the values are checked. Now it is the case that during normal use the product is far from meeting these values. The companies in the industry know each other very well, especially since they regularly exchange personnel and information. Now, what if one of the companies developed a small piece of software that would allow the product to distinguish testing situations from normal use and temporarily meet the values? And what if successively all the companies in the industry used such solutions—until the whole thing blew up? The prosecution is always happy about insiders who offer further, perhaps even decisive incriminating material—especially if one or the other suspect cannot be apprehended in any other way. And this is where the leniency program comes into play: punitive relief in exchange for information.

Prisoner's Dilemma

For the sake of good order: the extent to which seeking or negotiating leniency is possible, sensible, or even necessary must be determined in close consultation between organizational management (liability!), the CMT and the legal department. The question is a prototypical example of the prisoner's dilemma familiar from game theory. What if we do? But what if we don't, but someone else does? What if no one unpacks at all? Loosely based on Augustus, one thing is certain: the people love the betrayer, but they hate the traitor.

Spin-Doctoring and Smoke Grenades

When the public pounces on us and our alleged failings, it can help us to portray them as inherent in the system, inevitable, or possibly common in the industry.

To do this, we can proceed in several steps. First, our argumentation can target the framework conditions within which our organization must operate. These include, for example

- public support measures not granted;
- regulatory requirements that are declared to be misguided by our industry association or other "neutral" experts;
- competitive situations with non-European organizations, in particular those from the USA, Russia and China;
- and much more.

In short: In principle, we can take up everything that

- may have potentially contributed to the current situation (in whatever way and to whatever extent);
- may also apply to other, comparable organizations or industries;
- clichés and classic enemy images of the public are served.

Risk: Resentment of the Industry and Partners

Regardless of whether it is self-disclosure, spin-doctoring, or leniency: these strategies inevitably lead to third parties also coming into the focus of the public and/or investigating authorities. Rarely to their delight—after all, we wouldn't like to be dragged into the crisis of a partner (supplier, customer, etc.) or, even worse, a competitor.

3.2.5.6 Swapping a Scapegoat for an Identification Figure
Panacea Scapegoat
In Germany in particular, the call for a scapegoat quickly becomes loud. Demands such as "heads must roll" or "someone must take responsibility" become loud almost faster than we can count to three. As an organization, we must acknowledge this expectation and the resulting pressure. But we don't automatically have to give in to it. There's no question that it's always convenient to relieve a potentially responsible person of their duties, sign a generous severance agreement, and bind the then former employee to silence. We guessed it, the famous but follows. This strategy should not disregard the fact that not everyone is a good scapegoat. On the one hand, this can be due to the individual mentality and, on the other hand, to the area of responsibility that the person in question has (had) in our organization. There is a saying "the fish stinks from the head". This means nothing other than that the release of experts and members of middle management appears to be a rather transparent maneuver unless personnel consequences are also drawn at top management level at the same time—if only because of (political) responsibility. Otherwise, regardless of their actual culpability, those released will merely appear as pawns.

Rising Stars
In every crisis there is an opportunity, even if it is for personal advancement. When personnel consequences are unavoidable due to public pressure—and ideally also for factual reasons—there are always gaps in the hierarchy that want to be closed. In this way, crises offer the opportunity to bring in and promote committed individuals who are, ideally, demonstrably loyal to our organization—on the condition that they manage the crisis in the interests of the organization. A little cynically, we could speak here of an executive assessment center of a special kind.

Structural Changes
Replacing one head with another will usually not be enough. Most of the time, we need structural changes to regain or maintain the trust of stakeholders. Introducing them is one of the measures our new hopeful will find in the specifications. The structural changes must be aimed at ensuring that we do not fall into such a crisis (or any other) again. Where we should start will have to be examined in the context of crisis follow-up (see Chap. 6).

Either way, structural changes are costly and not very popular. But especially in combination with each other, they help to significantly reduce the probability of occurrence and impact of (cyber) crises. And perhaps there are (mis)changes that we had long recognized as useful but were unable to implement due to their unpopularity. The crisis could be our opportunity.

3.2.5.7 When We Are Blackmailed
Demands
Extortion is a common admixture of cyber crises. The motives and demands can be (roughly) divided into three categories:

- financial demands

   Example: The series of attacks with cryptolockers on German city administrations and hospitals in 2016
- Doing certain things

   Example: withdrawal of heavy machinery from the Hambach forest, see the DDoS example of RWE from 2018.
- Omission of certain things (as a special form of doing certain things)

   Example: airing a movie, see SPE's 2014 cryptolocker and data leak example.

It is possible for the claims to be combined, but in practice this is (so far) quite rare.

Motifs

We should be careful not to confuse the demand itself with the motive of the blackmailer. The demand is only one of often several forms through which the actual motive can express itself—or through which the motive camouflages itself.

Our strategy should therefore (explicitly!) also depend on the motive we suspect our blackmailer has:

- Is he ideologically motivated, i.e., a persuader?
- Does he have his back against the wall for some reason and doesn't know any other way to help himself?
- Is he making a demand without seriously expecting us to meet it—just to have a reason or a personal justification for taking action after all?
- Is he trying to prove something to himself or to us?
- Does he have a personal relationship with our organization and does his motivation stem from that relationship?
- . . .

Perpetrator Types

Motive and perpetrator types are closely related. If we have a hunch about one, we inevitably have a favorite about the other.

Roughly speaking, we can distinguish offenders into the following categories:

- Amateur vs. Professional
- Single offender vs. team
- Private sector or government background
- Free riders

The Combination Decides

Ultimately, a triad must be decisive for our strategy:

- The actual demand made and the object of blackmail (= the threat made, i.e., facts beyond our control)
- Our assumptions about the motive, the credibility of the threat, and the blackmailer himself (assumptions about things beyond our control)
- Our assumption of how well we will cope if the blackmailer carries out his threat (fact or assumption, depending on whether the event has already occurred and we have already been able to take countermeasures or not; i.e., in any case, things that we can influence ourselves)

Aids to Assessment
Orientation is provided by precedents, as recent as possible, of course. If, as in 2016, a wave of cryptolocker attacks sweeps across comparable organizations (at that time local governments) or the BSI issues a corresponding warning, this will (hopefully) directly influence our attitude.

From Practice: Haughtiness Comes Before the Event
Blackmail letters can reach us through a variety of channels, with social media and email being the most common. These letters are often written in English, but not necessarily in what we used to know as polished Oxford English in our school days. Rather, grammar, spelling, expression etc. would offer clear room for improvement. But beware: English and IT skills of the blackmailers do not necessarily correlate. We have experienced a case where a customer dismissed an extortion letter as untrustworthy due to the poor English (!). The demand was for a bitcoin amount that wouldn't have even impacted the client's P&L. A DDoS attack was threatened. Now we get to guess together how the story went on. On the bright side, the customer experienced a learning curve.

3.3   Reaction at Tactical-Operational Level

3.3.1 The Show Must Go on or: Restart of Processes and IT Systems

Continuity Management
When information—for whatever reason—can no longer be processed, we need to be able to act in two directions: We must use business continuity plans (the famous Plan B!) to get our critical processes back up and running in a timely manner, and work in parallel to restore the availability of information or information-processing systems. The specialist disciplines for this are called Business Continuity Management (BCM) and IT Service Continuity Management (ITSCM) or ICT readiness for business continuity (IRBC). We will look at them in detail in the respective chapters. For now, we will "only" deal with the reactive facet of these disciplines: the restart of processes and IT systems.

Emergency Operations Is Not Normal Operations

IT systems can be protected against failure in various ways. One possibility is to set them up redundantly (across at least two data centers). These are the famous cluster solutions. In normal operations, the components involved can share the workload in a so-called active/ active cluster, whereas in an active/passive cluster one side remains inactive and is only activated when the other fails. Emergency operations on the IT side therefore often means the loss of redundancy. While the infamous data center failure is often invoked at this point, it is neither the only, nor the most likely form of redundancy loss. It is much more likely that only individual systems (databases, network segments, control systems, etc.) lose their redundancy. Regardless of exactly what the loss of redundancy looks like, the consequence is not only increased risk, but sometimes also capacity limitations. After all, we now have to maintain production with only some of the resources (clusters, instances, etc.).

In normal operation, our (business) processes can access all the resources they need. These include applications, data, and control systems. Without these resources, we are dependent on workarounds. Such workarounds are both indispensable and only suitable for a limited time. The failure of IT systems can (if at all) only be compensated for with more work input, and by no means permanently. Workload and output reduction are the keywords.

In both cases—on the process and IT side—the consequence is similar: we only have limited (production) capacities available and thus lower output than in normal operation. This should make it clear that we can temporarily keep our stakeholders halfway happy by quickly switching to emergency operation—but only temporarily. Emergency operations are a temporary solution that must not, and cannot, become permanent.

Formal Requirement: Emergency

However, we cannot pull business continuation and restart plans out of our pockets and implement them on a whim. After all, the plans often contain specifications that specifically override regulations governing normal business operations. Therefore, a crucial prerequisite must be met: Someone (the → CMT, the → emergency management team, etc.) must have determined that a situation exists that cannot be handled by the regular organization— an emergency.

Dovetailing with Strategic Level

Unfortunately, there is no stop button in crisis management with which we can stop time and thus calmly analyze the situation from all sides. Due to the parallelism of events, decisions and measures at strategic as well as tactical-operational level, we must therefore ensure that the levels are closely interlinked. Above all, we must/should

- we alert or inform the different levels as simultaneously as possible;
- the respective steering committees (CMT, communication unit, situation center, emergency management team, contingency teams) continuously keep each other up to date;

- the working methods (see Sects. 3.2.1 and 3.2.2) of the steering committees should be compatible;
- we synchronize communication with our stakeholders (internal and external) across levels.

3.3.1.1 Restart: Critical (Business) Processes
Objective of the Business Continuation
The objective of business continuity sounds trivial at first: to ensure that in the event of a process interruption (e.g., due to the unavailability of data or IT systems), the process is restarted quickly enough to avoid serious damage to our organization. Mind you, no serious damage and not no damage. The latter would be at least an uneconomical, if not unrealistic goal.

Business Continuity Plans and Contingency Teams
To do this, we must activate the business continuity plans (BCP; vulgo: contingency plans) of our critical (business) processes as quickly as possible. And it is precisely for this purpose that we must formally establish the emergency at a central point (see above). Otherwise, we get uncontrolled growth, because individual process owners could switch to emergency operation depending on their whim. The contingency team of the respective process is responsible for the execution of the BCP (see also Sect. 4.1.4).

The contingency teams shall work through the BCP and regularly report intermediate statuses to the recipients defined therein.

From Practice: Recipients and Reporting Points
At the tactical-operational level, in addition to the contingency teams, we also have to deal with other emergency management committees, which are ultimately the central points of contact for our contingency teams (see again Sect. 4.1.4). We have to inform these bodies about, among other things:

- Interruption of the process including the reason for the interruption, i.e., the applications and information/data that are not available (among other things, the emergency or CMT needs this input in the event of an emergency or crisis in order to determine the emergency or crisis)
- Completion of emergency measures
- Significant delays that jeopardize the timely start of emergency operations
- Commencement of emergency operation
- Obstacles that jeopardize the required output of the emergency operation
- Re-availability of the information and applications that caused the process interruption
- Return to normal operation
- ...

Restart Times and Restart Sequence
Some processes need to restart faster than others. Some processes we may not even need at all in an emergency. We cannot determine whether a process is relevant to an emergency or not only during a crisis or emergency. We must do that beforehand, as part of the →
business impact analysis. In the event of an emergency, we need an overview of all our critical processes in the CMT and the emergency management team, including information on how much time remains for them to be restarted. This results in our restart sequence, which in turn determines how we deploy our (usually scarce) resources.

From Practice: Guiding Questions for the Coordination of Business Continuation
When we need to coordinate the initiation of emergency operations of our critical business processes, we can be guided by questions such as:

- Which information or applications are affected by the incident and at the same time relevant for the processes critical according to → BIA?
- Which processes are affected by the incident?
- How much time do we have before they have to at least operate in emergency mode again?
- Do we have BCPs for these processes and do they describe workarounds for the information and applications affected by the incident?
- Can we activate the BCP for all the processes concerned at the same time, or are there interdependencies so that we have to follow a certain sequence?
- If we don't have BCP or workarounds: How can we improvise?
- . . .

From Practice: Reporting Liberates. . .
The success or failure of the continuation of business is determined by the extent to which the individual emergency bodies (CMT, communications team, situation center, emergency team, contingency teams) know what the status is with the other bodies. Their own decisions and options for action depend on this. Therefore, the mutual exchange of information is the be-all and end-all. In practice, it has proven useful to use fixed roles in the individual committees to coordinate the flow of information and to practice the cooperation between the committees in advance. This is especially essential for cases where existing BCPs are ineffective or do not exist in the first place. Then we have to improvise, for which the best way is to pool all our resources. This requires a common picture of the situation across all levels—which brings us back to the point that "reporting frees up . . . and burdens the strategic level".

That's It?
In fact, there is not much more behind the activation of the BCP of the critical (business) processes. Thus, compared to crisis management at the strategic level, at least the reactive part of BCM is remarkably under-complex. There are clear scenarios (failure IT etc.) and

concrete resources to compensate. The means, we only need our process specific BCPs, which have been tested by our contingency teams in peacetime already, and which are just waiting to be activated. There's just one small catch: The reactive part is only the tip of the iceberg when it comes to → BCM, as we will see elsewhere.

From Practice: Nothing Works Anymore
Another catch: experience shows that in very many cases we simply won't find any viable workarounds to compensate for the failure of applications, control systems or data. The higher the level of IT penetration in an organization, the more difficult it becomes. Therefore, the restart of IT systems is crucial.

3.3.1.2 Restart: IT Systems and Data
Goal of the Restart and Restore
(Business) processes are absolutely dependent on data and on a wide variety of IT systems. If data or IT systems are not available (for whatever reason), the process suffers and may even be interrupted. The aim of restarting IT systems and restoring data is therefore to make the data and applications available again to the critical (business) processes within a time frame to be defined in advance. In this way, IT makes its contribution to business continuity (ISO 27031 also explicitly refers to IRBC, ICT readiness for business continuity).

Babylonian Language Confusion: Restart, Restore, and Recovery
Around IRBC, we need to distinguish between three aspects that play a role in IT emergency management:

- Restart
  Restart is the fastest possible activation of the "surviving" parts of a redundant IT system and is the subject of crisis management on the IT side. Restart is the transition from normal to emergency operation. We are talking about hours here, ideally only minutes or even seconds.
- Restore
  A restore is the recovery of data and can be done from backups on different storage media (hard disk, SAN, cloud, tape backup, etc.). We are talking here about hours, but possibly also days.
- Recovery
  The recovery of IT systems is the subject of crisis follow-up (explicitly not crisis management). This involves rebuilding a "broken" system from scratch. This is usually time-consuming and restores the original redundancy. We may be talking about days or even weeks here.

Restart Times
When restarting our IT systems and restoring data, we work against the time constraints of our critical (business) processes. If a process may be interrupted for a maximum of 4 h

(MTO; maximum tolerable outage), it must (with a small safety buffer) have activated the business continuation plans and started emergency operation after three and a half hours (RTO—recovery time objective). And if it needs a specific application to do this, then we have its recovery time objective with it. The sum of the time requirements of the individual, successive measures necessary for the restart must not exceed this time target.

Restart Sequence: Rule of Thumb
While we are hardly able to show a restart sequence that is valid across industries and companies for (business) processes, we are only slightly more successful in this respect for IT-side restarts.

Mentally, however, we can at least make the following distinctions:

- Hardware vs. Software
- Sequential vs. parallel switching operations

These help us to understand the systematics behind the restart sequence. Further orientation is provided by the OSI model, which offers a kind of template for IT networks with its layers. The seven layers of the model start very fundamentally with bit transmission (physical layer) and extend to the application layer. In between (from bottom to top) are the data link layer, the network layer, the transport layer, the session layer, and the presentation layer.

From Practice: Restart Sequence
Since the IT systems have highly complex interdependencies (n-to-n relationships) and technologies such as an Enterprise Service Bus (ESB; has nothing to do with transporting people but is used for data transfer) or dynamically distributed Docker containers shake up traditional restart wisdom (keyword: unique inheritance paths), we must once again work with a rule of thumb. This ensures that the IT systems restart from the general to the specific partly one after the other and partly in parallel, i.e., each system reaches the required re-systems at its own start. Accordingly, depending on the available technologies and assuming that power and hardware are intact, we can orient ourselves to the following restart sequence:

Step one:
   One of the most complex parts of the restart comes right at the beginning: We may have to (re)activate the network components, i.e., switches, load balancers and firewalls. Usually, we work our way forward segment by segment and activate the core switch, the central connection point between two data centers. Caution: Depending on the complexity of the network, restarting the network components and interconnecting the individual segments takes several hours and offers some of the greatest potential for error of the entire restart. No question: As in countless other places, a virtualization solution can offer advantages here as well.

Step two:

Only when the network is up and running can it continue—with the SAN (Storage Area Network) on the one hand and with the so-called basic services on the other. Behind these are protocols and other services (Active Directory, LDAP, DNS, DHCP, etc.), which are prerequisites for all other services and applications.

Step Three:

When the network components, the SAN and the basic services have "settled in", we have reached a central point. Whereas we previously had to operate the restart sequentially, we can now move on to parallelizing our other switching operations. For example, we can simultaneously restart

- Physical Windows clusters,
- Physical Linux clusters,
- ESX hosts,
- Cloud Services,
- Exchange Cluster,
- IBM mainframe (if still in operation),
- Appliances and
- Other (stand alone) systems.

These platforms and system groups are mostly essentially independent of each other, so we can parallelize the restart. This saves time that we should invest in the last important step.

Step four:

Before we release the systems, we should at least test their basic functionalities. To a certain extent, this can be done internally in IT, but only to a certain extent. Therefore, it makes sense to involve test users from the departments before the official system acceptance and release. Only when we have their "go" can we consider the restart to be successful with a clear conscience.

Subsequently, we need to perform these steps in the failed data center as well in order to tackle the swing back and restore redundancy.

Technology Groups

"Technology group"is a term of art behind which the following idea is hidden: Most (larger) companies today have huge IT landscapes, sometimes with several thousand applications. To consider each application individually (to secure it, to provide it with restart plans, to test it etc.) is almost impossible. Therefore, it is important to form sensible groups that offer more practicable quantity structures while at the same time providing a high degree of meaningfulness. For this reason, we group (wherever possible) all systems (applications, servers, databases, etc.) on their lowest common denominator. This lowest common denominator is sometimes the operating system, sometimes a specific hardware,

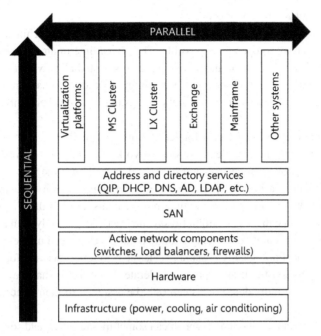

Fig. 3.6 Restart sequence of the technology groups

sometimes … just a technology group. If we can restart a technology group as a whole within a certain amount of time, the same must necessarily be true for the individual application that relies on it. A simple deduction. This is shown schematically in Fig. 3.6.

From Practice: Central Control of Restarting
In practice, it has proven useful to cast the individual steps for restarting a complete data center into a schedule based on the technology groups. The individual switching actions are numbered consecutively and called up individually or in groups by a central, coordinating unit (e.g. MoD, IRBC manager or IT emergency team). The basic rule is that no one begins a switching action without clearance from the central office. Coordination can be done through chats or web-based tools. It is important that all parties involved

- independently point out when they identify problems or delays;
- give their consent at neuralgic points so that the schedule can continue to be processed. These critical points include the restart of the network components, the basic services, the technology groups and the system acceptance tests (see above).

The central office records the times at which an individual switching action was called up and reported back as completed. This gives us a good overview of the time required for the individual steps. The schedule itself can initially be set up as an Excel file, and with increasing maturity we can fall back on more elaborate tools.

Restart Plans and Restore Concepts

We should automate the restart as far as possible, i.e., cast manual switching operations into scripts that are as easy to operate as possible. This saves time in an emergency, takes the pressure off the people involved and, above all, can be tested cleanly in advance.

However, the restore of data often fails without more or less extensive manual intervention, so that we should document and test the procedure in a comprehensible way.

From Practice: Grass Won't Grow Faster If You Pull on It

Depending on the size and complexity of our network, restarting the network components and basic services alone can take several hours and exceed our time limit. And we're not even talking about restarting the operating systems, let alone the individual applications or databases. We have to add up all these time requirements and run them against our time constraints. We can see this can get tight (to say the least). So, it's only human if we give in to the pressure and succumb to the temptation to parallelize or speed up the restart at points where it's just not technologically possible. A classic is to forego waiting for basic services to "settle in". Common to all attempts to accelerate the restart is that they produce error patterns in which the individual effects can only be assigned to their concrete cause with difficulty.

A lottery game, on the other hand, which can sometimes end well and sometimes badly, is the renunciation of (sometimes time-consuming) system acceptance and testing. Without such quality assurance measures, we should not release the restarted systems to our end users in the departments or customers. If all goes well, we've saved time. If not, well, reputation protection looks different.

From Practice: Using Time Reserves

Against this background, it is immediately obvious that we should use every time reserve we can find. Let's imagine that late one Friday evening, the re-cooling system in one of our data centers (data centers) fails. To protect against overheating, the systems in that DC will shut down in less than 45 min. Apart from the CSOC and the colleagues from IT operations/system control, no one is on site.

Prize question: How can we organize the restart in our fallback data center without having half the IT staff on hand? The answer is: by handing over the restart scripts from the IT production units to operations management. If we now also grant operations management the authority to start the scripts according to clear criteria and/or after approval by the manager on duty (MoD), we have gained valuable time.

3.3.2 Cybersecurity Incident Response

Events and Incidents

(Not only) in this chapter we work with the terms Events and Incidents. An event is any occurrence, while an incident is an occurrence with potentially negative effects on the confidentiality, integrity, availability, and authenticity of data and processes. In terms of set theory, Incidents are a subset of Events. Or: Not all events are incidents, but all incidents are events.

Cybersecurity Incident Response

Cybersecurity Incident Response (CSIR) is the process by which we can nip a cyber crisis in the bud and thus prevent it. Even if not, CSIR remains an essential part of the technical side of crisis management. To do this, we need clearly defined responsibilities, roles and tasks, as well as the best possible transparency about our systems, configurations and procedures. Always useful: information on where we can get help.

Typical Incidents

The most common types of incidents include

- Scans
  (a typical means for attackers to gain information; happens so often that we should at least automate evidence gathering)
- Compromises
  (any unauthorized access to an IT system or the information it processes is a compromise; sometimes difficult to detect in practice)
- Malicious code
  (worms, trojans, viruses, cryptolockers etc. are reported directly by (end) users or automatically by an IDS or intercepted by an IPS)
- DoS attacks
  (denial of service attacks flood systems with requests, overwhelming it; result: service is unavailable; difficult to defend)

3.3.2.1 Cybersecurity Incident Response Procedure

CSIR Process

The purpose of the CSIR process is to minimize the damage and can be divided into the following phases, for example:

- Identification
- Containment
- Elimination/Removal
- Recovery
- Lessons learned

Identification

The aim of this process step is to identify incidents and inform the people who can deal with this specific type of incident appropriately. We can gather these people, for example, in a → Cybersecurity Incident Response Team (CSIRT, see Sect. 4.1.4). But even the CSIRT cannot do without technical aids such as a tool for security information and event management (see Sect. 4.2.7).

Containment

The first priority should always be to take measures to contain the damage in the short term. This includes, for example, preventing (further) confidential information from leaking out or malicious code from spreading. The idea behind this is obvious: If we prevent the damage from spreading, we can keep the incident below the threshold that would require declaring an emergency or even a crisis.

We should also make backups of the images of the affected systems before cleaning them in the next step of the process. These images are the subject of the forensic investigation that we must also perform as part of incident handling.

In addition, we should take measures that enable us to provide the affected systems as quickly as possible and at least to a rudimentary extent until we have rebuilt them from scratch in the event of an emergency. This serves the IRBC, the provision of the IT systems without which our emergency-relevant (business) processes cannot function.

Elimination/Removal

In this step we take care of the removal of malicious code, malware, compromised systems etc. This creates the conditions for us to set them up cleanly again.

If we can already implement additional security measures—all the better. Otherwise, we will have to do this in the last two steps.

Recovery

The aim of the recovery phase is to restore the affected systems to their original state and reintegrate them into the productive environment. In doing so, we must pay particular attention to eliminating vulnerabilities by means of up-to-date patches and performing a thorough system acceptance. Likewise, we have to tackle the installation of the data backup in case the productive data was no longer available, or its integrity was questionable.

In doing so, we need to find answers to the following questions:

- When do we take the systems productive again? During the day, in the evening, at the weekend?
- What backup do we use and how do we make sure it's not compromised too?
- How do we test and verify that the systems are not only functional again, but actually clean?
- How long do we subject the systems to close monitoring to identify any conspicuous patterns of behavior?
- What tools do we use for this?

One thing is clear: At least for the first question, the Cybersecurity Incident Response Team cannot make decisions on its own but must coordinate with the IT emergency response team and/or the affected business functions.

Whether recovery takes place in the context of crisis management or post-crisis care depends to a significant extent on how the development of the crisis presents itself from the perspective of the CMT. What is important is that it takes place.

Lessons Learned
The lessons learned are discussed in Chap. 6.

3.3.2.2 Rules of Thumb for Cybersecurity Incident Response
Rules of Thumb
Since we don't have to go through every (painful) experience ourselves, we can use four rules of thumb to guide us. These are:

- Close monitoring of critical systems
- Do (NOT) shut down/shut down systems
- Communicate
- Document and save

These principles must be reflected in the → playbooks or (if there is no playbook for the specific situation) must be second nature to the cybersecurity incident response team.

Close Monitoring of Critical Systems
Two tools provide an introduction to the identification of critical systems: The Protection Needs Assessment (PDA, see Sect. 5.5) and the Business Impact Analysis (BIA, see Sect. 5.6.1). Very important: On this basis, we must identify all components that support the smooth operation of the critical systems. The latter include, for example, databases, firewalls, switches, routing, the connections between data centers and so on. This is where it helps us if our configuration management is as up-to-date and complete as possible and the IT architecture (or rather the enterprise architecture because we also want to keep an eye on the building infrastructures and production facilities) is cleanly documented.

Switch Systems Off?
While it may sound counterintuitive, shutting down systems for mitigation purposes is not always the best idea, even in the case of malicious code/malware-driven incidents. When systems are shut down and/or powered off, information is lost, such as that stored in the cache. However, it is this information that can be valuable when we are investigating the attack and trying to better understand the attacker's modus operandi. Both are important so that we can identify and close potential vulnerabilities. Therefore, it is often better to disconnect a computer from the network or isolate a network segment. In this way, we can

simultaneously prevent the spread of malicious code or malware, for example, and still obtain the information stored in the cache of the infected machines for IT forensic analysis.

If we do not have an orderly CSIR process in place, nor do we have a CSOC or CSIRT, the combination of shutdown/shutdown and disconnecting from the (W)LAN may be a viable option. Time is a critical factor, not only in the case of a spreading cryptolocker, so when in doubt, forensic analysis should take a back seat to containment. This also applies in the case that the encryption of data on a specific end device should be prevented at all costs.

Communication, Communication, and Again Communication

Communication is already important in routine situations and is not always easy. In the event of an incident—and we must bear this in mind—this applies even more. It is therefore important that we clearly regulate who communicates with whom, through what channels and on what occasions. In this way, we ensure dovetailing between the players involved in cybersecurity incident response at the technical level and cyber crisis management at the strategic level.

Documentation and Preservation of Evidence

Thorough documentation and backup of everything that happened on a technical level, as well as what we observed and did, is (unfortunately) essential. On the one hand, we need it for the (IT) forensic analysis and on the other hand, we can check afterwards where we acted expediently and where we acted inappropriately; in short: we can learn from it. Various stakeholders will also have an interest in clean documentation in the event of a case: Insurance companies, regulators and investigating authorities are among them. While Crisis Management has a dedicated role for documentation, this may not be practical for Incident Response, so each stakeholder will have to contribute themselves. This depends to a large extent on how the information and communication processes are designed and, above all, how they are practiced.

Important: Preserving evidence is not something we can do ex-post. Especially on a technical level, we need to collect evidence continuously—i.e., along the entire incident response process. Evidence includes, but is not limited to:

- Workstation computers, servers, other hardware
- Logs from security systems (SIEM, IDS, IPS, DLP, anti-virus software, etc.)
- Logs of network components
- Logs of the physical access system
- ...

Cyber Crisis Preparation

4

si vis pacem para bellum

4.1 Nothing for Regular Operations or: Emergency and Crisis Organization

Objective and Purpose of the Crisis Organization

What do the following—at first sight completely different—situations have in common?

- The diesel scandal in the automotive industry
- Attacks with cryptolockers on hospitals, for example in Neuss
- Accidents in (high-)risk environments, for example in a chemical park or power plants

At least this: To deal with them expediently, on the one hand we have to take the right measures for the immediate problem on an operational level, on the other hand we have to align these measures not only with the relevant target groups on a strategic level, but also make them known to you as well as interested third parties. Above all, someone needs to have the overview to coordinate the work of the different levels and roles, to make decisions and ultimately to take responsibility. Oh yes, and we should document the essential decisions and situation developments in a comprehensible way.

Organizational Structure

To get all this up and running in the shortest possible time is not possible with the line organization. For this reason, we need a special organization for the management of (cyber) crises, which is only activated depending on the situation: the emergency and crisis organization (ECO). This consists of at least a crisis management team (CMT) and can

© Springer Fachmedien Wiesbaden GmbH, part of Springer Nature 2021
H. Kaschner, *Cyber Crisis Management*,
https://doi.org/10.1007/978-3-658-35489-3_4

be expanded to include e.g., a communications team, a situation center, contingency teams, and incident response teams.

Rollers Instead of Heads

It is important that we staff the committees of our EOC according to roles, functions and tasks and, in doing so, break away from thinking in terms of specific people. Who is not familiar with the impulse to immediately think of a specific person in the face of a specific problem who can help solve it? This person helps quickly, reliably, and competently, knows what is important—and is the prime example of a single point of failure. Because often these people build up such a wealth of knowledge that they become head monopolies and others can no longer hold a candle to them. This becomes a problem when this person is not available—everyone is ill or on holiday. One or the other may even dare to retire or change employers.

In terms of crisis management, this means that we must not succumb to the temptation to think in terms of heads and simply let people do what they want. Instead, we must think in terms of roles and fill each role at least twice (substitution regulation).

Risk of Role Duplication

In practice, we regularly observe that several roles are bundled with one person. While this has the advantage of reducing the number of people who (want to or have to) have a say in the event of a crisis (which is a good thing at first), it also has the disadvantage that the work to be done in the crisis could exceed the capacity of a single person. In this respect, we should treat the bundling of several roles in one person with healthy respect.

From Practice: Roles Instead of People

Experience has taught us that we need to involve a considerable number of actors in the alerting, escalation, and management of cyber incidents. Thinking consistently in terms of roles rather than people has several advantages. We can

- Link decision-making powers and (IT) access rights to a role and in turn assign persons/users to the role;
- Define tasks and competences not only for one person but automatically for his or her deputies and use them for personnel development and recruitment (job advertisements!);
- Use the tasks of a role as a target within the framework of a training and awareness program (see Sects. 4.5 and 5.2) and prepare the role holders specifically for their tasks.

Important: This idea applies to all facets around cybersecurity in general and therefore also to cyber crisis management.

Multiple Levels of Crisis Management

Depending on the scope of the decision-making powers and capabilities, a distinction can be made between two or, if necessary, three levels of crisis organization. The top level is

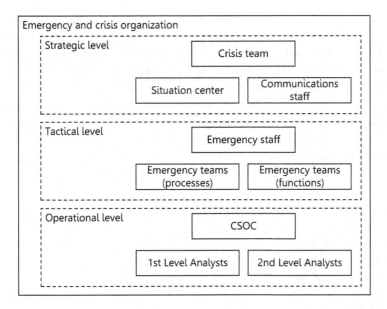

Fig. 4.1 Emergency and crisis organization

the strategic level. Below this is usually the tactical level, while the operational level refers to the immediate measures with local impact (see Fig. 4.1).

Disclaimer
The designations of the lower two levels are sometimes interchanged. This circumstance regularly leads to misunderstandings when consultants with solid half-knowledge are commissioned with the implementation of BCM and crisis organizations in the environment of people with experience from the fire brigade, disaster control, Bundeswehr, the police or other authorities.

Voluntariness Instead of Instructions
Whether at the strategic or operational-tactical level, experience shows that volunteers are the best choice for emergency and crisis management. Volunteers have a much higher level of commitment, are less likely to be absent in ad hoc situations, and are also less likely to withdraw in an emergency, for example due to unavailability or short-term illness. It is also clear, however, that we cannot always consider the wishes of the people concerned when it comes to key functions and qualifications.

What If Someone Does not Want to?
But what if someone does not want to be a member of the emergency and crisis organization (for whatever reason)? Then it is in our own interest to explore what the reluctance is all about. Often it is insecurity or even fear of not being able to cope with the situation.

What can I expect? What will happen if I make a mistake? We must and can counteract this fear. We have various instruments at our disposal for this purpose. Training and exercises help to reduce uncertainty about expectations in the long term. At the same time, participants build up specialist knowledge in crisis management and its related disciplines and acquire new skills that can also help them in their day-to-day business. The specialist knowledge and skills in turn not only increase confidence in their own abilities but can also make a substantial contribution to reducing personal stress levels in the long term.

Infrastructures and Tools
Emergency and crisis organizations often use the following infrastructure and tools:

- Crisis manual
- CMT's room
- Templates and posters
- Alerting tool
- Crisis management tool
- Governance suite
- IDS or SIEM tool
- . . .

4.1.1   The Rescue Team or: CMT

Core task of the CMT
The core task of the CMT is to keep the welfare of the organization as a whole in mind. Its guiding questions are:

- What is the situation?
- How does the situation affect relationships with key stakeholders and the strategic goals of the organization?
- What is the worst-case scenario that results from this?
- What do we need to do overall to prevent the worst-case scenario?
- Who does what until when?
- What support do we as a CMT/organization need to provide to those doing the tactical/ operational work?

Ergo: The CMT must initialize the CMT's working procedure and continue the crisis management process until we can return to normal operations.

Substitution, Stand-by and Availability Arrangements
At the latest when we deal with the question of whether our crisis organization is also capable of acting outside normal business hours, we have to deal with a substitution

arrangement. What use is the most fantastic CMT if the crisis is looming on Saturday morning, but no one can be alerted? Then a deputizing arrangement increases the chances considerably, especially if we combine it with an accessibility or standby arrangement. This can be designed in such a way that CMT members must be able to work in the CMT room or online within a certain time (for example 45 min) or be reachable at any time.

However, such arrangements are subject to co-determination and incur costs, as on-call services and availability must be adequately remunerated. For this reason, many organizations shy away from them, which is sometimes more, sometimes less understandable in view of the individual risk profile of the organizations. More on this in Sect. 3.1.3.

Interfaces

The CMT has interfaces within the organization, but also externally. Externally, depending on the division of labour with the other bodies of the emergency and crisis organization, these are the numerous stakeholders, which we deal with in detail elsewhere. Inside our organization, its interfaces are the management levels of the (business) functions, where its decisions are implemented, and measures are taken to manage the crisis. Other interfaces at the strategic level are the supervisory board and the works council, as well as the situation center and the communications staff. On the operational-tactical level, on the other hand, in the event of a cyber crisis, the following are mainly involved

- contingency teams,
- (business) emergency management team,
- IT emergency management team and
- Technical and support departments from the line organization

as major interfaces.

Conference Format

Once the crisis situation has been established, the question arises as to whether the CMT must meet physically or whether a decentralized set-up can be chosen.

Both variants have advantages and disadvantages. A physical meeting is usually not as quick to implement as a telephone or video conference, for example. On the other hand, it is more robust, face-to-face communication is more efficient and everyone has a view of the situation visualization.

The decentralised approach, on the other hand, allows the CMT members to remain closer to the operational units and thus to manage the implementation of the CMT's decisions more effectively.

But there is another aspect which is not entirely irrelevant to the question of whether the CMT should meet in person or merely meet by telephone: the frequency of meetings.

Meeting rhythm

Roughly speaking, we can distinguish three rhythms:

- Continuous
- On special occasions
- Regularly, but occasionally

A continuous meeting rhythm means that the CMT stays connected physically, by phone or by video conference until the crisis is over or at least a certain milestone is reached. That's one extreme. The other extreme is a purely occasion-based meeting rhythm. Here, the CMT only meets when there is a significant change in the situation. In between, we can have regular but ad hoc meetings. In this approach, the CMT meets at fixed times and works through all the process steps of the crisis management process once, starting with the control process step.

No question: Mixed forms between the last two variants are of course always possible.

Rule of Thumb

With increasing crisis duration, the meeting rhythm of a CMT usually shifts from continuous to regular to purely event-related meetings. The staffing of the communication team continues to dwindle until only the coordination function for crisis communication remains. The situation center—if it exists—remains continuously staffed until the end of the crisis, which has to be formally declared.

4.1.1.1 The Organizational Framework of the CMT
Basic Requirements

At the strategic level, the CMT is THE central body for crisis management. To do this, it must have clout. This presupposes that it is what one might call "competent and able to make decisions". Decision-making competence means that the crisis management team can make decisions at short notice and without consultation with, or even further approval from, the organization's management or senior management. Decision-making capability, on the other hand, means that on the one hand it must be regulated how a decision is reached in the event of divergent opinions within the CMT itself. On the other hand, the CMT must not become too large, as otherwise discussions can get out of hand and valuable time is wasted.

Budget

To ensure that the CMT can also raise money in case of doubt, organizations often provide a so-called crisis budget. Depending on the composition of the CMT (management!), it sometimes does not even have a fixed upper limit.

The budget itself is often provided via two different cost centres. One cost centre comprises the funds for financing ongoing operations outside times of crisis. This includes personnel costs (some organizations have separate Incident and Crisis Management or Business Continuity and Crisis Management units in their organizational chart for regular operations) and material costs (further training, external support for training, exercises and awareness measures, licence fees for a crisis management tool, consultancy for the further development of the crisis management organization, travel costs, etc.). The other cost center, on the other hand, comprises funds intended solely for dealing with an ad hoc situation.

From Practice: Crisis Budgets

It is sometimes the case that the expenses associated with crisis prevention, crisis preparation, crisis management and crisis follow-up are spread over several budgets. The spectrum ranges from personnel development budgets for training to material cost budgets for IT projects or consulting services to the line budgets of individual (business) functions. Some organizations, on the other hand, work with a special, central budget for the CMT. This (like so many things) has advantages and disadvantages. What is an advantage and what is a disadvantage depends on the perspective. So instead, we prefer to work with the terms properties or consequences. One property is that in this way we gain full transparency about costs. Another is that in this way we reduce the number of people who have a say in how the budget is used and thus in setting priorities.

Limitation of Liability

One concern that often preoccupies CMT decision-makers in particular is that of liability. Decisions made by the CMT can be far-reaching—after all, it is a strategic body that must have the entire organization and its well-being in mind. This concern can affect the quality of decision-making. A tendency arises to make defensive decisions, i.e., those involving the least personal risk to the decision maker. However, defensive decisions are not necessarily in the best interests of the organization (see Sect. 2.1). Senior managers therefore often have directors and officers liability insurance (D&O; a special form of professional liability insurance). Such insurance can help, but only as long as certain clauses do not apply. And not every CMT member (and certainly not members of the operational-tactical crisis organization) has such insurance. In practice, therefore, most organizations resort to the instrument of limiting the liability of CMT members. The limitation of liability (or indemnity) relates to consequences arising from crisis management decisions and actions. This reduces the pressure on the persons acting, which improves the overall quality of decision-making.

4.1.1.2 Manning of the CMT

Rule of Thumb

When putting together the CMT, we can follow a simple rule of thumb: As small as possible, as large as necessary.

Why the limitation by the "as small as possible"? There are several reasons for this. Firstly, many cooks spoil the broth, i.e., the work of the CMT does not necessarily get better just because more people are involved. Secondly, we have to keep the rest of the organization running—and the areas that are not directly involved in crisis management have to contribute to this in particular.

From Practice: Core CMT and Extended CMT

It therefore makes sense to divide the CMT into a core CMT and an extended CMT. The roles that are always involved in crisis management, regardless of the type of crisis, are represented in the core CMT. The extended CMT is made up of specialists and managers whose expertise adds value on a scenario-specific basis. A simple example of this: The role of the crisis management team is universal, whereas in the case of a hacker attack, the expertise of the pandemic officer is probably initially dispensable.

The separation into a core and an extended CMT has various advantages. These include, for example, the fact that we can create a focus within the framework of crisis training and exercises by taking particular account of the needs of the members of the core CMT. This in turn means that, irrespective of the specific crisis situation, there is always a fixed core of people involved in crisis management who are proficient in the initialisation and crisis management process, who bring with them appropriate routine and who radiate calm. With regard to stress and leadership aspects, this is a central point: the members of the core CMT can provide orientation, support and guidance for the remaining colleagues.

However, it is also clear that a great deal of responsibility rests on the core CMT and its members, since—unlike the members of the extended CMT—it can never remove itself from the line of fire. It is therefore all the more important that we prepare the members of the core CMT intensively for an emergency, whatever that may be.

Roles in the Core CMT

The composition of the core CMT is largely independent of the industry. It typically consists of the following roles:

- Head of CMT
- Executive member of the CMT
- Communication
- Law
- Protocol

To bring relieve to the CMT leader, one role is useful that we unfortunately rarely encounter: that of the managing member of the CMT (not: member of the management in the CMT). This role coordinates the staff's work along with the underlying processes and thus enables the CMT leader to concentrate on the essentials: maintaining an overview and making expedient decisions. For those of us with a military background, the CMT leader is the equivalent of the commander and the executive member of the chief of staff (J3), while the leadership of our organization (board, president, executive management, etc.) is the higher-level leadership.

A visualizer can also provide good services. It continuously translates the (usually complex) situation picture into a representation that conveys the essential information to the CMT members at a glance. He can work with both written and visual language. In the case of visual language, it is advisable to work with representations that can be understood equally by all CMT members—a clear disadvantage for the extensive and well thought-out visual language used in the official context. The tactical signs used there are absolutely well thought-out and very comprehensive, but unfortunately not immediately self-explanatory for people who do not have a background in the German armed forces, fire brigade, police, etc.

Roles in the Extended CMT

The extended CMT, on the other hand, consists of representatives of the areas and topics that are only needed in certain scenarios. These can be (in alphabetical order):

- Health, safety, and environment (HSE)
- BCM officer
- Business functions
- Compliance
- External advisors
- Facilities management
- Finance
- Money laundering
- IT
- Quality management
- Regulatory
- Safety
- Security/Corporate Security
- Pandemic Preparedness
- Staff
- Provider Management
- . . .

This list—see also Fig. 4.2—is still not complete. It does not have to be at this point, because it shows us why the division into a core and an extended CMT makes sense. It is hardly practicable to prepare so many role holders (first, second and, if necessary, even third cast members!) equally intensively for their tasks in the event of a crisis—and it is even less practicable to have all these roles meet in an emergency, irrespective of the specific scenario.

Tasks of All CMT Roles

With regard to the tasks of the CMT members, there is a lowest common denominator. Always related to their own area of responsibility

- Advising the head of the CMT, and
- "Translation" of the technical aspects -
  - linguistically for the rest of the CMT members and

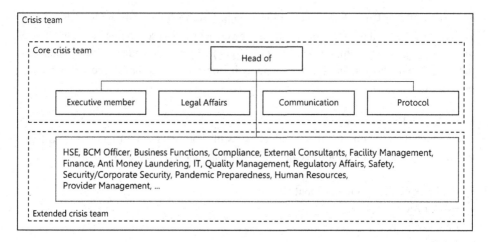

Fig. 4.2 CMT

- organizational, i.e. between the CMT and the tactical-operational level, the line functions or external agencies.

    The only roles with deviating tasks are those that are entrusted with coordination and support tasks instead of technical ones. These include the minute-taker and, if we provide for such roles, the visualiser and the executive member of the CMT.

Important Roles in a Cyber Crisis

But which roles should we assemble in the CMT in a cyber crisis? In practice, the following structure has proven to be effective:

- Core CMT
- Data Protection Officer
- IT
- Information Security
- Sales/Affected Business Functions/Customer Managers

    As well as depending on the situation

- BCM officer (if the availability of information is impaired and this has an impact on critical business processes)
- Regulation (depending on the industry)
- External experts (crisis consultants and—in the case of outsourced IT—representatives of the IT provider)

Decision-Making Authority

This composition ensures that the CMT always keeps an eye on the perspectives and thus the expectations of the key stakeholders and aligns its measures accordingly. After all, the goal must be to meet the stakeholders' expectations as well as possible in order to maintain their trust in our organization.

But enough about the decision-making competence (because we want to guarantee this through an appropriate composition and definition of the powers of the individual roles as well as of the entire body). Let's take a look at the quorum.

Quorum

After all, what use are all our decision-making powers if, in the end, we do not have a quorum? We can ensure the latter in two ways: First, by concentrating decision-making power with the CMT leader. This is the so-called Highlander principle ("There can be only one"), which is applied in the military and in blue-light organizations, among others. There the principle applies: responsibility is indivisible.

Second, by a democratic vote of all voting CMT members, with the CMT leader's vote counting twice in case of doubt. This is the US Senate model, where the vote of the Vice President of the US (also President of the Senate) breaks a stalemate.

Regardless of which process we establish, three principles apply:

1. We need to establish the procedure in peacetime, document it, and familiarize the people involved with it.
2. The procedure should be of a fundamental nature, i.e., based on the roles, and not dependent on the possible persons performing these roles on a case-by-case basis.
3. Even in the case of the Highlander principle, the CMT should always be a collegial body in which all participants can express their assessments and proposed solutions openly and without fear, and discuss them among themselves. This is the only way that the role holders can adequately fulfil their advisory role vis-à-vis the CMT leader.

4.1.1.3 The Crucial Question: Who Would Be Better (Not) to Be a Member of the CMT

Crux Question No. 1: Member of the Executive Board in the CMT?

One question we regularly encounter in our consulting practice is: Should top management be a member of the CMT or not? There are good reasons for both.

Pro

This is supported by the fact that the interfaces of the CMT are reduced, at least selectively. If the top management itself is part of the CMT, it does not have to be informed separately. Another argument in favor of this approach is that it takes account of the personal responsibility that members of the Executive Board predominantly have.

Contra

The argument against this, however, is that board members are needed more urgently elsewhere in a crisis. It can and must make a significant contribution to maintaining the trust of high-ranking stakeholders. The more important the stakeholder, the more intensive its support must be in times of crisis. Whether regulators, the media, suppliers, business partners and, in the B2B environment, customers: This is where board members are called upon. And not just once and sporadically, but in a way that is perceived by the respective counterpart as building trust. This costs time—time that we don't have if we as board members are actively involved in the immediate work of the CMT. Even if the board of directors takes over the communication in the direction of selected stakeholders, enough still remains with the CMT, as the quote from a CMT leader from a public administrative body shows as a summary after a cyber attack:

> My management level tried to keep some of the external pressure off us. Still, nearly 50 percent of my capacity went to bearding people who thought they had stakes in the matter.

Another practical aspect that speaks against membership of members of the board of directors in the CMT is their self-protection. In the CMT, ideas and approaches are discussed, rumors are evaluated for their credibility, and attempts are made to verify them. Possible failures become as much a topic as—this is human and happens again and again—potentially premature blaming of third parties. Now we come to the first part of the crucial point. If you know a lot, you can reveal a lot. But: we don't have to reveal everything, but everything we reveal must correspond to the facts. Against this background, we should divulge as little internal information from the CMT as possible and, above all, we should not engage in speculation. The second part of the crucial point is: A crisis is a stressful situation and going in front of the camera in such a situation is always a challenge even for PR professionals. It's even more of a challenge for people who have had no special training for it. It's human to say more (or different things) under such pressure than we've worked out in advance. And the more insight we've gained into the nitty gritty of crisis management through CMT membership, the more we can blurt out. With all the negative personal consequences.

But What About the Competency, Budget, and Accountability Issues?

A frequent objection is that without the membership of the management, the competences, or the scope of disposal are not sufficient. The underlying concern ("The CMT may not be able to act!") is understandable, but can be resolved quite simply by giving the CMT far-reaching competencies and an appropriate budget. Rules of procedure are an effective way of doing this.

This leads seamlessly to the question of accountability. KonTraG, VAG, MaRisk, ITSiG and HGB (to name a few of the relevant legal requirements) demand in very general terms that the management must take organizational measures to ensure the functioning of the organization (accountability). But nowhere does it say that the executive board members themselves and personally have to lead the crisis management.

Crux Question No. 2: Press Spokesman in the CMT?
Should the press spokesperson be a member of the CMT? After all, he must know what to tell the media in the form of simple statements, press conferences, or interviews.

Here, too, the following applies: Those who know a lot can tell a lot. Those who know too much can tell too much. Therefore, the press spokesperson should not be a member of the CMT under any circumstances, but "only" disseminate the core messages and statements released by the CMT. In order to know these, he does not have to be a member of the CMT, on the contrary. A proper briefing on the key findings and on the communication strategy is sufficient for this. Similar to the board members, the press spokesperson also has much better things to do during a crisis than to lose himself in staff work, namely, to show himself and thus contribute to maintaining confidence in the organization.

4.1.2   Situation Center

Aim and Purpose of the Situation Center
A situation center relieves the CMT by acting as an extended arm to the outside world, but above all within the organization.

The job of the situation center is to,

- monitor the implementation of the decisions taken by the CMT
and, if we don't use a separate communications staff.

- receive and process (inbound) incoming information and, if necessary
- coordinate outgoing information (outbound).

The situation centre is bound by instructions to the CMT and, as its extended arm, is usually authorized to issue instructions to all other bodies of the emergency and crisis organization on communication issues.

Manning and Technical Equipment
To this end, we can set up the situation center in the same way as the CMT with regard to the topics, i.e., assign a functionary to the side of a head of the situation center for each CMT role. Beyond this mirroring, however, other approaches are just as conceivable. This can make sense in particular if we want to coordinate outbound communication via the situation center. In this case, we need to plan additional capacities for this. Ensuring that all relevant internal and external stakeholders are informed in a timely manner and in a manner that is appropriate for the target group is an immensely important task that cannot be

performed in passing. Even if we do not assign this task to the situation center: We will not be able to avoid making a few organizational arrangements for it.

Either way, we need to provide appropriate technical equipment not only for the crisis management room, but also for the situation center. In the case of the situation center, the most important thing is communication and visualization capabilities. Enough telephones (with technical redundancies; from VoIP, satellite, analogue, to ISDN) including headsets, large monitors, beamers, smart or white boards and flip charts are particularly important.

Interfaces
The main interfaces of the situation center are:

- Crisis management team
- Communications staff
- Emergency management team
- Contingency teams
- External stakeholders (depending on the scenario)

4.1.3 Communications Staff

Aim and Purpose of the Communications Staff
The communications staff is the body that coordinates our crisis communications so that they are done

- quickly,
- target group-oriented,
- cross-stakeholder inconsistency,
- reliable and
- internally and externally.

It is bound by the instructions of the CMT and, as its extended arm, is usually authorized to issue instructions to all other bodies of the emergency and crisis organization on communication issues.

Tasks
In essence, the task of the communications unit is to develop the crisis communications strategy to relieve the CMT based on the objectives of the CMT's work as defined by the CMT.

- to design,
- implement or
- and to monitor their implementation.

To do this, the communications staff needs capacity for:

- (Social) media monitoring
- Inbound communication
- Outbound communication

To avoid misunderstandings: The people who represent these capacities do not necessarily have to be members of the communication staff. It is sufficient if they work with it. Even and especially in crisis situations, our stakeholders are happy to deal with the contacts they already know on our side. Trust is the key word.

Manning of the Communication Staff

However, we should assemble representatives of all line functions in the communications team who also have to communicate with our stakeholders on a day-to-day basis. They know their needs best. Typically, these are:

- Press/communication (external)
- Internal communication
- Distribution
- Regulatory affairs
- . . .
- IT (as interpreter for technical topics)

Such an interdisciplinary composition and good preparation (see Sect. 4.4) may become the decisive factor in crisis management.

Interfaces

The main interfaces of the communication staff are:

- Crisis management team
- Situation center
- Emergency management team
- Contingency teams
- External stakeholders
- Internal stakeholders

4.1.4   Emergency Bodies at the Tactical-Operational Level

Emergency Management Team

Depending on the size, location, business model, and risk profile of our organization, it may make sense for us to establish an emergency response team in addition to the CMT. If we set it up, it is the central steering committee for events in which we must coordinate a more or less complex restart of (business) processes and/or IT systems.

In principle, the emergency task force has similar tasks to a crisis task force, but with one not entirely insignificant difference: the emergency task force is responsible not only for crises, but also for events that we consider to be emergencies. Since the emergency usually comes before the crisis (is a preliminary stage, so to speak), we can also see the emergency unit as the CMT's little brother. In this context, the big brother (CMT) is authorized to issue instructions to the little brother.

Contingency Teams
Making the will of the CMT, the situation center and the emergency management team a reality is the task of the contingency teams. We should set up contingency teams for

- (Business) processes that we have identified as relevant to emergencies;
- IT and telecommunications systems that are indispensable in an emergency.

The contingency teams report to the emergency management team or the situation center (if we want to use such bodies), alternatively directly to the crisis staff (e.g. to the BCM officer and the IT representative). They consist of a leader as well as experts for the specific content-related tasks. For example, in an IT contingency team we gather specialists for databases, operating systems, networks, cloud, virtualization, etc., while in an emergency team for a banking-specific topic, such as payment transactions, specialists for transaction banking tend to play the decisive role.

To prevent prolonged stress or to compensate for the absence of individual persons, we should organize the contingency teams in the same way as the other bodies of the emergency and crisis organization on a role-based basis and fill each role with several persons.

On the one hand, the contingency teams need business continuation plans, restart and recovery plans, and restore concepts for their work. On the other hand, we should also provide them with infrastructural framework conditions under which they can pursue their demanding work over a longer period of time if necessary.

For more information, see Sects. 3.3 and 4.6.

CSIRT and CSOC
The (cyber) (security) incident response teams (CSIRTs) are on the move at the technical level (virtually in the depths of IT). In the event of an incident, they are usually the first to notice anomalies and thus the first to react—by taking operational countermeasures on the one hand and triggering the alert on the other.

To ensure an adequate response on a technical level, we first need the ability to detect anomalies—24 h a day, 7 days a week, 365 days a year. We need to assess these anomalies and follow up when they are appropriately critical. To do this, we can establish a CSOC, a Cybersecurity Operations Center. The CSOC is staffed in shifts by what are called first level analysts. If they discover an incident and an initial investigation substantiates the initial suspicion, they trigger the alert and hand over the incident to the second level analysts for further containment and analysis. first level and second level are bound by instructions to the IT emergency team.

The team of first and second level analysts should not only have extensive, but also in-depth IT and IT security know-how. This includes first and foremost knowledge about the correct response to incidents (incident response, incident handling), but also about the structure and security aspects of networks and protocols, operating systems, mobile devices, databases, cloud and virtualization solutions, hosts, etc.

For 24/7 shift operation, we need at least six full-time employees in the first level alone, whereby no one is allowed to drop out with this headcount and without even one shift being double-staffed (keywords: peaks, dual control principle). It is therefore better to have seven, if not eight or nine people. This is a cost factor that should not be underestimated, especially since the second level analysts are also added. On top of that, there are the costs for so-called SIEM tools, technical solutions for security information and event management, without which the CSOC cannot function. For this reason, many organizations refrain from building up their own staff for a CSOC and instead fall back on corresponding service offers from special service providers.

4.2   Infrastructures and Tools

4.2.1   Crisis Manual

Purpose of a Crisis Manual

The crisis manual is the central tool for the CMT—regardless of the specific nature of the crisis in question. It summarizes the information that the CMT actually needs in a real crisis in a short, concise, and to the point manner.

Typical Contents: Sample Structure

A crisis manual should provide the following information:

- Descriptions of the roles, tasks and competencies of the CMT members;
- A description of the process for initializing crisis management (alerting and first steps of the CMT);
- A description of the process by which each crisis is managed from initialization to its formal conclusion;
- Optional specific guidelines for selected high-risk scenarios, e.g., for
  - Situations involving injuries or even deaths,
  - Situations involving VIPs,
  - Searches by investigating authorities
  - ...

- Checklists, e.g., for the
  - Checking whether a crisis situation exists,
  - Situation report
  - …
- Templates, e.g., for
  - The visualization of situation images,
  - The crisis log/logbook,
  - The development of the worst-case scenario
  - …
- Universal communication modules, e.g., holding statements, Q + A, or lists with negative buzz words
- Contact lists:
  - CMT (core)
  - CMT (additional functions)
  - Other bodies of the security, emergency, and crisis organization
  - Internal stakeholders
  - External stakeholders
  - …
- Glossary

Crisis Manual Specifically for Cyber Crises?
Cyber crises are one of the typical high-risk scenarios that we can back up with more concrete action guides. However, a separate manual designed only for cyber crises is not really appropriate. After all, we need to familiarize CMT members with each crisis-relevant tool in such a way that they actually perceive it as a tool in an acute crisis situation.

Requirements for a Crisis Manual
When we set out to create the crisis manual, we need to keep the following requirements in mind:

- Availability
- Simplicity and essentiality
- Comprehensibility
- Acceptance

Availability
First, everyone who is to work with it must have immediate access to it—regardless of time and place. That means, if necessary, even at the weekend and at home. This sounds logical, banal, and downright trivial with today's technical possibilities, but in practice it has its pitfalls. For example, we regularly experience that crisis manuals are subject to a certain confidentiality classification due to their sensitive content. This is not only understandable, but even highly recommended. However, it becomes difficult when the classification

means that it is not allowed to leave the premises of the organization in paper form. This leaves only access to digital versions of the manual from home, which is only partially convincing in cyber scenarios (unless we assume files stored locally on a service note-book). Who says that the specific cyber scenario does not also restrict or even prevent access to the crisis manual?

Simplicity and Essentiality

The handling should be as simple as possible, so that in a crisis time and energy do not flow unnecessarily into finding the information that actually helps us. A clear structure and, if necessary, visual user guidance, for example by means of colors or picture elements, help us to do this.

However, it is at least as important that the crisis manual only contains information that is relevant for the immediate management of the event. In practice, unfortunately, we often find extensive risk analyses or information on dealing with events at incident or emergency level. This unnecessarily inflates the crisis manual and sometimes turns the search for crisis-relevant explanations into a search for a needle in a haystack.

Comprehensibility

The language used in the manual should be as clear as possible so that we immediately understand what is meant even in stressful situations. Academic-theoretical discussions and abstract formulations have no place in a crisis manual. Technical terms that are unavoidable but may not be equally familiar to all users of the manual must be explained in a glossary.

Acceptance

However, it is essential that the CMT members (especially the core CMT) accept the manual as a tool. Experience has shown that the criteria already mentioned are necessary preconditions for this. Whether they also pass as sufficient prerequisites depends on the concrete ideas and requirements of the CMT members. It is therefore advisable to involve this group in the development of the crisis manual—at the latest during the validation of the contents by means of a walk-through or a practical training session in which the participants have to work through simple but concrete cases with the aid of the manual.

From Practice: Good + good ≠ very good

Would you like a practical example of how good content can nevertheless become problematic? Well then, let's take a situation in which the crisis manual lacked simplicity and comprehensibility. Redundancies and competing methods are the keywords.

In the context of a mandate, we encountered the following situation: A client (an operator of critical infrastructures; the industry and even more so the name is irrelevant here) emerged from the split-up of a corporate group. From the group, the client had inherited large parts of the group's security organization as well as an extensive set of checklists that the CMT was to use for crisis management. Based on a crisis management tool (which had not been introduced), another checklist had been created to manage the overarching crisis management process, which was based on the classic management process. In addition, a new manager who had joined the company brought along FOR-DEC as a method for the crisis management process. This resulted in a further checklist.

Based on the draft of the crisis manual, the customer wanted to have its CMT leaders trained for the first time with external support specifically in the recording of CMT work. Since we had trained the CMT members of a competitor several times in the past, the customer approached us about this.

As part of the preparation, we first gained an impression of the draft crisis manual—after all, the CMT leaders should be able to use the crisis manual as effectively as possible in their crisis teamwork after the training. It quickly became clear: the individual checklists were

- all bundled and numbered in the appendix (good!);
- each thought out (good!);
- partly redundant to each other (already less good);
- only partially intertwined (bad);
- only partially intertwined with the leadership process checklist (bad);
- only conditionally interleaved with FOR-DEC (bad);
- partly in competition with each other (quite bad).

So all in all, it's a bit of a mess. So what to do? Since we rarely do ourselves any favors by strictly dictating anything ex cathedra to our own superiors, I suggested presenting the CMT members with two different possible combinations as well as the approach to initializing crisis teamwork from this book and letting them choose which approach or approaches they wanted to try out through practical exercises. Result: the participants settled quite quickly on one method and a few checklists, so that the company was able to adapt the crisis manual more and more to it. Those who participate accept.

Limits of a Crisis Manual
Despite all the useful features of a crisis manual, it can only help to think through the first few hours of a crisis in a reasonably concrete way—for everything else, the course of events varies too much from one crisis case to the next and goes beyond the scope of what can be prepared and written down with a reasonable number of resources. Also, even scenario-specific guidelines should only ever be understood as a guide, as the actual situation will usually always differ slightly from that assumed in the crisis manual.

However, the crisis manual can and must record the crisis management process by means of which any type of crisis can be managed. For the solutions that have to be developed within the framework of the process, the following applies: GMV—common sense. There is no substitute for it.

4.2.2 CMT Room

Purpose of a CMT Room

A fixed location prepared for the CMT has several advantages. First of all, the set-up times are reduced in order to get the CMT operational in an acute situation purely in terms of infrastructure. In addition, the equipment can be specially adapted to the needs of the CMT. The psychological component should not be underestimated either: By moving into the CMT room, the CMT members also leave their everyday business behind spatially and can thus concentrate much better on the essentials. Practical side effect: A predefined CMT room saves us having to discuss where the CMT should meet in the event of an emergency. But beware: In order to prevent the risk of a failure of the building or the basic infrastructure (electricity, water, heating/air conditioning), we should define an alternative room, equip it comparably and make it known among the CMT members.

Construction Requirements

- View and eavesdropping protection
- Access to a non-public underground car park
- Sanitary facilities within reach
- Sufficient space (at least 15 people)
- 24/7 access for CMT members
- Adjacent premises where CMT members can make undisturbed telephone calls
- Adjacent premises for the communication staff and the situation center
- Rest and retreat facilities
- . . .

Why These Requirements?

Some of the requirements are self-explanatory, others, from experience, not necessarily. The latter usually include the aspects "view and eavesdropping protection" as well as "non-public underground car park access".

Depending on the severity of a crisis or the extent of public interest in it, there are always cases where information is taken directly from the crisis management room. How? The answer is simple: journalists or interested third parties can lie in wait nearby and—using a good lens and a little luck with regard to the lighting conditions—photograph what we project onto the screen in the crisis management room. But that's not all:

If you have a little money in your hand and a certain elasticity towards legal restrictions (be careful, a euphemism!), you can use directional and laser microphones to listen in on conversations specifically through open (directional microphone) and even closed windows (laser microphone). We should keep these possibilities in mind when choosing and equipping a crisis management room.

Direct access to a non-public underground car park has the advantage that, if the worst comes to the worst, CMT members do not have to maneuver their way past waiting journalists—as is the case with an outdoor car park. This protects the CMT members from questions and deprives journalists of the opportunity to take pictures without reflective car windows.

Equipment of the CMT Room

The following equipment should be in our crisis room:

- Projector or comparable visualization option (e.g., smartboard)
- TV
- Fax
- (Network) printer
- PC/notebook with network access and prepared protocol template and, if necessary, access to the crisis management tool
- Telephone (landline; ideally with analogue connection)
- Satellite phone
- Patched network outlets
- WLAN
- Spare batteries for notebooks and mobile phones (depending on model)
- . . .

Beyond the ICT components just mentioned, we also need:

- FlipChart, whiteboard incl. pens and paper
- Table display with crisis staff rolls (printed on both sides)
- Physical copies of the crisis manual
- Extension cables, multiple sockets
- . . .

Alternatives to a CMT Room

We will not always have the chance (or need) to physically assemble the crisis management team, especially in the case of organizations set up in a decentralized manner across several locations. As an alternative, we should prepare options that enable a decentralized CMT meeting, i.e. virtual conference rooms for telephone or video conferences. Again, we always need to ensure is availability and manageability for all participants, while adequately reducing the risk of being overheard (intentionally or unintentionally). At the same time, we need to think about sharing essential information in real time. Standard tools such as Microsoft Teams and Sharepoint, Slack, Confluence, or even special crisis management tools can help here.

4.2.3 Templates and Posters

Purpose of Templates and Posters
The purpose of templates, posters and templates is quickly explained: to handle regularly recurring tasks and situations more efficiently in the CMT's working procedure. Such tools complement the crisis manual and the checklists contained therein.

Fields of Application
Typical templates and posters support with

- the initialization of the CMT's working procedure, e.g., through prepared cards and templates for
  - the situation assessment with the W-questions,
  - the most common stakeholders,
  - the basic (but to be specified) objectives,
  - the worst-case scenario;
- the visualization of the situation development;
- the presentation of the high-level communication strategy and
- keeping the CMT log (see Sect. 3.2.1)
- ...

4.2.4 IT-Supported Crisis Management Tools

Purpose of Crisis Management Tools
IT-supported crisis management tools help to set up crisis management across locations and time zones and to orchestrate all those involved in crisis management. In this way, more effective control of individual measures and distribution of relevant information is to be achieved.

As a rule, the CMT members themselves work less intensively with such a tool than the people in the situation center or in decentralized emergency management teams.

Advantages
Software-based crisis management tools usually offer functionalities such as:

- Workflows, e.g., for task management or action tracking along the crisis management process
- Telephone and video conferencing functionalities
- Information sharing system (press releases, social media posts, videos, audio files, etc.).
- Documentation/logbook function with time stamp
- Revision security

- Interfaces to alerting tools and GRC suites[1]

There are online and offline solutions, entire suites or lean applications that can be installed comparatively quickly and easily. Hosting can often be outsourced to the provider, as can (to a certain extent) the operation. In this way, the reliability is increased, but the effort in terms of control and costs increases.

Disadvantages

One disadvantage is the cost—both initial and ongoing. The running costs depend, among other things, on the number of users who are allowed to use the tool in principle and, above all, at the same time. In addition, there are initial costs for acquisition and company-specific configuration.

In addition, there is another practical disadvantage: A crisis represents an exceptional situation, which automatically brings with it an increased stress level. Who would want to handle additional tools in such a situation, which they usually use at best once a year for 1 or 2 h as part of an exercise? How realistic is it that such a tool can unfold its full (manufacturer-promised) benefit and represent a real added value under these general conditions? Of course, through a user interface that is as self-explanatory as possible, good training during the introduction of the tool and regular training sessions during the year in which the tool shall be used, this disadvantage can be levelled out to a certain extent. However, this results in additional efforts (time, costs).

Another critical point cannot be dismissed out of hand: What we record in such a tool is documented once and for all and can be directly traced by auditors, investigating authorities, insurance companies—in other words, anyone who subsequently makes demands on the organization or at least checks it. This regularly depends on nuances and formulations. Now the exciting question: Does everyone who has to work with the tool under stress in an emergency have the necessary intuition when it comes to weighing up exactly how a certain piece of information should be formulated? There is no question that this consideration is irrelevant from a purely formal legal point of view, since we must always assume that everything is done correctly and that all those involved act to the best of their knowledge and belief. Nevertheless, it is well-founded.

Principle

Since in cyber crises we always have to expect that exactly the IT tools we need for our crisis management will be affected, the old principle applies, especially to a strategic body like the CMT: as many technical helpers as necessary, but please as few as possible. The CMT must be able to do its work without any great technical aids.

---

[1] GRC stands for Governance, Risk and Compliance and focuses on BCM, ITSCM, ISM and Cyber Risk Management in the context of Cyber Crisis Management.

Against this background, small and medium-sized enterprises (SMEs) in particular should carefully consider whether the theoretical benefits to be expected are in a healthy relationship to the costs that are certain to be incurred.

4.2.5 Alerting Tools

Purpose of Alerting Tools

Alerting tools automate the alerting of the group of people needed to deal with a particular event, (hopefully) speeding up the whole process.

Advantages

Automated alerting saves time—and we have already seen how important the time factor is in crisis management. In addition to the time saved compared to a classic alerting based on a call tree (telephone cascade), common tools can also alert different groups of people depending on the scenario (after all, there are not only cyber crises). For this purpose, prefabricated voice recordings in combination with calls can be used as well as text-based alerts via SMS, e-mail, or messengers. All these variants contain instructions on how to proceed. Some alerting tools also provide a virtual conference room.

Another advantage over a call tree is robustness. With a call tree, if a crucial person is unavailable (for example, because they actually interpret free time as free time on an idyllic Saturday evening with no on-call hours), the entire phone cascade stalls and potentially crucial people cannot be contacted. An alerting tool, on the other hand, skips those who don't acknowledge an alert and moves on to the next contact. And if that is not reached either, to the next. And if this one is also not reached . . . The principle should have become clear.

Special Feature

It is important for all alerting tools to have an interface to personnel management systems (contact data!) and emergency planning tools. Ideally, such tools have their own alerting function or offer an interface to alerting tools. The latter is particularly recommended, as it reduces the number of IT systems required and thus the number of reciprocal interfaces, as well as the costs for acquisition, customizing, implementation and operation (license costs!). Not to mention the effort required to keep the data stock in different systems up-to-date and as complete as possible.

Disadvantages

In practice, we regularly encounter two disadvantages:

- The cost of having a sufficient number of end users can be quite significant—and ongoing.

- An alerting tool is only as good as the contact details it can access and the arrangement that forces us to respond outside normal working hours. If, for example, the members of the crisis organization do not release private contact details due to data protection considerations and an accessibility or on-call regulation is missing, even the best tool will only be of limited help on a Saturday evening.

Principle

As with a crisis management tool, the same applies to an alerting tool:

1. First of all, we should create the organizational and procedural basis before we think about technical support options or even spend money on them.
2. Its usefulness stands and falls with its availability in the event of a crisis and the acceptance of its users.

However, since alerting tools are generally easier to use and offer added value that is immediately comprehensible to all parties involved, they should be given priority over crisis management tools when it comes to acquisition and implementation.

Above all else: If a tool is to be used, then please use it properly. Including technical and organizational precautions that ensure that it actually works in the event of a cyber crisis.

4.2.6 Governance Suites for BCM, IRBC, and ISM

Information at the Touch of a Button

Governance suites, which we use to control the management systems for ISM, BCM, and IRBC, are central sources of information in the event of an emergency or crisis.

They provide us with answers to the following questions, among others, at the touch of a button:

- Which information classes/types/categories are processed via a specific IT system?
- What are the consequences if confidentiality, integrity, availability, or authenticity of a particular class/type/category of information is breached?
- In which order do we have to restart processes or IT systems to avoid a collapse of the entire workflow?
- How much time do we have before we must start emergency operations?
- How many employees do we need to bring in from the weekend or after hours for emergency operations?
- . . .

There is no question that the quality of the answers depends very much on the quality of the data base. The slogan "shit in, shit out" is all too true.

By the way: Some tools also support the coordination of the restart of processes and IT systems through live control options.

Benefits Beyond Crisis Management
But it is beyond crisis management that governance suites really come into their own. For example, they support us not only in the creation, but also and above all the documentation of:

- Business Impact Analysis
- Protection needs assessment (PNA)
- Risk assessments and risk treatment measures
- Business continuity plans
- Restart plans
- Recovery plans
- Tests
- Asset relations

It is precisely this documentation, in turn, that we rely on in crisis management—it provides the data basis on which we have to make decisions.

4.2.7   IDS and SIEM Tools

Intrusion Detection System
An intrusion detection system (IDS) automatically evaluates (network) data and can detect potentially harmful anomalies. We can distinguish between two approaches, knowledge-based and behavior-based detection. In simple terms, knowledge-based detection uses signatures similar to those used by anti-malware software. Behavioral detection, on the other hand, does not use signatures, but actually compares activities to patterns of behavior previously defined as normal or expected. In both cases, an IDS raises an alarm so that countermeasures can be initiated either automatically (this would be a so-called IPS, an intrusion prevention system) or manually by a CSIRT.

Security Information and Event Management Tools
Security Information and Event Management tools (SIEM tools) tie in with IDS/IPS solutions. They aggregate data from various corners of our IT landscape (IDS, IPS, anti-virus software, logs from host systems and firewalls, but also other network components and activities, etc.) and automatically compare them against pre-defined rules. In the case of potentially dangerous events, the SIEM tool generates an alarm, which the first level of the CSIRT can track using playbooks. The latter are an essential tool for our CSIRT and aim at minimizing the damage.

From Practice: Calibration Is the Be-All and End-All
IDS and SIEM tools are not all that useful out of the box. It is up to us to feed them with the information (signatures, rules) on the basis of which the tools do their work. In the case of behavior-based detection, they work with rules that we have to define ourselves. So, if we don't work properly with the rules, even the most expensive tool will be of no use to us. We should pay special attention to the calibration of the rules, otherwise our CSIRT will either get no alerts for tracking, or way too many. We are talking about false negatives and false positives here. Both are equally dangerous. If nothing is detected, the CSIRT can't track anything. If too many alerts pop up, the critical one may get lost in the shuffle. Therefore, it is important to achieve the best possible rate of positive-positives.

Example of Calibration Requirement
Let's illustrate this with an example. Let's imagine that we fear a brute force attack, in which an attacker wants to crack a user's account by automatically entering countless character combinations. A large number of failed attempts in a short period of time in the middle of the night leads to a different conclusion than slowly entered failed attempts on a Monday morning after the end of the holiday season. A rule that can be stored in the IDS, IPS or SIEM tool could therefore take into account, among other things, the time, number and time interval of the failed attempts.

4.3   Logistics Ensure Sustainability

The Misconception of a Quick End to the Crisis
When we slide into a crisis, we are usually completely caught up in the situation and find it difficult—in addition to worrying about the matter at hand—to take care of ourselves and our co-workers. And that's dangerous, because we don't exactly make the best decisions under pressure and fatigue (see also Chap. 2). That's why we should set a course in advance so that we don't have to worry too much about it in an emergency.

Wining and Dining
During normal working and business hours, the supply of sufficient food and especially drinks is no problem. At least if we only consider the CMT. But what about when we have to act on Sunday—and not just with the CMT, but with the entire emergency and crisis organization, i.e., additionally with the communications team, situation center, emergency team, contingency teams and incident response team?

Solutions that recur in practice are:

- Stockpiling
- Agreements with the operator of the company restaurant
- Agreements with operators of (fast) restaurants, caterers, and snack bars

No matter which solution we choose: Providing the members of the emergency and crisis organization with sufficient food and drink is elementary.

Retreats and Breaks
Especially when dealing with crises, it is incredibly important that we can retreat for a few minutes every now and then and turn our backs on the hustle and bustle. Regular, even short time-outs can noticeably reduce stress levels and thus significantly improve the quality of our decisions and work performance. Even a short phone call with family and friends can work wonders. The important thing is that we have a protected atmosphere for this, without spectators and listeners.

What to Do with Overtired Colleagues?
At some point, everyone gets tired. We can postpone this point to a certain extent or, when it is reached, temporarily mitigate it.

Temporary help:

- Oxygen
- Motion/exercise
- Caffeine (as well as teein, taurine, etc.)
- Capsaicin (the active ingredient that makes chilli peppers so beautifully hot)

We should be careful when using drinks and foods with particularly high sugar content. Sugar can give us a short-term performance high, but when blood sugar levels drop again afterwards, the hole we fall into is all the bigger—not an enticing prospect if we have to stay on post for several more hours.

In any case, in the long run, the only thing that helps is sleep. Therefore, we should consider to offer the members of the emergency and crisis organization

- rooms in nearby hotels,
- taxis or
- a ride home.

In any case, it is taboo to let people get into their own cars and drive longer distances. If someone has an accident, we have a crisis within a crisis—and that is the last thing we need.

Shift Handovers
In addition to these care-oriented aspects, there is also one that is aimed at the substantive quality of crisis management. We should think about how we organize the handover from one shift to the next in the case of longer-lasting crises, at least in the CMT, situation center, and emergency unit. Timely shift handover helps to ensure the quality of our crisis management. After all, the old maxim "After tired comes stupid" also applies to crisis management. The following procedure has proven its worth:

- Short, general briefing of the head of the respective body (CMT, situation center, emergency management team) of the shift still in office on the current situation to all members of the new shift
- Individual handover between the individual role holders
- Finally: situation report by the head of the respective body (CMT, situation center, emergency unit) of the new shift on the current situation; this is also the entry of the new shift into the crisis management process.

When handing over, we should proceed on the basis of the CMT protocol as well as the visualization of the crisis management team's work—and, above all, properly record the handover in the minutes.

Important: The "old" shift remains in charge until

- The handover to the new shift is documented in the log

AND

- Leader and Recording Secretary of the old shift have signed the portion of the minutes applicable to their shift.

4.4   Preparing for Crisis Communication

Variety of Options
To prepare for crisis communication, we can work in different places at the same time. We can

- Provide communication aids for our communicators;
- To ensure our ability to communicate in the event of an emergency;
- Train our communicators.[2]

To avoid misunderstandings from the outset: All options presented here are not mutually exclusive but complement each other.

Testimonials Can Help—or Hurt
Finding advocates in times of crisis is anything but easy. Especially those that our stakeholders consider to be

---

[2] See Sect. 4.5.

- credible,
- competent and best,
- non-partisan or impartial.

In fact, there are a number of experts who, depending on the topic, inevitably make their appearance in the media (professors, experts, publicists, lobbyists, etc.). Many of them do so (not only) out of a personal desire to communicate or because they are forced to do so by the interviewers, but also because they have personal, not too evident interests of various kinds—which usually have to do with the organization concerned or at least the industry. Knowing these can give us a good testimonial in an acute crisis.

But beware: malicious contemporaries have coined the pretty term "rent-a-mouths" for such experts. The solution is also available in the event of a cyber-crisis when communication can be an inherent problem in the system. On top of that, this solution does not tie up internal staff, so that they can take care of second or third level requests.

We can also increase first level capacity for communication via keystrokes in the short term. For this we have to

- create text modules (similar to those used in day-to-day business by first level support on the telephone or keyboard);
- select and train employees (in advance if possible!);
- provide access to the communication channels through which we want to receive and respond to inquiries.

Earmarked Accessibilities
In addition, we can offer input channels that are only provided for this one crisis. This ranges from microsites as a special form of web presence to social media presences to e-mail addresses or telephone numbers.

4.4.1 Communication Aids

Communication Aids
No matter how exactly we organize our crisis communication: In view of the different stakeholders and their information needs, we will not be able to avoid distributing the task across different shoulders. Account management, press spokesperson, provider management, internal communications, regulatory affairs, etc.—all these roles will have to keep their contacts happy in an emergency. And we should make that as easy as possible for them.

Key Messages
The basic equipment is a list of positive core messages—each consisting of a single sentence and verifiable with a neutral fact. With a little practice, we can formulate the

messages in such a way that we can use them for more than one stakeholder or information need (see below).

Example: Key Message

Key message	Proof
The security of our customers' data is very important to us	ISMS, certified according to ISO 27001, certificate number 234234
We have our security precautions regularly checked by external experts.	ISAE audit certificate, annual financial statement audit certificate

Crisis Communications Plan

We should translate these core messages into a crisis communications plan to which all those involved in crisis management (specifically, crisis communication) should adhere.

It is up to us whether we prepare such a crisis communication plan or only create one in the acute event of a crisis. Both have their advantages and disadvantages. While we have enough time for this in peacetime, we also shall think ahead to a wide variety of scenarios (cryptolocker, DDoS attack, data center/platform failure, data theft, etc.). In an emergency, it is the other way round—the scenario has then become very concrete, but time is short. Table 4.1 shows a possible implementation.

List of Negative Buzz Words

It is important that we avoid expressions with potentially negative connotations in our statements. These include:

- Event
- Disaster
- Crisis
- Breakdown
- Vulnerability
- Misfortune
- Failure
- Incident
- . . .

Especially if we use them repeatedly, such negative signal words can reinforce already existing negative attitudes in the addressee or worsen a neutral attitude. But be careful: Sometimes the German language simply does not allow us to use one or the other expression (anymore), so that a compulsive avoidance can be interpreted as gibberish and bumbling.

Table 4.1 Crisis communication plan in the event of a DDoS attack

Stakeholder	Information needs	Key message	Proof
Customers	When will access be possible again?	We are competent and work on the solution	If necessary, from individual customer history according to CRM
Customers	Is my data safe?	1. The security of our customers' data is very important to us. 2. We have our security precautions regularly checked by external experts.	1. ISMS, certified according to ISO 27001, certificate number 234234 2. ISAE audit, annual accounts audit
Data protection authority	Precautions too lax?	1. The security of our customers' data is very important to us. 2. We have our security precautions regularly checked by external experts.	1. ISMS, certified according to ISO 27001, certificate number 234234 2. ISAE audit, annual accounts audit
Data protection authority	Personal data affected?	According to the current state of knowledge, the confidentiality of the data is still ensured.	IT forensics testimony?
tbd.	tbd.	tbd.	tbd.

Sample Statement or Press Release

It is also helpful to have a sample statement at hand for different cases. Each sentence in it must

- be able to stand on its own, i.e., cannot be used against us even when taken out of context;
- contain at least a neutral, better a positive statement;
- be short and to the point so that it can be understood and rendered meaningfully by a layperson without an academic background.

We can have this statement released internally in advance and, if necessary, distribute it immediately via the homepage or other communication channels (Twitter!). On top of that, all those who shall communicate with the press can practice the statement in peace already in peacetime (press spokesperson, management). Positive side effect: If we add a headline, date, and place mark as well as a quote from a high-ranking employee to the statement, we have an initial press release at the same time.

Explicitly: Such a sample statement serves as a first, quick reaction. It is merely intended to show that we have understood that something is not going as it should. We have to continuously adjust the individual statements of the statement according to the development of the situation.

Example: Sample statement in the event of a DDoS attack, here as a press release with headline, date/location mark and citation as it is typically for Germany

   DDoS attack on SAMPLE-ORGANIZATION: Homepage access impaired
   SAMPLE CITY, DATE

   As of TOMORROW/TODAY/etc., unknown persons are attacking the internet presence of the MUSTERORGANIZATION. Due to the attack, customers currently have only limited access to their user accounts. SAMPLE-ORGANIZATION employees are already working intensively on the solution together with external experts.

   "We understand how upsetting the impact of this attack is for our customers. The security of their data is close to our hearts. We are working flat out to restore customers' access to their accounts as quickly as possible," says JANE DOE, press officer at SAMPLE-ORGANIZATION.

   At the present time, there is no reliable information on the expected duration of the attack or the background and motivation of the attackers. In order to determine these, the SAMPLE-ORGANISATIONORGANIZATION is working closely with the relevant authorities (and supporting them with its own experts).

Q&A

Furthermore, we can think ahead to some recurring questions or our answers to them. The same considerations apply as for the sample statement or press release. If we think of the questions and answers in advance, we can authorize their use in advance, thereby saving valuable time in an emergency and, above all, we can practice them.

Q:
   Why didn't you prepare for an attack?

A:
   The security of our customers' data is close to our hearts. Our information security management system is formally certified and regularly subject to external audits.

Q:
   Is it possible that customer data is also being stolen?

A:
   To steal customer data, an attacker would need access to our systems. We are currently subject to a DDoS attack. DDoS attacks are external and do not require access to our systems. Regardless, we use a management system for the security of confidential information. Our information security management system is formally certified and regularly subject to external audits.

Q:
   Is the rumor true that the attack is part of an extortion that you didn't take serious?

A:

>   Please understand that we do not comment on rumors. In all our decisions, we have the interests of our customers and shareholders in mind.

Further (Sample) Formulations

In addition to the press, there are other stakeholders who require information in the event of a crisis. These include, in particular, our customers and, in the case of cyber crises, data and consumer protection agencies. When communicating with them, our Customer Relationship Management (CRM) tool and hopefully existing text modules from routine operations provide a pool from which we can draw.

Dark Sites

On top of that, there are also dark sites. Dark sites are preliminary pages that can be prepared and activated instead of the normal web presence if necessary. A dark site is often kept in more muted colors than the normal web presence and should always make a statement about how we can be reached as an organization and what the current state of affairs is.

A classic field of application in cyber crisis management are DDoS attacks, whose target is usually web services. We can anticipate this case and have a dark site ready to pull out of the bag at any time.

Don't forget: In case of an event, we not only have to adjust our homepage, but also our social media profiles. Nothing looks more embarrassing than a perfect world representation in one place, when this very world is being shaken up in another.

More Helpers

In addition to all these little helpers that are used specifically in crisis communication, there are other tools that serve us well in the event of an incident. Namely, when it comes to explanations and background knowledge. We can make these available to stakeholders (especially journalists, bloggers, YouTubers, etc.). This makes it a little easier for them to do their own research and create posts. We should therefore hold out:

- Press kit (in digital form)
- Explainer videos (preferably kept simple) on
  - services, products
  - how to... e.g., change the password
  - ...
- Footage

4.5   Practice Creates Masters: Trainings and Exercises

What Use Is Training During a Crisis?
Employees who have been prepared for their crisis management tasks will act more confidently, quickly, and therefore more effectively in an emergency. Conversely, it can also mean: If we do not put our employees in a position to act quickly and correctly under the pressure of an exceptional situation—because nothing else is a crisis—our crisis management will run into the wall. And that's not all: if the worst comes to the worst, such failures can be considered organizational culpability and be prosecuted under criminal law.

4.5.1   Formats

Instruction, Training, or Exercise?
In everyday life, the terms often get mixed up and the common standards (ISO 223xx, BS 11200, BfV/BSI/ASW 2000-3, BSI 100-4 or 200-4) unfortunately do not offer satisfactory definitions or delimitations either. In this book, we therefore want to work with the following definitions:

- An instruction is a format that imparts knowledge without a great practical component.
- A training is a format that imparts knowledge and skills with the help of numerous practical parts. Through the practical parts, participants improve and practice both their individual and group skills.
- An exercise is a format that works exclusively with practical components. An exercise is always aimed at one or more teams whose cooperation is the focus. Through the practical parts, the participants improve and practice both their individual and group skills.

Trainings
We can design training courses for individual roles or entire teams—for example, the core CMT. They are particularly suitable for deepening theoretical knowledge and transferring it into action routines in a guided (!) manner. We can further consolidate these routines in in-depth, role-specific training sessions: Leading a CMT and managing crisis management, audit-proof documentation in the CMT protocol, visualizing situation pictures, the correct behavior when sounding the alarm, quickly initiating the crisis management team's working procedure, appearances in front of press representatives or in interviews or talk shows, etc. It is crucial that we do not lump all CMT roles together, as their respective training needs differ significantly from those of other roles.

By the way: Smaller scenario-based simulation games are ideal for use in training. Simulation games need a script that develops the situation on the basis of which the participants train.

Standardized (Open) vs. In-house Formats

Depending on our target group and objectives, as well as the budget available to us, there are standardized training formats from external providers for (cyber) crisis management—just as there are for many other topics—on the one hand, and on the other hand, the possibility of having the content taught company-specifically (in-house). Surprisingly, the latter is often much more cost-efficient, as we do not have to pay extra for each participant in an in-house training (not even the ever-popular travel expenses and possibly overtime for activities at a different location!) On top of that, the trainer can tailor the content of an in-house training much more precisely to the training needs of the participants.

Exercises

Exercises are always based on a specific scenario (analogous to a business game) and are aimed at teams (core CMT, extended CMT, contingency teams, entire emergency organization, etc.). They can remain at one management level (usually the CMT) or involve other parts of the organization. If it is an exercise in which only the CMT is exercised and the remaining parts of the organization are left out, it is usually referred to as a CMT exercise.

Providers of critical infrastructure in particular should consider not conducting exercises on their own, but rather involving associated companies (service providers, customers, cooperation partners) and authorities in the exercise.

Like all other formats, an exercise must always serve one or more specific goals—and we must never lose sight of these, both when designing the exercise and when observing the course of the exercise and the final evaluation.

Internal vs. External Coaches and Trainers

These different formats can be taught by both internal and external experts. In any case, we must ensure that the trainer or exercise instructor meets the following requirements:

- She/he needs didactic and methodological skills.
  After all, concrete contents are to be conveyed to specific target groups in an appropriate manner.
- She/he must have sufficient technical depth.
  A beautiful image applies here: If you have to give a lecture whose content is the size of a postage stamp, you must have knowledge the size of a sheet of paper at least.
- The target group must accept us as experts with regard to the topic.
  This requirement is often a problem for internal experts because the prophet unfortunately does not count for much at home. Above all, the prophet must be in a position to "recapture" EVERY participant if necessary. Especially with members of the

management or the first management level—the classic members of a CMT—this is sometimes not quite trivial.

• He should know the organization and/or the industry sufficiently well.

Depending on the topic and the target group, this may be a secondary point. A basic crisis management and communications training course is designed to convey generally applicable basics. In role-specific trainings or exercises, however, we should attach importance to this point.

Lack of Accreditations

It is important to know that (in Germany) there are no officially accredited training courses and training providers on the subject of crisis management. This leads to people who have never "tasted crisis air" themselves acting as trainers.

To avoid misunderstandings: A lack of accreditation does not mean that a course is automatically bad. But neither does it mean that it is guaranteed that the teacher meets minimum professional, didactic, or methodological requirements. In this way, the current certificates (unfortunately) play on the level of Loriot's famous yodelling diploma: you just have something of your own that looks nice on your CV.

4.5.2   Training Program

Training Program

If we want to take our emergency and crisis organization to the next level, a systematic training program is a good idea. In doing so, we think about

• the objectives we want to achieve with it;
• the target groups we need to prepare for their tasks in emergency and crisis management.

Principle 1: Didactics Determines Methodology

The structure of the training program, just like the structure of each individual measure, must follow a simple principle: Didactics determines methodology and takes precedence over it. This means that the objective determines which formats, contents, and methods we use. In this way, we reduce the risk of wasting our precious resources (time, money, participants' desire/interest, etc.) on individual measures that do not really meet the needs of the participants and our organization in the end.

Principle 2: From the General to the Specific

In practice, we encounter one phenomenon time and again with new clients: the desire to conduct a crisis management exercise (often based on an already established scenario). In the vast majority of cases, however, the intended participants have not yet had the chance to familiarize themselves with basic, scenario-independent crisis management methods. To avoid misunderstandings: Starting directly with an exercise can work if the level of difficulty is well hit as well as the expectations are not too high with regard to the learning curve and its transferability to other scenarios. It is therefore better to first practice the general procedures with suitable formats, e.g. basic training and (small group) training for the core CMT, before we bring the CMT together in its entirety and unleash it on a concrete scenario. And if it is to be an exercise, please moderate it.

Principle 3: From the Simple to the Difficult

If our CMT has not practiced together too often, let alone had to work together in an emergency, a CMT exercise involving a multiple protection target breach (i.e., a ransomware attack in which sensitive data is also released and the IT problems affect machine control systems so that employees working on them are injured or even killed) is not necessarily the best choice. Such a scenario can only overwhelm participants, making the learning effect manageable but the frustration all the greater. Neither is good if we want to push the topic of emergency and crisis management internally.

From Practice: Example of the Structure of a Training Program

What can a didactically sound training and exercise program look like? This is shown in Table 4.2, to which we have added a list of abbreviations.

Disclaimer, part 1: The table only shows an excerpt of a program—among other things, it is missing the timeline on which we intend to implement the individual measures. It also omits the initial stocktaking with which we determine the actual training and education needs, as well as separate measures for evaluating learning progress.

   Disclaimer, Part 2: This structure is of course not set in stone, but must be adapted to the specific organization.

From Practice: Particularly Recommendable Measures

The best quick wins for emergency and crisis organizations result when we particularly promote individual roles. These roles can become multipliers in two ways: on the one hand, by acting confidently in an emergency and thus becoming role models for other members of the emergency and crisis organization, and on the other hand, by reporting back to our organization on their (hopefully positive!) experiences with training and education. The roles that we have assembled in the core CMT are particularly suitable for this.

   On top of this, it always proves useful to turn those affected into participants. This means nothing other than not simply giving the CMT members (again: especially the core CMT) a certain method or a certain tool as a set but presenting it as a suggestion with the option of (co-)development. An experienced trainer will be happy to incorporate such an approach into a role-specific training or one for small groups.

   With this approach, by the way, we take all three principles of this chapter to heart by first focusing on the target group that will be at the center of all types of crises: the core CMT. We teach them the methods on which crisis management as a whole is based: Initializing the CMT's working procedure and going through the leadership process. If we

Table 4.2 Training program (excerpt)

Level	Format	TG	Goal: Participants …	Measure
0	I	3, 4, 5, 6	…know the basics of emergency and crisis management	Basic instruction
1	T	1	…can perform their tasks in the ECO*	Role-specific training
2	T	2	…practice the initialization + management of crises	Small group training
3	SE (C)	3, 4, 5, 6	…exercise themselves to cooperate – within the respective body – if necessary, under guidance – if necessary, with other bodies	Staff exercise for a single body of the ECO* with a simple scenario using coaching elements
4	SE	3, 4, 5, 6		Staff exercise for a single body with a simple scenario
5	E (C)	3, 4, 5, 6		Exercise for several bodies with a simple scenario using coaching elements
6	E	3, 4, 5, 6		Exercise for several bodies with a simple scenario
7	E	3, 4, 5, 6		Exercise for several bodies with a complex scenario
8	IE	3, 4, 5, 6		Integrated exercise for multiple bodies with a simple scenario and involvement of external stakeholders
9	IE	3, 4, 5, 6		Integrated exercise for several bodies with a complex scenario and involvement of external stakeholders

| *Formats*: C: Coaching elements IE: integrated exercise CSE: crisis management exercise I: Instruction | SE: Staff exercise T: Training E: Exercise | *ECO: Emergency and crisis organization | *Target Group (TG)*: 1 Single rolls 2 Crisis management team (core) 3 Communication staff 4 Crisis management team (complete) 5 Situation center 6 Emergency management team |

have confidence in our actions here, we can tackle more complex exercise formats with a clear conscience—from the general to the specific, from the simple to the difficult.

4.6   Create Conditions for the Continuation of Business Operations

Focus: Availability of Processes and Data and the Systems that Process Them
Especially in case of an emergency or crisis, our stakeholders expect us to be able to act, at least to a certain extent, and to maintain central pillars of our business operations. We need to identify these pillars and make robust provisions to ensure that they remain stable in the event of an emergency. This means we must

- identify and prioritize our critical (business) processes and determine the resources without which the processes will not work;
- describe workarounds for the most critical processes that ensure our operational continuity, at least temporarily, even if data or IT systems are not available to us (= BCP);
- on the IT side, translate the availability requirements of the (business) processes into an appropriate IT architecture;
- at least document the procedures for restarting these IT systems and restoring data and automate them as far as possible.

4.6.1   Prepare Emergency Operation of (Business) Processes

4.6.1.1 Criticalities and Resources
Business Impact Analysis
The Business Impact Analysis (BIA) is the foundation of BCM. We use it to determine which processes are relevant to emergencies and which are not. The decisive factor here is the maximum time that can elapse before the interruption of a process causes serious damage to our organization. This is the maximum tolerable outage (MTO). From this we must derive a time objective for the start of emergency operations (RTO; recovery time objective). This should be shorter than the MTO because we need to allow for a buffer for response times, errors and problems when starting emergency operations, etc.

Such prioritization along the MTO/RTO is essential for (at least) two reasons:

1. The MTO/RTO is the basis for the restart sequence as well as the central requirement for the Supporting Assets, especially IT (see Sect. 5.4).
2. Prioritization allows us to set priorities in safeguarding our operational continuity. Covering the entire organization indiscriminately would simply be completely uneconomical.

Establish Processes Relevant to Emergencies

If we want to carry out a BIA, we must make some determinations first:

- What are our most important products and services?

  This comparatively high level of abstraction is sometimes referred to as strategic BIA and provides an initial orientation. Such an orientation is important because it means that we do not have to examine all processes in the further course.
- Which processes pay into these products and services, or which processes do we want to include in the scope?

  Risk orientation ensures that expenses are limited.
- Which valuation periods do we use?

  The valuation periods should be synchronized with any availability or restart classes that may exist in the organization, e.g., from IT service continuity management or information security management. The following valuation periods have proven themselves across industries: ≤ 4 h, ≤ 8 h, ≤ 2 days, ≤ 5 days and ≤ 10 days. A process whose interruption does not cause serious damage within 10 days is not emergency-relevant.
- What types of damage should be the deciding factor as to whether or not there is an emergency?

  Typically, we should look at financial losses, reputation damage, and violations of contractual and legal obligations.
- What thresholds and damage levels do we want to work with?

  In order to avoid the inevitable trend towards the middle, we should work with an even scale, e.g., one with four levels (low, medium, high, very high). We must define the individual levels for each type of damage, i.e., with three types of damage and four levels of damage, we need 12 definitions.
- What exactly determines the emergency relevance of a process and its MTO/RTO?

  Here, a simple and therefore obvious procedure is offered: As soon as a level of "high" (or even "very high") damage is reached in any loss type within a certain time (e.g. 10 days), the process is emergency-relevant. Its MTO/RTO is automatically derived from the valuation period in which this loss is reached—after all, we want to avoid a high loss for our organization.
- Can/would we define the minimum output that a process must achieve even in emergency mode?

  We should pay attention to this so-called Minimum Business Continuity Objective (MBCO), among other things, if we can quantify the output, for example in terms of numbers of units, runs or euros. And, of course, if the expected losses are clearly linked to a certain output threshold.
- Which (supporting) assets do we want to look at, as they are likely to play a role in securing the business? For simplicity, please refer to Sect. 5.4.
- Should the BIA be linked to the Protection Needs Assessment (PNA) from the ISM, i.e., do we need to integrate the information and data as a further primary asset in the survey in addition to the processes (see Sect. 5.5 and again Sect. 5.4)?

The answers to these questions must be obtained primarily from the process owners (or, if we are not organized according to processes but along the organizational structure or products and services, from the managers or product and service owners).

Restart Sequence and Resource Requirements in Emergency Mode
When we have analyzed all processes in our scope, we have our BIA result. Assuming we have correctly inherited the restart times and criticalities of the individual processes along the entire process chain, the restart times of the individual processes more or less automatically provide us with the restart order.

But not only that. Now we can mutually relate and aggregate the BIA results of the individual processes (or products, departments, etc., depending on how we have aligned the BIA). This way we get the organization-wide resource requirements for emergency operations—including availability requirements for the relevant primary and supporting assets (IT!).

From Practice: Avoiding Complexity Voodoo
Unfortunately, in our day-to-day consulting work, we see time and time again that our clients have been talked into unnecessarily complicated methods for determining processes relevant to emergencies. A few negative highlights:

- Criticality is automatically determined by a (usually wickedly expensive) BCM tool, without users being aware of the basis on which the decision is made.
- The types of damage are weighted differently.
- In addition to or independent of the MTO/RTO, criticality classes are used in which the highest conceivable damage occurring at some time during the period under consideration plays a role.
  - Effect 1: Then we can debate forever which process is more relevant in an emergency:
    high damage after 4 h
      or
    very high damage after 2 days
  - Effect 2: What determines the restart sequence: MTO/RTO or criticality class?
- The number of valuation periods is unnecessarily high, i.e., more than five.
- The number of types of damage is more than four (financial damage, damage to reputation, infringements of the law and, where applicable, production backlogs).

Honestly: do these maneuvers offer any substantial added value that makes our organization more secure or saves costs while maintaining the same level of security? On the contrary, all of this is absolute hokum, as it has no useful effects whatsoever: It produces bogus inaccuracies, makes BIA unnecessarily complicated as well as its results opaque, and glorifies those who developed the methodology. Because no matter what the procedure looks like, in the end the result is "only" based on expert estimates and serves the purpose of getting critical processes into emergency operation in time. Therefore, we strongly advocate that the BIA (like everything else in the crisis management context) be designed to be as simple and robust as possible.

4.6.1.2 Business Continuity Plans
Purpose of BCP

Business continuity plans (BCP) describe temporary workarounds for emergency-relevant processes for the loss of resources that we have identified as necessary in the context of the BIA. Regardless of our organization's industry and the type of crisis, we should have BCPs in place for our emergency-relevant (business) processes for the following scenarios:

- Failure of buildings/sites
- Failure of machines/equipment
- Staff absenteeism
- IT failure
- Failure of applications and IT systems

In the context of cyber crises, the focus is on IT systems, IoT machinery and equipment, and service providers.

BCPs are the central tool for contingency teams that somehow must maintain (business) operations in the event of an emergency.

Content and Sample Structure of a Process-Related Emergency Plan (BCP; Excerpt)

1. Contingency team (roles!)
2. Contacts (internal, external)
3. BCP: Failure of applications and IT systems
    3.1 Application 1 (e.g., Internet telephony/Skype)
        3.1.1 Immediate measures to start emergency operation
        3.1.2 Measures to maintain emergency operations
        3.1.3 Measures for the return to normal operation
    3.2 Application 2 (e.g., accounting system)
        3.2.1 Immediate measures to start emergency operation
        3.2.2 Measures to maintain emergency operation
        3.2.3 Measures for the return to normal operation
    3.3 Application 3 (e.g., CRM tool)
    3.4 Application n
4. BCP: breakdown of machinery and equipment
    4.1 Machine/equipment 1 (e.g., stove and cooking infrastructure of the company canteen)
        4.1.1 Immediate measures to start emergency operation
        4.1.2 Measures to maintain emergency operation

4.1.3 Measures for the return to normal operation
4.2 Machine/plant 2 (e.g., printing line)
    4.2.1 Immediate measures to start emergency operation
    4.2.2 Measures to maintain emergency operation
    4.2.3 Measures for the return to normal operation
4.3 Machine/plant n
5. BCP: failure of service providers
    5.1 Service provider 1 (e.g., supplier)
        5.1.1 Immediate measures to start emergency operation
        5.1.2 Measures to maintain emergency operation
        5.1.3 Measures for the return to normal operation
    5.2 Service provider 2 (e.g., IT service provider)
        5.2.1 Immediate measures to start emergency operation
        5.2.2 Measures to maintain emergency operation
        5.2.3 Measures for the return to normal operation
    5.3 Service provider n
6. BCP: Failure of buildings/sites (mostly secondary for cyber crises).
7. BCP: Loss of personnel (mostly secondary for cyber crises).

From Practice: BCP Requirements
A BCP must meet some basic requirements. The first (and often non-trivial) requirement is that it must be available to all those who need to work with it. Also and especially in an emergency, i.e. in the event of a failure of central IT components. Therefore, we should not only think about online but also about offline solutions and/or order our emergency team members to have a printout in their drawer (and on their nightstand at home). In terms of content, it should be as concise as possible, but as detailed as necessary. Experience has shown time and again that a plan that is too complex or too extensive is confusing in an emergency and, in case of doubt, causes more confusion than it is useful. In other words, it is hardly manageable, especially not for someone who has not defined the plan or the workarounds himself. In short, the BCP must work in an emergency, even if a knowledgeable third party is supposed to work with it. This brings us to the last (and perhaps most important) requirement: we must test it (see Sect. 4.7).

As an aside, if we are toying with implementing a BCMS and getting it certified to ISO 22301, we need to demonstrate that we meet these requirements (among many others).

4.6.2   Enable Restart of IT Systems

4.6.2.1 Technical Solutions
Technologies
In IT landscapes, we encounter various technologies, all of which have their advantages and disadvantages in terms of restart (and, of course, failover).

Cloud Solutions: No Internet, No Nothing

If we focus solely on the questions of safeguarding against failure and speed of restart, there is one clear favorite among all these technologies: Off to the cloud! This means that the restart is not our responsibility, but that of the solution provider. Through appropriate contracts, we as an organization can contract with various service providers or for selected services all-round carefree packages. There are only two not entirely insignificant snags:

1. Once our availability problems are not home-made, but related to the internet connection, we have no chance to do anything to get the services restarted. Oh stop, there is something we can do: wait, pray, and activate the business continuation plans.
2. Even though we have outsourced the provision of the service and thus the responsibility for its restart to a service provider, the responsibility for everything that our stakeholders expect from this service still remains with us. To reiterate: We cannot outsource the responsibility, neither in moral, nor in legal terms.

Virtualization: No Interruption, No Restart

Virtualization solutions in which the virtualization layer spans more than one data center are the preferred solution from an ITSCM or IRBC perspective. Such a design completely automates the restart of the virtualized systems—if a failure occurs at all and a restart becomes necessary. In this case, the virtualized systems start up so quickly that the user is usually unaware of it.

Cluster: Robust IT Operation

We can think of clusters as federated solutions in which at least two instances (called nodes) jointly provide a service. The nodes should be evenly distributed across our data centers, i.e., in a four-node cluster, two nodes should run in one data center and two nodes in the other.

Clusters come in different varieties:

- Physical vs. virtualized
- Active-active vs. active-passive

Physical means that we (and independent of the operating system running on it) connect hardware components together for a common purpose, even across two data centers. Alternatively, we can virtualize the clusters and thus benefit from the advantages of virtualization solutions described above.

In an active-active cluster, all nodes are active at the same time and share the work. If one of the nodes fails, the rest take over the work. Therefore, the individual nodes must always have free capacities in order to be able to increase their own "work volume" at any time. An active-passive cluster also has two or more nodes, but only half of them are active while the others are waiting to take over.

Cluster solutions are designed to provide robust IT operations. If one or more nodes fail and a restart becomes necessary, it usually requires at least selective manual intervention, which we should document in restart plans.

Redundantly Set Up Systems

With redundantly set up systems, the system exists twice, ideally once each at different locations. If one fails, the other can take over. Like clusters, this usually does not happen automatically, but must be initiated manually. More on this in Sect. 4.6.2.2.

By the way, a classic example of a redundant system is often the IBM mainframe, our good old mainframe (which, of course, does not necessarily have to be redundant).

4.6.2.2 Organizational Preparations: Restart Plans and Restore Concepts
Restart Plans

If a particular system is required by an emergency-relevant (business) process, we should prepare all its components (application side, databases, middleware, basic services, operating system) for restart. The means of choice are restart plans. In contrast to BCPs, restart plans have a decisive advantage: we can cast them to a large extent in scripts, i.e., automate them. In this way, often only a manual trigger is required, and the rest happens all by itself (except for the system acceptance that concludes the restart). And, above all, faster than if we try to intervene manually. On top of that, such restart plans are more robust, i.e., independent of human shortcomings—assuming, of course, that the scripts are error-free (which we can and must find out by testing).

Restart of Stand-Alone Systems

However, we can only use restart plans if our systems are set up redundantly (or even better virtualized). Unfortunately, there are often still systems that are solitary or stand-alone for a variety of reasons. This means that they have no redundancy, which makes it much more time-consuming to compensate for their failure. In principle, there are two options: We can

- try to restore the system in place;
- to convert the test machine to the productive one in the hopefully existing test environment.

For the recovery, we may have to rebuild the system from scratch. For this purpose, so-called recovery plans are a useful thing. With a little luck, we will be spared having to create these recovery plans separately. In the operating documentation (e.g., the operating manual) we have a wild card that already describes the necessary steps if necessary.

When converting the test environment to the production environment, we usually have to migrate larger amounts of data, since production data has no place in the test environment. In most cases, we also must reconfigure the connections to surrounding systems.

Both variants cost time and are prone to failure, making them unacceptable for time-critical systems from IRBC's point of view.

Backup and Restore Concepts
We can distinguish three types of backups:

- Full backups

  (as the name suggests—a complete data backup)

- Differential backups

  (differential backups save the differences in the data stock since the last full backup).

- Incremental backups

  (incremental backups save the differences in the data stock since the last backup—regardless of whether this last backup was a full or incremental backup).

From Practice: Combining Backup Strategies
Since the individual procedures differ considerably with regard to the storage requirements and also the amount of time we have to plan for the creation and, above all, the import of the backups (the famous restore), the procedures are often combined. One full backup per week and incremental backups on the days in between have proven to be effective. Suppose we always do the full backup on Saturdays and are forced (for whatever reason) to restore on a Friday. In this case, we need to import the full backup and the incremental backups from Sunday, Monday, Tuesday, Wednesday, and Thursday. That's a total of six backups, which adds a certain amount of time or complexity when restoring. Alternatively, we can work with differential backups between the full backups. This increases the storage requirements and the time required for creation, but reduces the complexity and time required for restoring—after all, instead of up to six separate backups, we only need to import a maximum of two, namely the last full and differential backup in each case.

Synchronous Data Mirrors
Synchronous data mirrors distributed across multiple locations are the most desirable option from an IRBC perspective—but also the most expensive. This involves mirroring copies of changes to the dataset in real time from the database on which the change is made to a database at another location (usually a second data center). The distance between the locations can be a stumbling block, however, as fiber optic lines reduce latency significantly but do not make it disappear.

Data Safe
A data safe at a third location (in addition to the locations of our data centers) may be worth considering to prevent a complete loss of data. However, such a data safe is generally not suitable for ensuring a timely restore. If our restore concepts provide for something like

this, we should check practically and on the living object how much time the procedure takes.

4.6.3   Creating a Framework for Cybersecurity Incident Response

In Detail at Another Place: CSIR(T), SIEM and More
In order to be able to act in an emergency, we should set up a team that can react quickly on a technical level. This is the so-called Cybersecurity Incident Response Team (CSIRT, see Sect. 4.1.4). We need to provide the CSIRT with technical solutions that enable them to detect potentially dangerous events in the depths of our IT landscape (see Sect. 4.2.7).

For the actual incident management, we should develop process descriptions in the CSIRT that can be used to track common incidents in a standardized (and thus quick) manner. These are the so-called playbooks or runbooks. On top of that, we should identify the IT systems that are particularly critical and/or exposed to special risks and should therefore be closely monitored during operation. The starting point is the requirements of the (business) processes (see Sects. 4.6.1 and 5.7).

4.7   What Works and What Does Not: Tests

Aim and Purpose of Tests
Tests serve a single purpose: they verify that our measures (procedures, technologies and tools) actually work to the extent we require for our cyber crisis management—starting with prevention, continuing with preparation and ending with immediate crisis management.

And What About Audits?
To avoid misunderstandings: Of course, tests are not the only way to convince ourselves of the effectiveness of our countermeasures for cyber crises. In addition to tests, there are (unfortunately, every now and then) also serious cases—and audits, as we will see in a separate chapter (Sect. 5.8).

Test Program
"Measures" is a broad term here, which we will replace with that of "test object" from now on. These test objects include, for example:

- Technical components and functionalities
- Organizational arrangements (procedures, plans, templates, etc.)
- Assumptions (time requirements, resource requirements, etc.)
- ...

Then we have to figure out which test object

- with what *specific* goal,
- how (theoretically or practically),
- how often (cycle) and
- by whom (internal or external testers)

is to be reviewed.

If we map these points in a multi-year plan and provide them with responsibilities and reporting mechanisms in the direction of top management, we are doing a lot right. For the sake of good order: We are probably familiar with such a test program from the audit planning of our internal audit.

From Practice: Risk Orientation Strongly Recommended

Given the quantity frameworks of test objects and review needs, we will once again not be able to avoid a risk-based approach. Important information about the risks that we need to keep an eye on with our test program comes from cyber risk management, the protection needs assessment, the business impact analysis, the BC Risk Assessment and, of course, the audits.

And: The intensive treatment of a test object through close test cycles including increased practical forms of verification can certainly be a measure within the framework of cyber risk management.

Tests

While audits usually have a somewhat broader perspective, tests are usually directed at a single, concrete test object. This can be, for example, a specific process, a specific technical functionality, etc. Which test format we choose in each individual case also (but not only) depends on the test object. Basically, we can distinguish between purely theory-based and practical test formats. Theory-based test formats include, above all, the notorious desk tests, while a colorful bouquet of designations and systematizations is customary for practical test formats.

Disclaimer: Unfortunately, even recourse to common standards does not really help if we want to resolve this Babylonian linguistic confusion: ISO 22398 and the BSI glossaries on basic protection and emergency management tend to contribute to this.

Theoretical vs. Practical Test Formats

Once again, the principle applies: from the easy to the difficult. This means that if we want to approach the subject of tests, we are well advised to start with desk tests first, as these are

- easier to organize and
- less risky

than practical tests.

But compared to practical tests, they also have considerable disadvantages. They

- are less meaningful and
- are increasingly considered insufficient by auditors.

Our test program should therefore start with desk tests for the individual test objects and then successively replace them with practical test forms. This is not the only reason why multi-year planning is a sensible thing to do.

Let's now take a look at the tests that are most important when it comes to cyber crisis management. Without these tests, we come to

- prevention,
- preparation,
- coping and
- (aftercare)

of cyber crises.

Penetration Testing

Pentests on supporting resources identify any gaps in our security measures and thus show us risks that could be potential crisis triggers. Not only can we (have) pentests performed on all types of IT components (web applications, databases, operating systems, hosts, network components, etc.) as well as IoT components, mobile devices, machines and equipment, but we should also not ignore physical perimeters and, above all, the human factor. When we talk about IT components, vulnerability scans, among others, are a common method, while when it comes to the human factor, social engineering is the tool of choice. In the case of the latter, we can of course again make use of technological support (e.g. by means of phishing e-mails), but also of good old-fashioned conversation (in person or by telephone).

Test of Technology and Physical Access

The best CMT room (even at an alternate location or virtually) with the best equipment is useless if our CMT can't get to the site, the building, or the room itself when in doubt. After all, we have to expect that we'll need to get the room and equipment up and running outside of business hours—that is, when no one from facilities management or other indispensable support functions is on hand. It's equally annoying when the PCs or notebooks in the crisis room are busy for the first hour pulling up the last 9 months' worth of pending updates. We should also regularly check the connection to the multifunction devices, the functionality of the LAN ports, etc.

Of course, this does not only apply to the CMT room and the CMT members, but one-to-one to all other rooms and bodies of our emergency and crisis organization (communication unit, situation center, contingency teams, etc.).

Test of the Alerting Procedure and Tools

Periodic testing of anything related to our ability to alert is essential. The tests must provide information on the following questions:

- Do all instances involved in alerting actually dare to escalate a potential crisis case and alert the next instance?
- Are the contact details still up to date?
- Does our on-call or reachability policy apply?
- Does our alerting tool work and can the members of the crisis organization stored in it handle it?
- Does our call tree take effect in a reasonable amount of time?
- Is the virtual conference room actually ready 24/7?
- Does the moderator who has to unlock a conference call with a PIN have the PIN at hand when needed?
- Does the dovetailing between IT emergency management, cybersecurity incident response, BCM and crisis management work?
- ...

Test of the Business Continuity Plans

When critical IT systems fail, the emergency response teams of critical business and support processes must fall back on the workarounds they have (hopefully) documented in the business continuity plans. So much for the theory.

In the course of tests we have to find out whether

- the contingency team is sensibly composed (roles, number of persons);
- those who have to switch to alternative IT systems also have the necessary access rights (keyword: IAM, emergency user);
- the process descriptions documented for the individual phases (start of emergency operation, emergency operation, return to normal operation) are comprehensible to a knowledgeable third party;
- the time specifications for the maximum tolerable downtime and the required restart time are realistic and sustainable;
- ...

In short, we need to put organizational arrangements to the test.

Test of the Restart and Isolated Operations of IT Systems as Well as the Recovery of Data

What applies to organizational measures applies equally to the technology that is supposed to make us more robust against emergencies. This means that we also have to test whether we can restart the IT systems (at the level of individual systems and components through to data center swings and black building tests) in the time frame that we are given as a requirement from the critical processes. Getting systems back up and running is only half the battle. We must also master the recovery of lost data.

IRBC tests must therefore verify that our

- restart schedules (scripted and manual) work;
- technical solutions (redundancies, cluster, virtualization and cloud solutions) are suitable for meeting the availability requirements;
- IT systems can maintain production even if only one data center "survives" (islanding capability);
- our restore procedures will take effect;
- . . .

IRBC Test Scenario "Failure of a Data Center"
Let's assume we have two data centers. In the data centers we have, among other things, redundant clusters (partly active/active, partly active/passive), virtualized components, stand-alone systems and, of course, a physical infrastructure. A common test scenario is the assumption that one of the data centers fails (e.g. the famous, improbable meteorite that strikes, in the case of older data centers a CO_2 flood, the failure of the recooling system, etc.). Consequently, we have to manage the restart of the systems in the "surviving" data center, which on the one hand are relevant to the emergency, but on the other hand are not fully automated.

From Practice: Test Results and How to Deal with Them
In an ideal world, we collect all test results in the context of cybersecurity or resilience at a central location that has sufficient capacity to track the open points. Technically, this can be easily solved using common tools that are used, for example, in IT for tracking so-called "problems" (the corresponding ITIL® process is appropriately called Problem Management). In reality, however, the tests are prepared, executed, and tracked in the silos of the line organization (ISM, ITSCM, BCM, etc.).

4.8 Insurance of Cyber Risks

Purpose of Cyber Policies
As with any insurance, cyber insurance aims to mitigate (residual) risks; specifically, to transfer them to a third party. As such, it is one of our risk mitigation measures (just like the other measures described here in Chap. 5) and is a useful intermediate step before a risk owner gets around to accepting his residual risk.

Insurance Claim
For the insurance to apply (the fine print!), there must usually be at least one threat, if not a violation of our protection goals (confidentiality, integrity, availability, authenticity).

Often, however, another condition must be met for us to qualify for the insurance benefit. The cause of the breach of the protection objective must be a security incident.

Typical examples of security incidents are:

- Spreading of malware in or by means of our ITC systems (Trojans)
- Electronic access blocking of or by means of (!) our ITK systems (Cryptolocker, Ransomware)
- Access to our ITC systems
- Unlawful misuse of our ITC systems (pharming, bot-net integration)
- ...

Possible Contents of a Cyber Insurance Policy
A cyber insurance policy can cover a wide variety of aspects—as always, it's a question of money. This applies in particular to the amount of the damage or the costs that the insurer covers. As a rule, a distinction is made between compensation for damage,

- which we ourselves incur (self-inflicted damage) and such,
- incurred by our customers, partners, etc. because of the security incident (third-party damage).

Insurable own damage includes, but is not limited to:

- Business interruptions
- Recovery of IT systems incl. data
- Consequences from phishing and pharming
- Property damage to our IT and telecommunications systems
- IT Forensics
- Costs for external consulting in crisis management and crisis communication
- ...

Third party losses we can insure include:

- Contractual claims for damages (e.g., according to PCI-DSS, due to delayed service provision, etc.)
- Invasion of privacy
- Infringement of intellectual property rights (name, trademark, and copyright)
- Claims for exemption and defense
- Costs according to legal liability regulations
- ...

The extent to which these benefits are already included in the basic offer (and up to what amount of damage) varies from insurer to insurer.

Organizational Requirements

From insurer to insurer (or scope of benefits to scope of benefits), the prerequisites that we ourselves must create in our organization to benefit from a policy also vary. These range from simply filling out a questionnaire, which can be quite clear, to proving that our management systems for information security and business continuity management are properly implemented and certified (ISM according to ISO 27001; BCM according to ISO 22301). Various insurers also reserve the right to send their own auditors to verify the arrangements and our information on them.

Model Conditions of the GDV

The German Insurance Association (GDV) provides sample terms and conditions for cyber insurance on its website. (GDV) provides sample terms and conditions for cyber insurance on its website. This gives us a first, quite useful orientation, in case we do not want to blindly trust the offer of an insurer (or our insurance broker).

Cyber Crisis Prevention

5

5.1   Starting with an Analogy

Analogy: Traffic Safety and Cybersecurity

Cybersecurity is often equated with IT security and reduced to the latter. Anyone who has even a little idea can only shake their head. Equating cybersecurity and IT security is like reducing traffic safety to the proper tires of a vehicle. Traffic safety needs rules—the road traffic regulations. Cybersecurity also needs rules—including the German legislation such as BSIG, VAIT, MaRisk, and the like. Drivers and cars are not simply unleashed on humanity—without TÜV and driver's license tests it does not work. Tests and audits are the equivalent in the cybersecurity context. In order to (be able to) drive our car, we need to take driving lessons at the beginning of our driving career and remain continuously alert on the road later on. This is nothing but a call for training and awareness measures with cyber risks in mind. Keyword risks: On the road, we consider our own skill, the weather conditions, the condition of our vehicle, and most importantly, whether we are driving alone or with passengers dear to us in a hectic and dangerous environment, among other factors, when we drive. We do nothing different with cybersecurity in mind when we operate a cyber risk management program. There is no question that a securely designed vehicle with a complete overview of all installed parts and their specification is elementary. So are information, IT security, and asset management. But it is not everything. If we want to move around in road traffic, we must always have a plan B in our pocket in case our vehicle breaks down or—heaven forbid—we have an accident. Extricating ourselves from the vehicle, securing the scene of the accident, administering first aid, calling the emergency services and police, organizing a tow truck and subsequent repairs, and dealing with rubberneckers at the scene of the accident. So what does this mean for the cybersecurity analogy? Well, we need effective incident response as well as effective stakeholder and issue management, business and IT service continuity management or ICT readiness for business continuity and, last but not least, crisis management (!).

Governance

The main burden in the prevention of (cyber) crises is therefore borne by governance systems, as they are already required by regulation or at least lived practice in many industries:

- Stakeholder management and issue management
- Asset management
- Information Security Management
- Business and IT Service Continuity Management
- Cyber risk management

In this book, we look at the essential components of these governance systems so that we can form an opinion about the extent to which we might want to adopt similar measures in our organization. The entry and exit points of this section are two aspects that are not themselves governance systems but play a major role in each: Awareness and Audits.

Disclaimer

Of course, governance or management systems include a basic set of documentation—in particular, a scope document, a policy describing the context and intent of management, and role and process descriptions, etc.—in short, documents that establish the system and anchor it in the written order of any organization. And it is just as natural to integrate the management systems reciprocally.

We do not cover any of the governance systems exhaustively here (not even close) and therefore deliberately neglect the comparatively formal aspect of the documentation required in each case, as a detailed consideration would go far beyond the scope of a book on the management of (cyber) crises. Each of these systems offers enough material for a book of its own, and for some of them there is already more literature than even the most diligent reader could cope with.

Certification of Management Systems

We can operate some governance systems on the basis of certifiable management systems. These include a BCMS according to ISO 22301 as well as an ISMS according to ISO 27001.

Certification has numerous advantages: It

- builds trust with key stakeholders, reducing their and our effort in third and second party audits;
- requires a professional implementation of the respective topic;
- is an asset you can use to your advantage in crisis communication;

- can shift some of the public's attention and anger to the certifying body in the event of an emergency;
- creates the prerequisite for a cyber risk policy or can reduce its premiums.

The disadvantages are limited, as the additional costs are manageable compared to normal operation (at a semi-professional level).

5.2   Danger Recognized, Danger Averted: Awareness

. . .and that Helps Us with Crisis Management Because. . .?
Good awareness helps employees to identify potential crises early enough so that they can be contained as they arise. Awareness is the contribution of each individual employee to crisis prevention and thus the individual counterpart to a structured early warning system in the form of stakeholder and issue management (Sect. 5.3).

Objective: Recognize Dangers
Crises do not always come suddenly, but often insidiously. This is dangerous because we find it difficult to correctly classify potentially negative consequences in gradual developments. That makes sense in principle, because otherwise we would all be in a state of permanent alert—that would be everything, but not healthy. It also means that we sometimes miss the point of action. Therefore, it is essential to recognize in the first place that we are dealing with a potential crisis trigger. And also to know what to do in such a case. Otherwise, the damage will gradually build up until it may be too late.

Anticipation of Damage
Damage of all kinds is another matter entirely. As a rule, damage does not develop in a linear fashion, but at an ever faster rate. And that brings us to the second problem. We humans are bad at dealing with non-linear developments—we tend to massively underestimate them. This means that we have to do everything in our power to identify potential trouble spots as early as possible so that we can initiate countermeasures in good time.

The Frog in the Cooking Pot
The importance of awareness is illustrated by the following example (for all animal lovers, this is a thought experiment only): Let us imagine two things, namely a pot of water standing on a stove as well as a frog. In the first case, the action starts with bubbling water in the pot and the frog somewhere outside the pot. When the frog lands in the water (for whatever reason), it will immediately try to hop back out. He recognizes sudden heat as a threat. In the second case, the action starts under different auspices. Now the water in the pot is a pleasant 15 °C (for a frog) and he paddles happily along in it. If we now increase the water temperature very gradually, the frog can acclimatize to a certain temperature. But only up to a certain temperature and not beyond. The point at which further acclimatization

is no longer possible is the point at which the frog suffers damage. The crucial question is: Does the frog recognize the temperature at which it becomes dangerous for it?

Awareness Program

If we want to prevent ourselves from becoming like the researcher in the continuously warming water, we must help our employees to achieve an appropriate level of sensitivity. To do this, we can borrow from what was said in the section on training. We need to think about goals, target groups, didactics, and measures. We can even take to heart two of the principles described earlier: "Didactics determines methodology" and "From the general to the specific".

Differences to Trainings

However, there are two major differences that we should keep in mind: Target group and content differ significantly between training and awareness measures.

In the case of training, we can restrict ourselves to the members of the emergency and crisis organization and the tasks they have to perform in it. For awareness measures, the scope is broader, both in terms of target groups and topics. In terms of awareness, we need to include everyone who works for our organization, even service providers if necessary. After all, anyone can find themselves in a situation where they observe or experience something that could result in a crisis. The spectrum here ranges from topics from the context of information security (the famous phishing e-mail) to the increased volume of complaints on the customer complaints hotline.

5.3   Early Warning System: Risk Communication, Stakeholder Management, and Issue Management

. . .and that Helps Us with Crisis Management Because. . .?

What would it be like if we could catch wind (not randomly!) of potentially dangerous developments so early that we could still take action in time and under the radar of public perception to prevent the likelihood of occurrence or impact of negative developments for ourselves and our stakeholders? That is precisely the goal of risk communication, stakeholder and issue management: to dispel the embers before they become a fire.

Examples

For simplicity, let's imagine the following situations:

- Our customers are becoming increasingly sensitive about the protection and use of their data. Their expectations of us as an organization that processes their data are growing.
- Competitors are forging ahead and setting new standards, for example with regard to investments and cybersecurity measures.

- At the political level, trends are emerging that restrict our discretionary powers in cyber crises or tighten reporting requirements.
- Judicial rulings set precedents for data breaches.
- Service providers in our industry (or even from us) have problems with data protection issues, IT security, their own service providers or are in the focus of external auditors or regulators, have to put the brakes on costs, which in turn has an impact on investments in cybersecurity.
- . . .

Even though this book is about cyber crises, crises can come at us from many different directions, and cyber risks are just one of them. Therefore, our stakeholder and issue management should not be limited to cyber risks.

And How Is that Supposed to Work?
To do that, we have to:

- have a clear picture of our stakeholders;
- have a clear picture of the issues that are of concern to our stakeholders;
- have a clear picture of the issues that are real pain points for our business model;
- bring these individual images together and use relevant starting points for our interests;
- we will take up these points of departure in our risk communication, which we will pursue with our stakeholders on an ongoing basis wherever possible.

The approach is somewhat reminiscent of the prototypical risk management process.

From Practice: Interweaving Crisis Management with Risk Communication, Stakeholder and Issue Management
In crisis management, we have already thought about relevant target groups in at least two places: in the → initialization of the crisis management team's working procedure and → crisis communication. Whereas there we looked at stakeholders from the perspective of the specific crisis situation, we now have to adopt a fundamental, scenario-independent perspective. This means that if we have already managed a crisis using the suggestions from the Crisis Response chapter, we can draw on the insights gained about stakeholders at that time. However, if we do not yet have such experience, we may be able to draw on insights from different areas, such as sales, legal, communications/PR, marketing, data privacy, regulatory affairs, compliance, and public affairs. When a crisis actually hits us at some point, our crisis management team (CMT) will benefit considerably from this preparatory work.

5.3.1 Stakeholder and Issue Management

Identification of Stakeholders and Issues

First, we need to identify our stakeholders—identify, mind you, and not yet rank or evaluate them in any way. This can be helped by the rough sorting we learned about in Sect. 3.2.1 Setting the Course: Initializing the crisis management team's working procedure. A typical representation would be a MindMap, but tables (Excel is the perennial favorite) and database-based CRM tools also serve their purpose. We should refine this sorting until, ideally, we find specific individual people in it. Because these are the people we need to deal with.

Stakeholder Assessment and Analysis

Once we have identified our stakeholders, we can set about looking at their

- worldview;
- attitude toward our organization, industry or business model;
- attitude towards cybersecurity and data protection issues;
- red lines;
- ability to exert influence

and thus, the risks we run when we make trouble with the respective stakeholder.

We need to dress these considerations up in concrete questions. Who is critical of us, our business model or our industry? Who is sympathetic, who is neutral? Who is influential and how?

How Do We Get to Know the Opinions of the Stakeholders?

To learn more about the opinions and attitudes of our stakeholders, we can make use of numerous sources:

- Big Data and Artificial Intelligence (AI)
- (classic) quantitative data (development of customer numbers, key financial figures, company value, etc.)
- Qualitative data, which we can collect via various formats:
  - Common methods of customer surveys
  - Round tables and customer events, if necessary, with the presence of management
  - (Anonymous) questionnaires
  - Interviews conducted by neutral (external) third parties (but please not by auditors or law firms—this inevitably creates reservations on the part of the interviewee, a defensive attitude, or a tendency to say only what is absolutely necessary. Unfortunately, auditors and law firms often have an aura reminiscent of the Holy Roman Inquisition).
  - ...

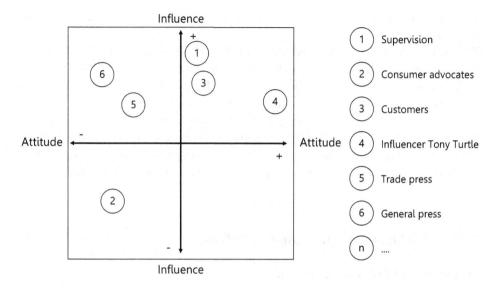

Fig. 5.1 Stakeholder map

From Practice: Visualization of the Result

We can visualize the result in a coordinate system so that we can quickly give our management a high-level impression. On one axis we map the stakeholder's attitude towards our organization, on the other its influence. Based on Fig. 5.1, an additional color coding can show which issues are of concern to the respective stakeholder.

Stakeholder and Issues Management

Once we have answered these questions, we need to find starting points to work with the stakeholders and issues. First starting points can be found by asking the following questions: Why are our critics critical, our friends friendly and the neutrals neutral? How can we get the neutrals on our side and contain the influence of the critics, so that in the event of a crisis we are not faced with an overwhelming number of critics all by ourselves (credo: make friends before you need them)? Who takes care of which stakeholders and issues?

Stakeholder-Issue-Matrix

The result is a stakeholder-issue matrix from which we can prioritize both the stakeholders and the issues. We should prioritize because a considerable number of people and issues quickly accumulate—and taking care of all of them is simply illusory. The issues and people that we have prioritized can now be assigned to people who are responsible for managing the stakeholder or the impact of the issue on the stakeholders.

From Practice: Confidentiality of Stakeholder Assessments and Stakeholder-Issue Matrices

The moment we assign a natural person information about his or her stance on a certain topic or, more generally, his or her world view, we are dealing with personal data that must be handled in accordance with the provisions of the EU DSGVO. This obliges us to limit the group of people who have access to the stakeholder assessment or stakeholder-issue matrix. Beyond the formal legal obligation, however, we also have a vested interest in ensuring that our assessment does not spread further afield. After all, from time to time we experience a media outcry when yet another case becomes public in which an organization has classified certain customers (or even journalists, heaven forbid!) for internal use.

5.3.2   Risk Communication (And Its Pitfalls)

Monitoring and Risk Communication

In any case, the basis of caring includes at least two components: Monitoring of the respective issue or stakeholder and risk communication with the stakeholder about the issue.

Monitoring means keeping an eye on a stakeholder or issue. We can do this in many ways:

- (Social) Media Monitoring
- Attendance at events
- Direct contact maintenance
- Legal monitoring, i.e., the monitoring of laws and regulations that relate to our own issues and are currently being prepared at the various political levels (local, state, federal, EU).
- . . .

Risk communication is nothing other than entering a conversation with key stakeholders on topics that are important to us but are not viewed positively by key stakeholders. The aim of this exercise is to,

- impart knowledge (many of the stakeholders are laymen in the respective field and have no rational reasons for their skeptical attitude);
- become visible themselves as people (and not just as an organization);
- build confidence and reduce fears.

No question, even this approach has limitations—especially vis-à-vis activists and ideologized stakeholders.

Well-Meant Is the Opposite of Well Done

As well-intentioned as we are: We should expect that people will misunderstand what we do with the best of intentions—or that our actions will have unintended side effects. Science (specifically: Otway/Wynne) speaks here of "paradoxes".

Prototypically, seven such paradoxes can be observed again and again, which we should know and consider:

- Reassurance-arousal paradox
- Information targeting paradox
- Information cultures paradox
- Information demand paradox
- Body language paradox
- Credibility-complacency paradox
- Credibility-authenticity paradox

No. 1: Reassurance-Arousal Paradox

We want to reassure our stakeholders—and achieve the opposite. A prime example of this problem does not originate from the cyber environment but has been persistently in the media for some time. The then German Federal Minister of the Interior, Thomas de Maizière, became the focus of public attention when an international football match between Germany and the Netherlands in Hanover was cancelled in November 2015 due to fears of attacks. In view of further attacks in Paris just a few days earlier, people across Europe were worried anyway, so the German government's objective was clear: the population should not be unduly alarmed. When members of the press asked for details about the threat situation, Federal Interior Minister Thomas de Maizière was understandably reticent and gave selective evasive answers—only to explain: "Some of these answers could unsettle the population. Indeed, speculation about suspected threats ran high, and the Süddeutsche Zeitung noted, "An interior minister is doing exactly what he pretends to want to prevent: He unsettles."

No. 2: Information Targeting Paradox

The information targeting paradox describes the problem that a piece of information triggers exactly the opposite of what we want to achieve in the addressee—a more general variant of the example we just used.

No. 3: Information Cultures Paradox

The information culture paradox picks up on the fact that every organization has its own habits in dealing with information. We can see this in the

- Choice of the language of certain stakeholders, the appropriate terminology and the channels used;

- Answer to the fundamental question of whether our organization communicates at all or otherwise views its communication as a necessary evil and keeps it to a minimum.

In other words, we make ourselves suspicious if we never inform our stakeholders about anything, but suddenly unleash communication frenzy via Facebook, Twitter, phone calls, etc. Communication frenzies unfold.

No. 4: Information Demand Paradox

The information demand paradox describes the risk of overloading our stakeholders with information. As a result, the recipients of the information are no longer able to filter out the information that is actually relevant in the mass of information. The consequences: They either lose interest in the crisis (which would be good) or are simply annoyed by it (which would be bad). So it all comes down to the quantity of communication. To exaggerate a bit: Since we don't want to launch a DDoS attack on our stakeholders, we should avoid an *information overload* with our stakeholders to be on the safe side. Therefore: no digital speech diarrhea, please!

No. 5: Body Language Paradox

The body language paradox states that the unconscious (non-verbal) information can differ significantly from the consciously sent information (verbal and non-verbal). In journalism, there is the term text-image scissors for this phenomenon.

Since we rarely end up on TV but will pretty much use our social media channels for crisis communication, we should keep this point in mind. Those who step in front of the camera are often completely focused on their messages and less on their body language, facial expressions, gestures, clothing, hairstyle, articulation, etc. Therefore, it is advisable that another person is present (quasi as a coach) when recording a video message and makes sure that the recording cannot boomerang.

Against the backdrop of the body language paradox, by the way, it makes sense to broaden our perspective from pure body language to our overall reaction. The overall approach to communication allows conclusions to be drawn about how much our cyber crisis—regardless of the messages dressed up in words—has actually affected our organization. Which brings us back to the information targeting paradox.

No. 6: Credibility-Complacency Paradox

The credibility-complacency paradox refers to the fact that trust in the people who control a risk eclipses the attitude towards the risk itself to the extent that our stakeholders become indifferent to it. Trust in us overrides everything.

Conversely, this also means that if we trust a service provider too much, we may systematically underestimate the risk inherent in its operational organization. This is a clear argument in favor of governance that also includes the management of service providers—especially from a security and continuity perspective (more on this in Chap. 5).

No. 7: Credibility-Authenticity Paradox

The credibility-authenticity paradox is also about trust. Often, the objective truth of a message is less important than trust in the sender. Conversely, this also means that if our basis of trust is shaken, our messages will no longer get through to our target groups—no matter how true they are. Then it is all the more important that we back up our messages with facts that can be easily and quickly verified.

Read More

If you want to learn more about risk communication with, shall we say, complicated stakeholders, you should read "The Art of Risk Communication" by Otto-Peter Obermeier. The book is not only instructive, but also enjoyable to read for long stretches. In it, Obermeier uses the following stakeholder typology, which we can also use as a guide:

- Nopes ("not on planet earth"): Fundamentalists
- Nimtos ("not in my term of office"): Bureaucrats
- Nimbys ("not in my backyard"): Activists
- Nimbles ("not in my bottom line"): Company

Especially when it comes to cyber and data protection issues, we encounter representatives of each type again and again.

5.4   Not Sexy, but Fundamental: Asset Management and Structural Analysis

...and that Helps Us with Crisis Management Because...?

Even though this may sound at least spiritual, if not esoteric, it also applies to information, IT systems, etc., as well as their protection goals and needs: Everything is connected to everything else. The clearest possible picture of the interrelationships is crucial:

- in the immediate event of a crisis for the CMT as well as for resuming business operations, restarting IT systems, restoring data, or cybersecurity incident response;
- for setting up and operating an information security management system, perhaps the most important preventive measure against cyber crises. Without knowledge of the context, we cannot take effective security measures. And without security measures, we can turn our crisis organization into a regular organization.

Primary Assets and Supporting Assets

For asset management, we can follow the breakdown from ISO 27005 (which we should definitely do). Asset is a collective term for what we can also call tangible and intangible goods. In other words, things of value that we can put our hands on—or not.

When we speak of primary assets, we mean those that we cannot take into our own hands. They are the ones that set the pace. There are exactly two types of primary assets in the cyber context: processes and information. These are characterized by the fact that we cannot attack them directly, but we cannot protect them either.

However, we can attack and protect the so-called supporting assets, by means of which the primary resources are processed, i.e., are given life. There is a whole range of these supporting resources. IT systems come to mind first and foremost, of course. But they also include buildings, people (roles!), machines and equipment, paper documents, service providers, and so on. You can't do without supporting resources—they are the skeleton around which any organization is built.

Asset Relationships and Enterprise Architecture

"Built" means that ideally we have or know two things:

- A list of all components that we have installed for any purpose at any place at any time and
- the corresponding architecture plan.

Asset management is nothing else. It gives us information about which (supporting) resources we have in use where and for what purpose.

Structural Analysis and Information Network

The basis for this is the structural analysis that is often carried out in connection with the → protection needs assessment or the business impact analysis.

- Primary assets to primary assets (i.e., information and processes),
- Primary assets to supporting assets; and
- Supporting assets among themselves

can be determined. These dependencies are sometimes also called relations. This is very reminiscent of the classic enterprise architecture—the information network is just a special perspective on it. And this is exactly what we should know as precisely as possible if we want to prevent or manage cyber crises.

From the Practice: Illustrative Example "Sales Process"

Let's take our sales process (primary asset) as an example. The sales process requires different types of information (also primary asset). This includes information about the customer himself (his buyer history, potential needs, etc.), but also information about our products and services (features, marketing materials, price lists, etc.). The salesperson (role, i.e., a supporting asset) prepares the sales call in the office (supporting asset) by getting a final overview of the information on his tablet (supporting asset) in the CRM system (supporting asset) and then gets into the car (supporting asset) to drive to the customer (stakeholder). The CRM system with all its components (database, middleware) is hosted and operated by an external service provider (supporting asset) on its own hardware (supporting asset). The hardware, in turn, is located in the data center (supporting asset) of a specialized data center operator (supporting asset), where the IT service provider has rented space (supporting asset).

Such dependencies inevitably become complex. Our company has more than just the sales process with its few supporting resources. It always gets exciting when a resource has dependencies in several directions. A very banal example is the car of our salesperson. This could be, for example, a company-owned pool vehicle that other roles (for example, fitters, other salespeople, etc.) can also access. In that case, we most certainly have a department somewhere in our organization that handles fleet management—from acquisition to contract to workshop management. These colleagues also have to deal with the supporting resource "car", but they process completely different types of information than our salesperson, of course they also use other IT systems than the CRM for this purpose and they are located in other offices, maybe even at a different location. The car, on the other hand, is probably parked (when it is not being driven) in a company-owned area (parking lot, garage), which is kept in good condition by other colleagues (facility management) or possibly an external service provider.

From Practice: Tool Suites for Asset Management and Governance

And now let's just mentally transfer the example of the car to the CRM system, which in turn requires different databases and servers (physical, virtualized), network components, a (WAN) connection from the data center to our location, etc.. All of these components need to be patched and maintained on a regular basis. Each of these components usually serves more than one purpose, making the relationships in IT systems difficult to manage.

Therefore, nowadays we can no longer avoid an IT-supported solution for asset management that goes beyond mere Excel sheets. Especially since we have so far completely ignored the aspects that are crucial from a cyber perspective: the questions of confidentiality, integrity, availability, and authenticity of the information (protection requirements!) that we process with our supporting asset.

A good tool is characterized primarily by its underlying data model. The data model MUST be able to handle multidimensional relations, protection needs, criticalities as well as their inheritances for primary resources and supporting resources. In short: It must be able to consistently link ISM, BCM and ITSCM, because all these disciplines are based on a (hopefully common) asset management (more on this in the following chapters).

From Practice: ITIL®, CMDB and Asset Management

Anyone involved in ITIL® will be familiar with the Configuration Management Database (CMDB) from the Configuration Management process. In it we (hopefully) find much of the information we need for clean asset management, at least for the supporting resource IT. Unfortunately, experience shows that a reliably maintained CMDB is the exception rather than the rule (and that is a euphemism).

5.5   Indispensable: Information and IT Security Management

...and that Helps Us with Crisis Management Because...?
Information Security Management (ISM) is probably the most important preventive measure when we talk about cybersecurity and cyber crisis management. Its symbolic effect on our stakeholders should not be underestimated: Crisis communicators are happy if they can refer to a certified ISMS in case of an emergency.

Basic Idea of ISM
The basic idea of ISM is as follows: If we want to create security for our business-critical information, we must concretize this comparatively abstract goal and then take appropriate measures. To do this, we proceed in several steps. We must

1. Agree on protection or security objectives to be defined for each type/category of information;
2. Define the level of protection to be achieved based on the protection or security objectives and systematically implement it using concrete specifications and architecture blueprints for the security configuration of our supporting resources.

In this way, we can ensure an appropriate level of security for our resources (both primary and supporting) in a risk-oriented manner.

5.5.1   ISM in Fast Forward Mode

Concretization: Protection Needs and Security Objectives
Depending on whether we proceed according to a system from the Anglo-American or German-speaking world, we have the choice between an approach with three and one with four protection goals. Both approaches work with

- confidentiality,
- integrity and
- availability.

This gives rise to the acronym CIA.
In the German-speaking countries, the protection goal of

- Authenticity

which refers not only to the content, but also to the sender and receiver of a piece of information. If we pick up the first letters of the German terms, we can work with the acronym VIVA. We will encounter it one or two more times in this book.

Protection Needs Assessment

Now we have to answer the question of how bad a breach of these protection goals would be in the case of each individual type/category of information (personal identifiable data (PII), special types of PII, financial data, marketing documents, production secrets, data with security relevance, etc.). The procedure for this is the protection needs assessment or protection needs analysis (PNA).

In terms of potential damage, it is useful to consider legal and contractual breaches, but also reputation damage and financial losses on a multi-level scale (e.g., low, medium, high, very high).

If we are in an industry where information security breaches can turn into safety issues, it is important that we also consider the risks to life and limb. These industries include not only almost all critical infrastructure providers (especially in the healthcare, logistics, and energy sectors), but also all other users of IoT machines and systems, such as automotive manufacturers and suppliers, the manufacturing and chemical industries, etc.

From Practice: Dovetailing and Integration of PNA and BIA

It makes sense to use the same parameters, damage types and amounts, and evaluation periods for availability as in the business impact analysis. Ideally, we even dovetail the surveys and thus halve the effort for all parties involved.

Interim Result: Need for Protection

So far, we have the following intermediate result: per information type/category and protection goal (VIVA), we know the amount of damage (danger to life and limb, violations of the law, etc.) that we shall expect. This is the so-called protection requirement.

Through structural analysis, we also know which supporting resources process these information types/categories.

From PNA to Protection Levels to Specifications and Blueprints

Now we can set about translating the need for protection into a level of protection. This means nothing other than that for each combination of

- protection goal,
- protection needs and
- supportive asset

define minimum requirements that are as concrete as possible. Catalogues with individual specifications as well as blueprints for the protection of (ICT) systems are suitable for this purpose.

In this way

- we don't have to reinvent the wheel for every single type/category of information or supporting asset;
- we create comparability with regard to the achieved and targeted level of protection;

- we facilitate the tracking of the implementation status for all parties involved (risk owner, auditor, etc.).

After the PNA Is Before the PNA

ISM is a cyclical management process, usually designed for one run per year. In this respect, we cannot avoid repeating (better: updating) the SBF—but with the difference that the repetitions mean significantly less effort than the initial implementation. Especially if we have documented the results including derivation and justification in a comprehensible way. BIA and IRBC gap analysis send their regards.

5.5.2   Fields of Action for Information Security

ISO 270xx vs. BSI Basic Protection (BSI Grundschutz)

While in the international arena almost exclusively ISO standards as well as the US-American NIST CSF play a role in the context of cybersecurity, Germany continues to try a national special path. This is the BSI Grundschutz. In its latest amendment, however, it is moving ever closer to the management system approach of the ISO standards and enables "ISO 27001 based on BSI Grundschutz" certification. Therefore, we also focus on the fields of action that ISO 27001 identifies.

Fields of Action

According to ISO 27001, if we want to operate an ISMS, we have to deal with the following topics:

- Information security guidelines incl. specifications of the (top) management
- Organization of information security (internal, teleworking, mobile devices)
- Security around the human factor (before, during and after employment)
- Asset management (responsibilities, classification of information, handling of data carriers)
- Control of accesses, accesses and accesses (requirements of the identity and access management for users, responsibilities of the users, control of the access/access to systems and applications)
- Cryptography
- Physical and environmental security (security zones, equipment)
- Operational security (processes and responsibilities, protection against malware, backups, logging and monitoring, technical vulnerability management)
- Security of communication links (secure networks, information transmission)
- Acquisition, development and maintenance of IT systems (security requirements, security in development and support processes, test data)
- Relationships with suppliers and service providers (information security, service provision)

- Information Security Incident Management
- Information security aspects of BCM
- Compliance (compliance with legal and contractual requirements, information security reviews/reviews)

Numerous topics also play a role in the management of cyber crises (albeit to varying degrees) and are therefore reflected in this book.

5.6   Focus Availability: Continuity Management

5.6.1   Business Continuity Management

BCM Focus: Availability of Processes
Business Continuity Management (BCM) deals with the question of how we can keep time-critical processes and activities, including the necessary information (primary assets according to ISO 27005), available to the extent that no serious damage occurs to our organization, even in the event of a failure of central resources (supporting assets according to ISO 27005). The common standard for BCM is ISO 22301.

What Use Is BCM During a Crisis?
In an acute crisis, BCM keeps the CMT's back free by preparing emergency operations for time-critical processes and activities. In this way, it helps to meet the expectations of key stakeholders. At the same time, it provides immensely important information: What are the most important products, processes and services that we offer as an organization?

What Are Important Elements?
We best manage BCM using a cyclical process embedded in a Business Continuity Management System (BCMS). Its essential steps are:

- Business Impact Analysis (BIA)
- BC Risk Assessment (BC RA)
- BC strategies for typical failure scenarios
- Preparation/updating of business continuity plans (BCP)
- Tests, especially of the BCP

Business Impact Analysis
The BIA has a central purpose: to find out our emergency-relevant processes and to determine the requirements for their emergency operation. Since the BIA also provides us with, among other things, the order in which we need to send our processes into emergency operation mode, we can find more about this in the chapter → Preparing Emergency Operation of (Business) Processes.

BC Risk Assessment

As part of the BIA, we elicit, among other things, the (supporting) resources without which our emergency-relevant (business) processes would not function. The BC Risk Assessment is there to analyze,

- for what reason the individual resources may fail, i.e., to answer the question of threats;
- how long the resource is likely to be down depending on the cause of failure (=threat);
- what damages are associated with it;
- which risk treatment measures make sense;
- at what point we can bear the residual risk.

These steps are covered in more detail in Sect. 5.7.

BC Strategies

The resources that we looked at more closely in the BC Risk Assessment also play a decisive role in the BC strategies. However, rather than each resource separately, they are grouped into resource types. The common resource types are:

- Staff
- Buildings/Locations
- IT
- Service provider
- Machinery and equipment

We consider the individual resource types each on a comparatively abstract level as a so-called failure scenario. For each failure scenario, we should identify basic courses of action to limit its probability of occurrence and impact. With regard to cyber crises, the focus is inevitably on IT, certain service providers, and machines and systems connected to the IoT. The common approach is to,

- provide redundancy and shift production to multiple locations to reduce the likelihood of failure;
- to get a grip on the effects by means of business continuity, restart, and recovery plans as well as restore concepts.

Business Continuity Plans

BCPs, also known as "contingency plans", have only one purpose: to identify and document workarounds and temporary solutions that enable us to maintain our emergency-relevant processes, at least temporarily, even if central resources fail. We discuss them in more detail in Sects. 3.3.1.1 and 4.6.1.

Tests

Having BCPs is all well and good, but only half the battle. The decisive question is: Do they really work? Apart from serious cases, this question can only be answered by tests, tests and more tests. More on this and on test forms, objectives, etc. can be found in Sect. 4.7.

5.6.2   IRBC/IT Service Continuity Management

ITSCM/IRBC Focus: Availability of IT and TC Systems
IT Service Continuity Management (ITSCM) ensures ICT readiness for business continuity (IRBC), i.e., that our critical (business) processes can rely on IT and telecommunications solutions to the extent required. Our goal at this point is therefore to keep IT (supporting resource!) available to the extent that its failure never causes serious damage to the organization.

What Use Is IRBC During an Emergency or Crisis?
In an acute crisis, IRBC keeps the CMT's back free by making their required IT systems available again for the time-critical processes and activities within a predefined timeframe. In this way, it helps to maintain business operations.

What Are Important Elements?
Just like BCM and ISM, we best manage IRBC using a cyclical process. Its key steps are:

- IRBC gap analysis
- IRBC strategy options
- Creation/updating of restart and recovery plans as well as restore concepts
- Test of the plans and restore concepts

IRBC Gap Analysis
With the IRBC gap analysis, we find out whether we meet the availability requirements of the (business) processes for our IT and telecommunications components. To do this, we first need the results of the business impact analysis and the protection needs assessment with the required recovery time objectives (RTO). We compare these with the recovery times that we are able to maintain (recovery time actual, RTA). Second, we must also do this with the maximum data loss times (recovery point objective, RPO). Ideally, our achieved recovery and data loss times are smaller than the required ones. If not, we should discuss with the process owners and information owners whether the availability requirements we can offer are still sufficient in case of doubt. Then all the process owner or information owner has to do is correct their availability requirement and we are off the hook IRBC-wise. However, if they are indeed insufficient, the process owner or information owner can choose between two options: Either he provides the funds so that we, as an

internal service provider, meet the availability requirement, for example, by switching to a different technology, or he evaluates and accepts the risk resulting from the TARGET-ACTUAL deviation of the availability requirement.

IRBC Strategy Options and Principles
Based on the results of the GAP analysis and the understanding we have gained of our IT landscape, we can now address the question: How can we prevent the likelihood of a failure (and, if the worst comes to the worst, its impact)?

To this end, we can be guided by various principles, These include:

- The redundancy principle

  (supporting assets must be available several times)

- The distance principle

  (assets resources must be far enough apart that they are not hit by the same physical event)

- Poka Yoke Principle

  (Technologies and processes must be foolproof to prevent humans from making a mistake in the first place).

- . . .

For those who want to learn more principles and strategies, we recommend "IT-Sicherheit mit System" by Klaus-Rainer Müller. Müller describes more than 30 (!) different principles, which are not only focused on availability, but also on the remaining protection goals.

Fundamentally, we must always ask ourselves the question of make-or-buy. Can we operate our IT more reliably and cost-effectively ourselves than a specialized service provider can? Where do we use cloud solutions with a view to availability requirements and where does this make us too dependent on the WAN connection?

Either way, which strategy options we should choose depends on several factors:

- our industry and how it is regulated (critical infrastructure providers vs. "normal" organizations)
- the specific availability requirements that we must meet
- the investments we can (or want to) make

Highest Availability vs. High Availability
We will not be able to avoid taking a closer look at (at least) two of the principles described above: the principle of redundancy and the principle of distance. In practice, we usually quickly end up with the questions "Do we have to build our data centers with high availability?" and "Are our data centers far enough apart?"

The BSI operates with the concepts of maximum and high availability. The following availability requirements are hidden behind this:

- Maximum availability (VK*4): 99.999% p.a.
- High availability (VK3): 99.99% p.a.

The BSI has published its ideas on the design of data centers that meet these requirements in the High Availability Compendium.

*VK is the official abbreviation for the German term Verfügbarkeitsklasse (English: availability class).

Distance Between Two Redundant Data Centers
Until the end of 2018, the BSI still recommended that our data centers should have a minimum distance of five kilometers. The BSI has pulverized this distance, at least for data centers in the high and maximum availability categories. Under the label of geo-redundancy, we are now at a minimum distance of 100 km, which the BSI accepts. However, the actual recommendation for geo-redundant data centers is 200 km. The BSI has also recognized that these distances are hardly feasible with the current state of the art (latency times!) depending on the operating concept (keyword: synchronous operation with IBM mainframe). Therefore, the same paper that specifies the distance contains an opening clause that explicitly refers to technical reasons.

From Practice: Classic 99.9% Availability Trap in SLA and UP
Service Level Agreements (SLA) or Underpinning Contracts (UP) regulate the availability we can expect from an (IT) service. We often find assurances that the service provider must keep the service available 99.9% of the time—measured over one (calendar) year. Table 5.1 shows how far we are from what our emergency-relevant (business) processes actually require.

Restart Plans and Restore Concepts
Restart plans and restore concepts are often referred to as "IT contingency plans". They describe how we provide our IT services within the required recovery time in the event of an IT system or its data failing. We discuss them in more detail in Sects. 3.3.1.2 and 4.6.2.

IRBC Tests
IRBC gap analysis, restart plans, or restore concepts—whether we meet the availability requirements in an emergency, can only be answered by tests that are as close to reality as

Table 5.1 Availability rules in SLAs

Availability (%)	Failure (%)	Failure (h)	Failure (min)
100	0	0	0
99.999	0.001	009	5
99.99	0.01	0.9	53
99.9	0.1	8.8	526

possible (analogous to the BCP, see above). More on this and on test forms, objectives etc. can be found in Sect. 4.7.

5.7 Cyber Risk Management

. . .and that Helps Us with Crisis Management Because. . .?
Cyber risk management primarily helps us to coordinate the various preventive measures by forming a bracket, as it were, around all the technical and organizational measures with which we want to reduce the probability of occurrence or impact of a cyber crisis. A structured cyber risk management program makes risks transparent to us so that we can decide where to deploy precious resources to achieve the best possible risk reduction. In other words, cyber risk management enables efficient resource allocation thanks to transparency about risks.

Process Steps
As with most types of risk management, we always go through three steps at regular intervals in cyber risk management:

- Risk assessment
- Risk treatment
- Acceptance of (residual) risks

Basic Idea
The basic idea is to get an all-around view of possible threats to our primary resources by systematically scanning the supporting resources to see how these threats can exploit any vulnerabilities. Once we have a combination of vulnerability and threat, we need to think about how we want to deal with that risk (which is then the subject of risk treatment).

Relevant Standards
The relevant standards are ISO 31000, ISO 27005, ISO 27001, and ISO 27032. This sounds extensive, but it is not so bad—the procedures described in them are almost identical. We orient ourselves on them here.

5.7.1   Preliminary Work

Asset Management and Protection Needs Assessment
Before we can get down to cyber risk management, we need to set up two things: asset management and the protection needs assessment from information security management. Unfortunately, we can't do without it, because for the risk assessment we need to know not only potential threats, but also and above all their docking points in our organization—and those are the assets. And since it would be completely uneconomical to treat all supporting resources in cyber risk management in equal detail, we cannot avoid a filter that helps us with a risk-oriented approach—which in turn is the protection needs assessment.

From Practice: Using Interfaces
When setting up our cyber risk management, however, we should not try to completely reinvent the wheel within the organization. After all, we have certainly already taken measures in one place or another that can help us wonderfully and that we should definitely take into account (also out of respect for the said departments).

Typically, we encounter the following points, sometimes individually, sometimes combined in different ways, but rarely complete and synchronized with each other:

- IT Risk Management
- BC Risk Assessment (also called RIA in the distant past)
- Risk assessments based on ISO 27001
- Operational risk management

5.7.2   Risk Assessment

Components of the Risk Assessment
The risk assessment (often translated as risk evaluation) already consists of several components:

- Risk identification
- Risk analysis
- Risk assessment

Admittedly, the individual points sound like synonyms at first. But on closer inspection we will see what differences there are and how one step builds on the other.

5.7.2.1 Risk Identification
Identification of Assets
Unfortunately, a complete and up-to-date (information) architecture is rarely available in practice. But there are ways to find reasonably reliable approximate values. First of all, a

process map helps us to document all processes of our organization including their mutual interfaces and, ideally, roles and IT applications. If we supplement this process map with statements about which process processes which information and how urgently we need to process it with regard to

- confidentiality,
- integrity,
- availability and
- authenticity

then we've come a long way. Because now we can focus everything else on the really critical processes and information (and the supporting assets that process them).

This focus (in the sense of prioritization) is important because otherwise we would have to secure all of our supporting assets to the extent that the most stringent requirement for any single resource demands. That would be a guarantee for exploding efforts—in terms of time, personnel deployment, and costs.

Scope of Cyber Risk Management
Instead, we should focus on the supporting assets that play a role in our organization in handling the critical processes and information from all types of supporting assets:

- IT (hardware and software)
- Persons (roles)
- Service providers and suppliers
- Locations, buildings
- Machinery, equipment
- . . .

Threat/Hazard Catalogues
The first question is what threats or dangers we need to consider. These certainly differ from category to category. While a DDoS attack is undoubtedly a relevant threat for some IT assets, it is not relevant for people or building infrastructure (or at least not immediately). On the other hand, a fire is a threat to a building, but not to an application—but again to the hardware through which it is delivered. If we have outsourced part of our information processing to a service provider or are dependent on the supply of a supplier, its failure will also affect our organization.

Conversely, however, it is also true that a hazard without exposure also entails no risk. Expressed in our road safety analogy: a certain road can be as slippery as it wants to be—if we don't drive along it, the slipperiness doesn't matter.

From Practice: BSI Threat Catalogues
To ensure that we do not have to start from scratch in the initial compilation of potential threats, the BSI, for example, has done some good preparatory work—at least for IT assets.

Unfortunately, the BSI provides less help for the other categories. Here we have to invest a little brainpower ourselves (or ask an experienced service provider if we can invest money instead of time).

Where Do We Stand with Which Combination of Resource and Threat?
Since we cannot plan and build our organization from scratch, we always start from a status quo. This means that we have usually already implemented countermeasures of some kind for a considerable number of combinations of asset and threat. We must not disregard these, on the contrary.

Identification of Vulnerabilities
Thus equipped, we can now turn our attention to the vulnerabilities that remain. Which resources do we know about their individual vulnerabilities? Are our employees chronically eager to provide information on the phone and accordingly susceptible to social engineering? Do they often work on their laptops on the train, but without adequate privacy protection? Do we use software that has been tried and tested over many years but is no longer supplied with security patches by the manufacturer?

And the Consequences?
As a final step, we try to identify the fundamentally conceivable consequences that could occur in each case. What would be the effect on a purely technological level? And how would such an event affect the information and processes themselves, i.e., ultimately the reputation, the earnings situation or applicable laws and contracts?

Result of the Risk Identification
The result of the risk identification is the allocation

- of threats/dangers,
- countermeasures,
- vulnerabilities, and
- consequences

to the individual supporting assets. With this, we have identified the individual risks. Mind you, identified—not analyzed and not assessed.

5.7.2.2 Risk Analysis
Subject of the Risk Analysis
Risk analysis is about three things:

- a more precise assessment of the impact side of each risk (i.e., the amount of damage)
- the estimation of the probability that the risk will materialize
- the determination of the risk resulting from the combination of the amount of damage and the probability of occurrence

From Practice: Avoiding Fictitious Inaccuracies

Risk analyses tempt us to use arbitrarily complex models and calculations. However, since we usually have to work with expert estimates due to the lack of valid and reliable statistical values, even the most complex models only produce pseudo-accuracies. We can therefore spend a lot of time on the most beautiful Monte Carlo simulation, but this will only bring us closer to the truth to a limited extent. Ergo, a simple but robust model does not necessarily have to be worse.

Impact Assessment and Probability of Occurrence

When assessing impact, we need to consider non-linear damage trajectories, for all the types of damage that can be considered. Typically, these are our usual suspects: financial impact, reputational damage, and consequences from breaches of law or contract.

When estimating probabilities of occurrence, we can take a look in the rearview mirror and use frequencies as a guide, e.g., at least annually, every 2 years, every 5 years, and every 10 years or less.

Risk Evaluation

The risk is usually determined from the product of the impact (amount of damage; S) and the probability of occurrence (W) and plotted in a matrix (risk map). A risk map shows the respective scale of probability of occurrence and amount of damage on the x- and y-axis.

Figure 5.2 uses a four-point scale and shows the risk values of the individual combinations of impacts and damage levels.

From Practice: Uniform Scales

In practice, several risk scales often exist side by side. One from BCM, one from IT risk assessment, one from risk management, and one from... The problem should be clear: Many cooks spoil the broth, which leads to the fact that the scales and results often do not quite fit over each other. So we need a body within the organization that sets the pace and has some kind of directive authority or methodological sovereignty. It usually works out well if this body is based in risk management. Ideally, this is done by the unit that is responsible for managing operational risks.

Result of the Risk Analysis

The result of the risk analysis is a risk value resulting from any combination of supporting resource, vulnerability, countermeasure, and consequences.

We have thus now identified and analyzed the individual risks, but not yet assessed them.

5.7.2.3 Risk Assessment

Set Priorities

Having identified and assessed our risks so far, we now need to look at assessing them. Which of the risks

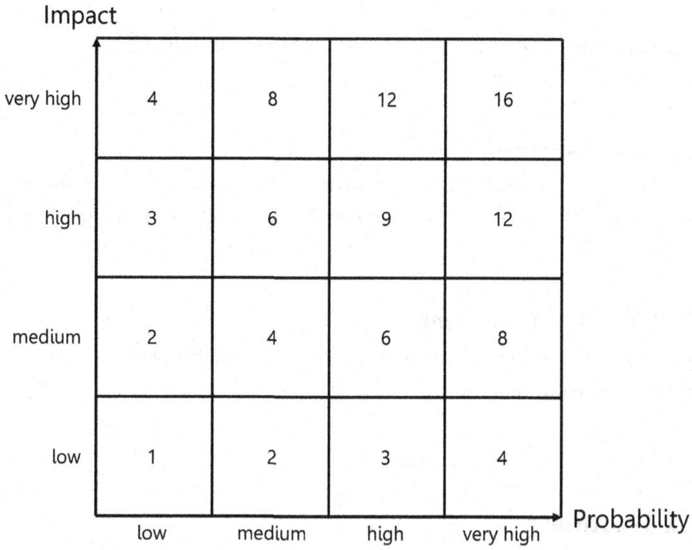

Impact

	low	medium	high	very high
very high	4	8	12	16
high	3	6	9	12
medium	2	4	6	8
low	1	2	3	4

Probability

Fig. 5.2 Risk map

- must,
- should, or
- can

we subject to a more extensive risk treatment?

To answer this question, we must

- rank the risks (or, more generally, prioritize them), and
- determine the criteria according to which further risk treatment is mandatory, advisable, or simply possible in principle.

Prioritization and Thresholds

Prioritization is not particularly complicated. Since each risk has a risk value, we can sort the risks according to their risk value. The higher the risk value, the higher the priority.

We can define the threshold values of the individual categories (must, should, can) on an organization-specific basis. As is so often the case, there is no right or wrong here, but once again the distinction between appropriate and inappropriate. The higher we set the threshold values, the fewer risks we have to deal with. At the same time, this also implicitly means that there tends to be a higher risk appetite, while lower thresholds are evidence of a risk-averse orientation of the cyber risk management program.

Risk Owner

Every risk needs a clear responsible party—the risk owner. Without such a clear assignment, responsibility diffuses, and the risk remains (almost certainly) unaddressed or stuck with the person who controls the cyber risk management program. However, the role of risk owner also provides latitude. Unless treatment of the risk is mandatory, he or she is the one who decides not to treat it.

Result of the Risk Assessment
As a result of the risk assessment, we now have a prioritized list of all resources, sorted by their risk value. For some of them, the risk owner must initiate a risk treatment, for others he should or can do so.

Completion of the Risk Assessment
Incidentally, with the risk assessment we have also completed the part that the ISO standards refer to as risk assessment.

5.7.3   Risk Treatment

Treatment Strategies
In addressing risk, there are some prototypical strategies that we can use either individually or in combination. The essential strategies are:

- Avoidance
- Mitigation
- Transfer
- Acceptance

Risk Avoidance
The most thorough way to deal with a risk is to simply avoid it. In road traffic, there is the risk that I react too late when a drunk person stumbles in front of my car. I can eliminate this risk by not using the car to get around, but by walking myself or switching to public transport, for example—not particularly attractive alternatives for many of us. The situation is similar with cyber risks. Risk avoidance has its price.

From Practice: Risk Avoidance
Let's imagine that we have to go on a trip. Let's say, to China or to the USA. In both cases, we should expect to be thoroughly checked upon entry for reasons of national interest (whatever that may look like in concrete terms). During this check, our laptop, our smartphone and/or our tablet is in the middle of it instead of just being there—and with it data that we quite justifiably regard as confidential. This applies not only to data stored locally, but also to data that may reside somewhere remote or in the cloud, but that we access via our mobile devices (second-order, so to speak). We can avoid this risk to the confidentiality of information by either no longer traveling, or by switching to virgin

mobile devices for travel that our organization provides specifically for such purposes—with all the convenience sacrifices that entails. Once again we see: There is no free lunch.

Risk Mitigation

If we want to mitigate a risk, we have two starting points: its probability of occurrence and its impact. If we can bring either one or the other to zero, we have completely mitigated the risk, that is, in a sense avoided it. The measures we take to reduce the probability of a cyber crisis occurring can largely be subsumed under the aspect of information security management, flanked by tests, audits, training and awareness measures. We combat the effects through cyber (security) incident response and crisis management. However, there are also hybrid forms, i.e., approaches that address both the probability of occurrence and the impact. These are stakeholder and issue management, business continuity management and IT service continuity management. More details are provided in the respective chapter.

Risk Transfer

A risk management strategy that is convenient in theory but rarely works well in practice is risk transfer. Behind this is the idea of transferring the risk, and thus its costs, to someone else.

From Practice: Risk Transfer

It is tempting for organizations to outsource a particular task to a service provider. There may well be cost reasons for this. Often, there is also the desire to no longer be responsible for the risks associated with the task. However, at least the latter does not work, as the ultimate responsibility in the case of outsourcing always remains with the outsourcing organization. Regulators have clear ideas on this, as BaFin's MaRisk and BAIT, among others, show. Expressed by means of a RACI matrix: The R is definitely with the outsourcing recipient, but the A remains with the outsourcing organization. This means that the risk transfer fails.

Another way of playing the game, which basically works better, is to transfer part of the risk to insurance companies. We look at such cybersecurity policies in Sect. 4.8.

5.7.4 Acceptance of (Residual) Risks

Risk Acceptance

Love it, change it or leave it. Risks that we cannot mitigate or avoid must be accepted. At some point in the risk treatment process we come to the point that, despite all mitigation measures for any given risk, neither its occurrence nor any harm whatsoever can be ruled out. Any further risk treatment would cost a great deal of money, but would hardly reduce the risk any further (somewhat unwieldly, we could also speak of infinitesimal marginal utility). In other words, we have turned a gross risk into a net risk. This is significantly lower than the original risk, but it is not zero—the famous residual risk that we have to live with.

From Practice: Risk Acceptance

The risk of a DDoS attack on our online services could be avoided by not having a website for our organization. However, this is not very effective for marketing reasons. The question is how do we mitigate the risk of the website being crippled by a DDoS attack? About the probability of occurrence? Hardly, since the website is supposed to be public by definition, but at the same time the motivation of an attacker can be very different. Then perhaps about limiting the impact? To this end, we can try to identify the IP addresses in the event of an attack and let all requests coming through these IP addresses go nowhere (blackholing, sinkholing). Likewise, various service providers offer to make more bandwidth available to an attacked organization at short notice. Due to the additional capacity, the website remains available (at least) to a limited extent for the duration of the attack. The problem with this is the cost. While attackers can rent DDoS capacities for small money on the basis of botnets in the darknet, the costs for a short-term, temporary bandwidth increase are incomparably higher for the attacked party. In practice, this regularly leads to the acceptance of possible damages from a DDoS attack.

Acceptance Criteria

We have to define the organization-specific criteria on the basis of which a risk owner may accept a (residual) risk. To do this, we can use the results of the risk analysis and risk assessment, i.e., we can rely on the risk value determined. This always involves profitability aspects. When dealing with risk, we can sink as much money as we like without being able to completely eliminate the risk.

Residual Risks Are Managed in Terms of Impact

The residual risks, which we ultimately accept and ideally even back with equity, are an important variable for cyber crisis management. Since we must expect the risk to materialize at some point, we must deal with the consequences at the appropriate time. Depending on the type of risk and how early we become aware of it, we can prevent it from developing into a real crisis by means of a rapid initial response (cyber security incident response) and/or targeted stakeholder and issue management.

But if we cannot avoid this, we need our

- Emergency and crisis organization,
- Business continuity plans (BCM), and
- Restart plans (ITSCM/IRBC).

5.8   Our Cyber Resilience and What It Is Like: Audits

...and that Helps Us with Crisis Management Because...?
The basic objective of audits is to verify the effectiveness of a management system or set of measures, or their conformity to a certain standard or other target. This gives us, among other things, an idea of the weak points, the associated risks (the starting points of crises!) and, above all, the measures we need to take to mitigate the risks. And: the results of audits and tests are very often an argument with which we can convince the management of one or another investment.

Added Value (I)
In addition, in the event of a crisis, we can make excellent use of positive testimonials from external auditors as evidence that we have done our homework.

- in principle (if we have regular checks carried out) and
- good (if the tests give us a good report)

have made. So, if we as management want to emphasize in the context of crisis communication that we have adequately fulfilled our organizational responsibility, testimonials are the means of choice. And, of course, also if stakeholders want to make claims against us in the aftermath of a crisis due to alleged (gross) negligence or if the provider of a cyber insurance wants to make sure of our preventive measures before concluding a contract.

Additional Benefits (II)
If we organize our crisis prevention along the disciplines presented in this book and adhere to the respective ISO standards, we inevitably operate a management system, if not several. At the very least, the ISO standards ending in 01 (e.g., 22,301, 27,001, etc.) require this. A key aspect of any ISO-based management system is regular verification of the effectiveness of the measures—through audits and testing. This means that when we conduct audits, we are moving within the management systems.

Audits
Through audits, we can put our finger in open wounds in each of the sub-disciplines that contribute to cyber crisis management:

- Crisis Management (BS 11200, BfV/BSI/ASW 2000-3)
- Business Continuity Management (ISO 22301)
- IT Service Continuity Management (ISO 27031)
- Cybersecurity Incident Response (ISO 27035)
- Cybersecurity Management (ISO 27032, NIST Framework)
- Asset management (e.g. ISO 27005)
- Information and IT security (ISO 270xx, BSI 200-x)

- Cyber Risk Management (ISO 27005, ISO 31000)
- Stakeholder and issue management
- Training and Awareness

If we systematically and repeatedly audit all these sub-disciplines and put their results in context with each other, we will get a feeling for how our cyber resilience is doing. In doing so, we can conduct the audits against internal as well as external specifications, i.e., measure against different target state specifications. In addition to the standards that have already been mentioned many times, external requirements also include best practices, maturity levels, benchmarks (very popular!) and, last but not least, regulatory requirements.

Audit Program
Similar to the tests, trainings or the topic of awareness, it makes sense to systematically initiate our transparency efforts. Which sub-discipline do we have to audit and how often? Do we use internal or external auditors? We should map the answers to these questions in a multi-year plan. But be careful: Our audit program must be flexible enough to allow for repeat audits and follow-up audits.

From Practice: Working Through the Findings
An audit (much like a serious test) leads to findings—always and inevitably. This means a continuous need for rework. Such rework sometimes overwhelms the line organization, since day-to-day business does not stand still and very few organizations can afford excess capacity in IT and the (supposedly unproductive) governance functions (where, in turn, the bulk of the rework occurs). As a result, the only way out is often to apply for a formal project with a separate budget—which is usually only approved when the pressure is great enough. Keyword: cost-benefit consideration under risk aspects.

From Practice: High Demands on Auditors
Since the cyber disciplines are all regulated by separate standards and are also distributed across different functional areas in most organizations, the audits should focus in particular on the interlocking of the topics. If it breaks anywhere, it's at the interfaces (vulgo: silo boundaries). This increases the demands on the auditors because they must be equally well versed in several disciplines (and in each case in several standards and practices).

Post Crisis Care: Follow Up

6

6.1   The View Outwards: Repairing Stakeholder Relationships

Inventory

There are a few questions we should answer for each stakeholder who has appeared in our orbit during the crisis. Where are we in our relationship with him? And where do we want him to go from here? What have we done well in his direction and what have we done poorly? Have we truly understood his interests and needs? Have we aligned our actions with them?

And especially if we were not successful in one or the other point: What was the reason? How can we do better next time? What can or must we do to at least meet the stakeholder's needs now? Set up customer loyalty programs? Increase investment in IT security? Engage independent reviewers? Set up a whistleblower hotline?

What Do Our Stakeholders Continue to Need?

After we have, so to speak, put the first, quick band-aid on the wound of the respective stakeholder in the context of crisis management, we now have to deal with the question of wound healing. This means nothing other than taking responsibility for direct and indirect consequences, even beyond the duration of the actual crisis. To avoid misunderstandings: taking responsibility also means accepting legal consequences, including liability claims. In the short term, this may not be appealing either to our management or to our shareholders. But that is precisely the point: short-term thinking geared to quarterly figures inevitably leads to our continuing to stick plasters on the wounds—or even to pouring salt on them in the end. Under no circumstances does it lead to a lasting recovery in our relationships with our stakeholders.

© Springer Fachmedien Wiesbaden GmbH, part of Springer Nature 2021   187
H. Kaschner, *Cyber Crisis Management*,
https://doi.org/10.1007/978-3-658-35489-3_6

Victim Care Strategy
This applies in particular to the case where we have pursued the victim care strategy. Here we would like to remind you once again of the central idea: trust is the sum of promises kept. And how is stakeholder trust supposed to return if we have only followed up our words with actions in the short term? Focusing crisis management on defending against liability claims is the surest way to squander the last vestige of trust and completely ruin your reputation.

6.2   The View Inwards: People, Processes, and Technology

The View Inwards
When looking inwards, our goal is to find starting points that we can use to reduce the probability of occurrence and impact of future crises. It is about systematically taking stock of what went well and what went badly. In short, the focus is on the famous lessons learned, which we use to systematically examine structures, processes, teams and tools for weaknesses and potential for further development.

Risk Inventory and Action Tracking
We should assess vulnerabilities systematically. The best way to do this is to transfer them to our cyber risk management, where we have (hopefully) set up appropriate processes. This way, we can subject them to systematic risk treatment.

Lessons Learned
To implement the lessons learned, we offer topic-specific workshops, which we can hold with different groups of participants depending on the topic. The following topics are available:

- Human factor
- Alerting and escalation
- Interaction of the levels of emergency and crisis organization (strategic, tactical, operational)
- Crisis management at strategic level (crisis unit, situation center, communication unit)
- Crisis management at tactical level (emergency staff and emergency teams)
- Crisis management at operational level (CSIRT)
- Crisis communication
- Infrastructure, Technology, Tools, IT Solutions

There is nothing wrong with summarizing some of the topics in a workshop. Either way, we should not wait too long—about 2 weeks after the end of the crisis is a good deadline by which we should have carried out our lessons learned.

A positive side effect of the lessons learned is that they can serve as a blueprint for us should we ever find ourselves in a similar situation again.

6.2.1   Human Factor

Fears and Anxieties
Fears and worries are almost omnipresent emotions, especially on the customer side, but also among our own employees. Someone who is afraid behaves differently than someone who is not afraid. They are often closed to factual arguments and tend to make impulsive decisions and actions.

- Have we taken the fears and concerns of our stakeholders sufficiently seriously?
- Have we shown the stakeholders that we really take their fears and concerns seriously?
- Are we currently showing our stakeholders that we still take their fears and concerns seriously?
- What internal or external stakeholders have indicated fears and concerns?
- How did we handle it?
- . . .

Grief and Anger
Similarly, strong emotions are sadness and anger. Dealing with stakeholders who are sad or angry is often anything but easy.

- Have we found the right responses (verbal and non-verbal) to grief and anger?
- Which internal or external stakeholders have shown signs of grief and anger?
- How did we handle it?
- . . .

Where Did We Experience Excessive Demands?
For those teams, individuals, situations, etc., where we find excessive demands, we need to go into further detail. In particular, we are interested in:

- What could have happened because of the overload?
- What caused the overload?
- How can we prevent the situation from happening again?
- . . .

How Did the Overwhelmed People Deal with It?
How people react to excessive demands varies from person to person, but can still be classified schematically (see Chap. 2). We can and must ask:

- Did they consciously perceive the excessive demand in the situation itself as such?
- Have they articulated their overwhelm to any authority/role?
  - If yes, to which and what has this body/role done to provide relief?
  - If not, why not?

- What can we do to ensure that, in the event of renewed excessive demands, those affected are relieved more quickly and better?
- ...

6.2.2   Alerting and Escalation

Core criterion: Robustness
Alerting and escalation form the entry point into crisis management. This is where we gain or lose precious time. For these two reasons, we must pay special attention to analyzing our performance in alerting and escalation.

We can do that by asking:

- Were we fast enough at all levels (crisis team, emergency teams, CSIRT, etc.)?
- Are our alerting and escalation processes robust?
- Were all persons involved in alerting and escalation confident in their actions?
- Have the criteria on the basis of which the escalation should take place proved successful?
- Where did we lose time?
- How did we find out about the incident? By luck? Through designated channels (internal, external)?
- Is our current regulation regarding (on-call) standby and availability arrangements appropriate?
- ...

6.2.3   Interaction Between the Levels of the Emergency and Crisis Organization

Interaction Internally and Externally
The cooperation within a body is one thing, the interaction between the bodies is another (especially across levels). When things break down somewhere, it is often at the interfaces. This is true not only in the normal course of business, but even more so in the event of a crisis. That's why the interfaces are of particular interest when we do some navel-gazing.

To this we can ask:

- How did the interaction within the strategic/tactical/operational level work?
- How did the interaction between the levels work?
- How did the interaction of the individual levels with the line organization work?
- How did the interaction of the individual levels with external partners (service providers, authorities, etc.) work?
- ...

6.2.4   Strategic Level

Crisis Management Team (CMT), Situation Center, and Communication Unit
If we want to examine how we have done at the strategic level, we should look at different issues:

- our processes (initialization of crisis management, crisis management process)
- the path we have chosen, i.e. our strategy
- our bodies (crisis unit, communication unit, situation center)
- the tools we used (or urgently needed)

Initialization of the CMT's Working Procedure

- Did we begin the CMT's work by following a structured process and did it work for us?
- Have we identified the objective of our crisis team, the key stakeholders and our worst-case scenario?
- Have we aligned our actions with this?
- Did we make a strict distinction between fact and conjecture?
- Did we start logging in time?
- Have we formally established, documented, and communicated the crisis situation?
- Was the core crisis management team able to provide guidance to the remaining CMT members in initializing the CMT's working procedure?
- How has the initialization process worked?
- . . .

Crisis Management

- Did we follow a consistent process in the CMT (and other emergency and crisis organization bodies)?
- How did the cooperation of the emergency and crisis organization bodies with external bodies (e.g., authorities, service providers, etc.) work?
- Was the core crisis team able to provide guidance to the remaining crisis team members as they went through the crisis management process?
- How has the crisis management process worked?
- . . .

Choice of Strategy

- Did we have a clear strategy for our crisis management?
- Did the strategy work? If not, why not?
- Do we need to make structural changes in our organization?

- Establish or further develop governance systems (see Chap. 5)?
- Issue or further develop compliance guidelines?
- Set up whistleblower hotline?
- Improve error culture?
- Breaking up hierarchies?
- Change processes, responsibilities and competencies?
- …
• …

Organizational Precautions

• Was the composition of the crisis unit, situation center and communication unit (roles, functions) and staffing (persons) appropriate?
• Did the crisis team, the situation center and the communications team have the necessary technical tools at hand?
• Were all persons sufficiently qualified for their role or prepared for the tasks?
• Was the infrastructure fit for purpose (technology, tools, premises, IT)?
• Did we have cyber risk insurance and did it step in?
• Do we need to equip the committees with additional tools (methodological, technical)?
• …

6.2.5   Operational Level: BCM and IRBC

Analysis Objects
At the operational level, we need to look at how our continuity organization has performed. This includes both business and IT service continuity. In doing so, we should take an overall perspective, which in turn should be fed by the experiences of the individual emergency teams.

BCM
From a (business) process perspective, we can ask:

• Did we start emergency operations in time (actual time reached, RTA)?
• Were the results of the BIA regarding restart times correct (RTO)?
• Did we have a handle on the interdependent processes?
• Did we have sufficient resources for emergency operations?
• Was the output of the emergency operation sufficient?
• Were the workarounds workable?
• Did the overall coordination of the switch to emergency operation work?
• …

IRBC/ITSCM

From an IT perspective, we can ask:

- Were we able to provide the applications needed for business operations (emergency and normal operations) again in time?
- Were we able to restore the data needed for business operations (emergency and normal operations) in time?
- Did we have a handle on the interdependent systems?
- Did the overall coordination of the restart work?
- ...

Preparatory Measures and Tools

- Was the composition of the BCM and IRBC teams (roles, functions) and staffing (people) appropriate?
- How did the cooperation in the emergency staff and within the different emergency teams work?
- Did all these bodies have the necessary technical tools at hand?
- Were all persons sufficiently qualified for their role or prepared for the tasks?
- Was the infrastructure fit for purpose (technology, tools, premises, IT, etc.)?
- ...

6.2.6   Tactical Level: CSIRT and Cybersecurity Incident Response

Analysis Objects

At the tactical level, we need to examine the Cybersecurity Incident Response Team (CSIRT), its procedures and tools. It is a good idea to look at these in isolation from the analysis of the specific cybersecurity incident, which we must of course also analyze.

Cybersecurity Incident

The analysis of the specific cybersecurity incident should include the following aspects:

- When and by whom was the problem discovered?
- How widespread was the incident (network segments, number of systems, clients, customers, etc.)?
- How was the incident contained?
- How could the cause be eliminated?
- What activities were necessary for this?
- ...

Organization and Tools

A look at the CSIRT and its tools or preparatory measures must not neglect the question of possible technical measures. Their implementation can sometimes be cost-intensive. In this respect, dovetailing with cyber risk management is once again a good idea, as it offers us a holistic view of our cyber risks and answers the question of whether the necessary investments have the best cost-benefit ratio compared to other security measures.

- Was the composition of the CSIRT (roles, functions) and staffing (people) appropriate?
- Were all persons sufficiently qualified for their role or prepared for the tasks?
- How did the cooperation in the CSIRT work?
- Did the CSIRT have the necessary professional tools at hand?
- Was the infrastructure fit for purpose (technology, tools, premises, IT)?
- What rework/developments of our IDS/IPS or SIEM tool are required?
- Are there technical solutions we should implement (black-/sinkholing, bandwidth increase, DLP, DMZ etc.)?
- ...

Disclaimer

For the sake of good order, depending on how you read it, this step is sometimes part of the CSIR process.

6.2.7   Crisis Communication

Crisis Communication

No matter how good we were at practical crisis management, in a professionally managed crisis, crisis communication is an integral part. When we review our crisis communication, we should ask ourselves:

- Did we have and implement a communication strategy?
- Have we monitored their impact, e.g., by means of social media monitoring?
- Have we properly coordinated our communications across stakeholders and aligned them with the communications strategy?
- Was our communication appropriate to the target group, quick, empathetic, and factually sound?
- Which stakeholders did we reach, and which did we not reach (in terms of content, emotion, technology)?
- Were we accessible to our stakeholders?
- How prepared were we? Did we have sample statements, stakeholder matrices, text modules, etc. at hand?
- Were we equipped in terms of personnel (quantitative, qualitative) for the communication work?
- ...

At a Glance: Seven Deadly Sins of Cyber Crisis Management

7

No. 1: Losing Stakeholder Focus

We must never lose sight of the fact that our customers (or other stakeholders) see themselves primarily as victims. They see first and foremost the problems that arise (or have already arisen) for themselves as a result of the event. Our problems, on the other hand, are at best a side note to them. Therefore, our decisions must never appear to put our own interests above the needs and expectations of our most important stakeholders.

No. 2: Neglect Prevention and Preparation

The effort in terms of time and costs is constant in the management of (cyber) crises: Either we invest in the prevention of (and preparation for) crises, or take the money in hand when an unpleasant event occurs. Therefore, it makes a lot more sense to invest in prevention and preparation, because at this stage we have the two crucial things that we would desperately need in a crisis, but certainly don't have: Silence from nosy stakeholders and time, time and more time.

No. 3: The "too … illusion"

Few things are more dangerous than the following attitude:

We are too
- insignificant,
- uninteresting,
- small,
- big.
- powerful,
- well prepared, and/or
- adept at crisis management
- …,

© Springer Fachmedien Wiesbaden GmbH, part of Springer Nature 2021
H. Kaschner, *Cyber Crisis Management*,
https://doi.org/10.1007/978-3-658-35489-3_7

Than that we need to worry about cyber crisis management and everything related to it any more.

This illusion (not to say hubris) is the surest way to get caught cold, because given the

- constantly growing number and complexity of (IT) systems,
- interdependencies in the supply network, and
- different types of perpetrators and their motivations

a cyber crisis is not a question of if, but merely of when and how. This is shown by the countless precedents that occur every month, if not every week—across all countries and industries.

No. 4: Public Blame Games

Few things make us look less confident than engaging in public mudslinging with service providers (or even customers, heaven forbid!) when our stakeholders, quite rightly, actually expect solutions from us. Even if our cyber crisis is the fault of one of our service providers and there is no doubt in the public's mind about it either: Attacking and discrediting him is taboo! Our customers have entrusted us with their data, not our service provider. So we bear the responsibility for our customers' data. Entrusting the service provider with the processing of the data was our own decision. If he does not perform this task as we would like him to, we have to look at our own nose: What does the service or outsourcing contract say? Did we adequately manage the service provider? These are the questions we should be asking. But please ask them internally and not publicly.

No. 5: Salami Tactics

In court, it may sometimes be a sensible strategy to only come out with the truth in bits and pieces: to admit just as much as can be proven. The problem with crisis management (more precisely: crisis communication) is that we are facing a different kind of (arbitration) judge. All of our stakeholders sit in judgment over us, not just representatives of the judiciary. In this respect, we should think carefully about whether we choose the salami tactic, because it is like a ripe salami in a crowded train compartment. It smells. And in the case of the tactic, not delicious, but of attempted cover-ups.

No. 6: Internal Communication Forgotten

Who doesn't dream of learning via one of the relevant online media that the organization we've been working for years has been hacked? And that data from the payroll department has been leaked as a result of the attack? That's probably not an attractive notion for very few of us. Therefore, when we inform our external stakeholders about significant events and also progress in crisis management, we should always inform our employees as well. At least at the same time, if not out of pure decency with a small-time lead. There is one caveat we must keep in mind here: If we are listed on the stock exchange, we must publish certain information by means of an ad hoc announcement.

No. 7: Words Instead of Deeds

"Trust is the sum of promises kept", "Threats have to be carried out" or "underpromise and overdeliver". No matter which of these proverbs we follow - we do it right. Nothing alienates our stakeholders more than big announcements that fall flat and fizzle out. That's why it's better if we hold back on big promises. No one will be angry if he gets a better result in the announced time or the announced result faster than promised. On the contrary, he will be pleased. After all the hardships, aren't these conciliatory prospects?

Appendix A: Read More

Requirements for crisis unit members	Enzensberger, Hans Magnus (2008): Hammerstein oder Der Eigensinn. Eine deutsche Geschichte, Frankfurt (Main): Suhrkamp
IRBC: High availability	Federal Office for Information Security (2013): Quick Reference Guide https://www.bsi.bund.de/SharedDocs/Downloads/DE/BSI/Hochverfuegbarkeit/QuickReferenceGuide.pdf; jsessionid=7DA885B08F891D3175B03DD491D383B0.2_cid360?__blob=publicationFile&v=1
IRBC: Policy options and principles	Müller, Klaus-Rainer (2014): IT-Sicherheit mit System. Integratives IT-Sicherheits-, Kontinuitäts- und Risikomanagement—Sichere Anwendungen—Standards und Practices, 6. Auflage, Wiesbaden: Springer Vieweg.
IRBC: RZ distances	German Federal Office for Information Security (2018): Kriterien für die Standortwahl höchstverfügbarer und georedundanter Rechenzentren, Standort-Kriterien HV-RZ, Version 1.0 https://www.bsi.bund.de/SharedDocs/Downloads/DE/BSI/Sicherheitsberatung/Standort-Kriterien_HV-RZ/Standort-Kriterien_HV-RZ.pdf?__blob=publicationFile&v=5
ISO standards	The international ISO standards describe cyber crisis management, i.e. the management and prevention of as well as preparation for cyber crises, using various standards from different series. The following is a selection to get you started. The 27,000 series in particular contains numerous others, including industry or technology-specific standards. The four-digit year after the colon indicates the version of the standard in effect at the time this book was published in its German edition. In all cases, the publisher is the International Organization for Standardization (www.iso.org).
	ISO 19011:2018 Guidelines for auditing management systems

(continued)

© Springer Fachmedien Wiesbaden GmbH, part of Springer Nature 2021   199
H. Kaschner, *Cyber Crisis Management*,
https://doi.org/10.1007/978-3-658-35489-3

ISO 22301:2019 Security and resilience—Business continuity management systems—requirements
ISO/TS 22317:2015 Societal security—Business continuity management systems—Guidelines for business impact analysis (BIA) At the time of publication of the German edition of this book, the standard was under revision and will be called ISO/NP TS 22317 in the future. Security and resilience—Business continuity management systems—Guidelines for business impact analysis (BIA) bear.
ISO/TS 22318:2015 Societal security—Business continuity management systems—Guidelines for supply chain continuity At the time of publication of the German edition of this book, the standard was under revision and will be called ISO/NP TS 22318 in the future. Security and resilience—Business continuity management systems—Guidelines for supply chain continuity bear.
ISO 22398:2013 Societal security—Guidelines for exercises
ISO/IEC 27001:2013 Information technology—Security techniques—Information security management systems—Requirements
ISO/IEC 27005:2018 Information technology—Security techniques—Information security risk management
ISO/IEC 27031:2011 Information technology—Security techniques—Guidelines for information and communication technology readiness for business continuity At the time of publication of the German edition of this book, the standard was under revision and will in future bear the name ISO/IEC WD 27031 Information technology—Guidelines for ICT readiness for business continuity.
ISO/IEC 27032:2012 Information technology—Security techniques—Guidelines for cybersecurity At the time of publication of the German edition of this book, the standard was under revision and will in future be called ISO/IEC WD 27032 IT Security Techniques—Cybersecurity—Guidelines for Internet Security.
ISO/IEC 27035-x:2016 Information technology—Security techniques—Information security incident management "-x" means that there are multiple parts under the number 27035, all

(continued)

	covering different facets of incident management. At the time of this book's publication, there are two parts, and a third is in preparation.
	ISO/IEC 28000:2007 Specification for security management systems for the supply chain At the time of publication of the German edition of this book, the standard was under revision and will be called ISO/AWI 28000 in the future. Security and resilience—Security management systems for the supply chain—Requirements bear.
	ISO/IEC 31000:2018 Risk management—Guidelines
Crisis management (maxim)	Sunzi (2013):Die Kunst des Krieges*. Aus dem Chinesischen übertragen und mit einem Nachwort versehen von Volker Klöpsch, 5. Auflage, Berlin: Insel Verlag. *The Art of War The quote used in this book is found in the above edition on page 58.
Crisis communication	Höbel, Peter/Hofmann, Thorsten (2014): Krisenkommunikation, 2. Vollständig überarbeitete Auflage, Konstanz: UVK.
Crisis management	The British Standards Institution (2014): BS 11200:2014. crisis management—Guidance and good practice. This standard provides a system or process-oriented framework for setting up crisis management. The definition of "crisis" from the chapter "To whom this book is addressed, what it covers and how it is structured" can be found in BS 11200 on page 2 in paragraph 2.4 (translation by the author of this book).
National standards	The national standards describe cyber crisis management, i.e. the management and prevention of and preparation for cyber crises, on the basis of various standards from different series (BSI Grundschutz and Wirtschaftsgrundschutz). The download of the standards is free of charge. In all cases, the publisher is the Federal Office for Information Security. Exceptions are marked separately.
	Overview: https://www.bsi.bund.de/DE/Themen/ITGrundschutz/ITGrundschutzStandards/ITGrundschutzStandards_node.html [accessed Dec 30, 2019]
	Guideline for basic security according to IT-Grundschutz Download: https://www.bsi.bund.de/SharedDocs/Downloads/DE/BSI/Publikationen/Broschueren/Leitfaden_zur_Basis-Absicherung.html
	BSI Standard 200-1: Information Security Management Systems (ISMS) Download:https://www.bsi.bund.de/SharedDocs/Downloads/DE/BSI/Grundschutz/Kompendium/standard_200_1.html; jsessionid=E0E723AD65E870E3D4D8641C2918E011.1_cid351

(continued)

	BSI Standard 200-2:
	IT-Grundschutz methodology
	Download:
	https://www.bsi.bund.de/SharedDocs/Downloads/DE/BSI/
	Grundschutz/Kompendium/standard_200_2.html
	BSI Standard 200-3:
	Risk management
	Download:
	https://www.bsi.bund.de/SharedDocs/Downloads/DE/BSI/
	Grundschutz/Kompendium/standard_200_3.html
	BSI Standard 100-4:
	Emergency Management
	Download:
	https://www.bsi.bund.de/SharedDocs/Downloads/DE/BSI/
	Publikationen/ITGrundschutzstandards/BSI-Standard_1004.pdf?__
	blob=publicationFile&v=2
	At the time of publication of the German edition of this book, the
	standard was under revision and will in future be known as BSI 200-4.
	BfV/BSI/ASW: Standard 2000-3
	Establishment and operation of an emergency and crisis management
	system
	Download:
	https://www.wirtschaftsschutz.info/DE/Veroeffentlichungen/
	Wirtschaftsgrundschutz/Standards/Notfall_Krisenmanagement.pdf;
	jsessionid=B8C3BDD11FEDB4F27C560B7A16E187A2.2_
	cid365?__blob=publicationFile&v=3
Risk communication	Obermeier, Otto-Peter (1999): Die Kunst der Risikokommunikation.
	Über Risiko, Kommunikation und Themenmanagement, Munich:
	Gerling Akademie Verlag.
Risk perception	Munzinger, Paul (2015): Warum sagt er das? In:https://www.
	sueddeutsche.de/politik/thomas-de-maiziere-warum-sagt-er-das-1.
	2742900.
	[published: Nov. 18, 2015; accessed Dec. 27, 2019]
	Otway, Harry/Wynne, Brian (1993): Risiko-Kommunikation:
	Paradigma nd Paradox, in Krohn, Wofgang/Krücken, Gerd (eds.):
	Riskante Technologien: Reflexion und Regulation. Einführung in die
	sozialwissenschaftliche Risikoforschung (pp. 101-112), Frankfurt/
	Main, Germany: Suhrkamp.
Social Media and	Lobo, Sascha (2019): Realitätsschock. Zehn Lehren aus der
Shitstorm	Gegenwart, 2. Auflage, Cologne: Kiepenheuer & Witsch.
	Lobo covers the topic of "social media" in the above issue on pages
	291–329.
Sony Pictures	A nice overview including an extensive collection of links can be
Entertainment (Hack)	found on the English Wikipedia page:
	https://en.wikipedia.org/wiki/Sony_Pictures_hack
	[accessed Dec 30, 2019]

(continued)

	Depending on your interests, some of the articles below may be informative.
	Cook, James (2015): Security researchers have discovered more information on how the Sony hackers managed to stay undetected, in: https://www.businessinsider.com/security-researchers-discover-hacking-tools-used-in-sony-pictures-hack-2015-11?r=DE&IR=T. [published: Nov. 23, 2015; accessed Dec. 29, 2019]
	Frizell, Sam (2015): Sony Is Spending $15 Million to Deal With the Big Hack, in:https://time.com/3695118/sony-hack-the-interview-costs/ [Published: Feb 04, 2015; Accessed 30 Dec. 2019]
	Schirrmacher, Dennis (2015): Wikileaks publishes documents from Sony hack, in:https://www.heise.de/security/meldung/Wikileaks-veroeffentlicht-Dokumente-von-Sony-Hack-2610817.html [published: Apr 17, 2015; accessed Dec 30, 2019]
	Zetter, Kim (2014): Sony Got Hacked Hard: What We Know and Don't Know So Far, in:https://www.wired.com/2014/12/sony-hack-what-we-know/ [Published: 04 Dec. 2014; Accessed 30 Dec. 2019]
Stress Management	Kaluza, Gerd (2018): Stressbewältigung. Trainingsmanual zur psychologischen Gesundheitsförderung, 4., korrigierte Auflage, Berlin: Springer.
	Strang, Axel/Günthner, Christian (2005): Krisenintervention. Psychosoziale Unterstützung für Einsatzkräfte, Stuttgart: W. Kohlhammer.

Appendix B: Abbreviations and Glossary

The definitions are those of the author. Where this is not the case, the source is shown separately.

Actor	see stakeholders
Alerting tool	IT-supported tool for accelerating and automating the alerting of the crisis team. Different people can be contacted via different channels (telephone, SMS, mail) at the push of a button via predefined distribution circuits. Can be part of a crisis management tool or a GRC tool suite, but does not have to be.
Assets	Also called resources; according to ISO 27005, a distinction is made between primary assets and supporting assets. Primary assets are information and processes, whereas supporting assets include IT systems, roles/people, service providers, machines/equipment, building infrastructures, paper-based documents, etc. Important to understand: primary resources cannot be attacked—attacks can only be made against supporting resources. Therefore, the immediate protective measures must also start with the supporting resources.
Asset management	Asset management is the management of primary resources and supporting resources. It provides us with information about which resources we have in use where and for what purpose. The interdependencies (relations) of the resources, which are recorded by means of the structure analysis, are central. All other management systems (ISMS, BCMS, etc.) are based on a common asset management.
Audit and testing	Generic term for the structured review of the appropriateness, completeness and effectiveness of measures or their conformity to defined target specifications. A test and audit program derives concrete verification measures from the target specifications and risk exposures.
Authenticity	One of the protection goals in information security management; refers to the fact that there must be certainty about who is actually a participant in an information exchange (mainly on a technical level).

(continued)

© Springer Fachmedien Wiesbaden GmbH, part of Springer Nature 2021
H. Kaschner, *Cyber Crisis Management*,
https://doi.org/10.1007/978-3-658-35489-3

Actor	see stakeholders
	The reason is clear: anyone who successfully pretends to be someone else can—usually unnoticed—connect to information flows that are not intended for them. In order to legitimize themselves, users and also IT systems must provide special proof. This includes, for example, crypto certificates (PKI), 2-factor authentication (have or be principle) or at least the combination of user ID and password. Authenticity is the key protection goal when it comes to information warfare and fake news campaigns.
Availability	One of the protection goals or basic values in → Information Security Management and the central protection goal in → Continuity Management.
Availability requirements	Requirements for resources in terms of time, quality and quantity that must be met during their → restart and → recovery. Important categories of availability requirements are → RTO or → WAZ, → MTPD or → MTA, → RPO and → MBCO. Availability requirements are determined in the → BIA.
Awareness	Refers to sensitivity and attention to risks, developments or events/ situations. Plays a decisive role in the prevention of or reaction to crises. Often mentioned in connection with training and, like training, ideally controlled by a programme. See also Training and Awareness
BaFin	Federal Financial Supervisory Authority; supervisory and regulatory authority for the financial sector in Germany, which includes fintechs and insuretechs in addition to banks and insurance companies.
BAIT	Banking supervisory requirements for IT; issued by → BaFin as the competent supervisory authority. The BAIT specify the → MaRisk in more detail.
BCM	See Business Continuity Management
BC RA	BC Risk Assessment, see Cyber Risk Management
BCP	See Business continuity and recovery plans
BfArM	Federal Institute for Drugs and Medical Devices; responsible for • Medicinal products for marketing authorisation • Medical devices for the central recording, evaluation and assessment of risks and the coordination of measures
BIA	See Business Impact Analysis
Black Building Test	In a Black Building Test, a building is completely de-energized to simulate its failure and to test the effectiveness of emergency preparedness measures.
BNetzA	Federal Network Agency; supervisory authority for companies in the electricity and gas, telecommunications, postal and railway sectors; already required certification of an ISMS in accordance with ISO 27001 for network operators at the time of the draft bill for the → IT Security Act—the first authority ever in Germany to do so.

(continued)

Actor	see stakeholders
Botnets	A botnet consists of the interconnection of a large number of Internet-enabled (end) devices—from baby monitors and traditional PCs to surveillance cameras and refrigerators. Attackers take over these devices and connect them together in order to use the collective computing power to carry out → DDoS attacks themselves or to rent out the botnet on the darknet for DDoS attacks. Important: Unsecured devices or devices secured unchanged with the factory password favor takeover by third parties. The owners of the taken-over devices often do not even notice that their device is being misused.
BSI	Bundesamt für Sicherheit in der Informationstechnik
BSIG	Also BSI Act; Act on the Federal Office for Information Security; central part of the→ IT Security Act conceived as a shell law.
Business Continuity Management	BCM is a cyclical management process by means of which an organization ensures the availability of its critical processes, activities, products, departments, etc., also and especially in emergencies (e.g. cyber attacks). Key process steps: → BIA, → BC RA, maintenance of → CFP, performance of → tests. Essential output: critical → resources incl. → availability requirements, → CFP of critical processes.
Business continuity and recovery plans	Documented (and hopefully proven) workarounds for the time critical processes, activities, products, departments, etc. The BCP/contingency plans must include workarounds to compensate for the resources relevant to the emergency. These are usually IT applications, buildings, roles and staff, service providers, and machines/equipment.
Business Impact Analysis	Through the so-called BIA, the time-critical processes, activities, products, departments, etc. of an organization are determined. The result of the BIA is a list of these, including recovery targets (times, quantities, qualities). Essential process step of → BCM.
Call tree	See telephone cascade
CMDB	Configuration Management Database; directory of all IT assets, also called Configuration Items (CI). Ideally, various information is stored for each asset, in particular mutual dependencies, processed information types/categories, protection class/basic value per protection goal or basic value of information security and who is responsible for an asset.
CMT	See Crisis Management Team
Confidentiality	One of the protection goals or basic values in → information security management; describes the fact that not every piece of information is intended for everyone's ears (or eyes).
Contingeny plan	See business continuity plan
Contingency Team	Contingency teams can be formed to coordinate the emergency operation and restart of processes (business emergency teams) as

(continued)

Actor	see stakeholders
	well as the restart and recovery of failed resources. Similar to the crisis team, they are not standing teams, but are activated on an ad hoc basis.
Core Crisis Management Team	See crisis management team
Crisis	See event categories
Crisis communication	An integral part of crisis management, which must be continuous and address both the factual and emotional levels, depending on the addressee.
Crisis infrastructure	The crisis infrastructure includes all infrastructural measures available to the crisis organisation for the management of crises, i.e., among other things, the crisis management room, the situation centre room, the crisis manual, an alerting system or even a crisis management tool.
Crisis log	The crisis log is the central documentation tool for the crisis team. It records incoming and outgoing information, decisions, responsibilities and times. It therefore has considerable probative value when investigating authorities, auditors and other auditors examine the work of the crisis management team after the crisis has been resolved.
Crisis management	Crisis management • Serves the protection of (im-)material goods (first and foremost people); • Cannot be planned in detail; • Must take place at different levels; • Must also include issues such as issue and stakeholder management, business continuity, incident response, etc. • Consists of measures to prepare for, prevent, contain and follow up crises.
Crisis management process	The crisis management process is a scenario-independent procedure for managing (acute) crises. It is structured, role-based, documented in the → crisis manual and should be second nature to the crisis team members. In Germany, it is usually based on the → management process, and much less frequently on → FOR-DEC.
Crisis Management Team	The crisis management team (CMT) is the central coordination and decision-making body at strategic level. It is divided into a core CMT and an extended CMT. While the core team consists of the roles that are always required in crisis management, regardless of the scenario, the extended team contains additional roles that reinforce the core team on a case-by-case basis. The CMT is not a standing body, but only meets in the event of a crisis (ad hoc).
Crisis management tool	A crisis management tool is an IT-supported, often web-based tool that is intended to support the crisis management team and the situation centre in their work. The functionalities range from task control and documentation to the distribution of communication elements. Interfaces to alerting and GRC tools are also typical.

(continued)

Actor	see stakeholders
Crisis manual	A crisis manual describes the tasks and competencies of the crisis team members as well as the processes for initiating crisis team work and crisis management. In addition, it can also include checklists and guidelines for selected concrete scenarios together with text and communication modules for crisis communication as well as templates for visualising and documenting the crisis team's work. Stakeholder lists including contact options and a template for the → crisis team protocol are indispensable.
Crisis room	A crisis room provides the CMT with an appropriate infrastructure. This includes, above all, sufficient space, visualisation and telecommunications facilities, in particular access to the intranet and internet. In the case of distributed crisis teams, the crisis team can also be set up virtually, e.g. using IT-based crisis management tools or simply telephone conferences. It is crucial that all infrastructures are as robust as possible, i.e. that they also function in the event of a failure of the basic supply (electricity, water, cooling/air conditioning) and (at least parts of) the IT.
Cryptolocker	See Ransomware
Cyber Insurance	Insurance benefit that takes effect in the event of a breach of one of the → protection goals; often linked to the condition that the breach results from a safety incident.
Cyber Risk Management	Cyber risk management is a systematic approach in which cyber risks are first assessed and then dealt with on the basis of the assessment. The assessment ("Cyber Risk Assessment") consists of the steps identification, analysis and evaluation. The typical treatment options are avoidance, mitigation, transfer or acceptance of the (residual) risks. Ideally, cyber risk management is set up as a management system and closely interlinked with other governance disciplines, for example via the → BC RA, IRM and OpRisk. The relevant ISO standards are ISO 27032, ISO 27001, ISO 27002, ISO 27005 and of course ISO 31000.
(Cybersecurity) Incident	See event categories
D&O insurance	D&O insurance is a special form of professional liability insurance for senior executives. D&O stands for Directors & Officers. D&O insurance reduces personal liability risks.
Data	Uncontextualized → information
DDoS attack	Distributed denial of service; form of attack in which IT systems (for example the website) are deliberately flooded with requests so that they are no longer accessible to the user. → Bot networks are often used for such attacks. Threatened protection goal: availability.
Disaster	See event categories
EBA	European Banking Authority; European Banking Authority
Emergency	See event categories

(continued)

Actor	see stakeholders
Emergency operations	Temporary form of operation with limited capacities ($\rightarrow$ resources) due to adverse events. Emergency operation must meet $\rightarrow$ availability requirements.
Emergency organisation	The emergency and crisis organisation includes the structural and procedural measures that an organisation has taken to prevent and, in particular, manage crises. These include the crisis team and the situation centre as well as the alerting procedure and crisis team processes.
Event categories	**Incident** An incident is a non-standard operating situation of a service that can cause or causes a reduction in the agreed quality or availability (oriented to ITIL®). In the context of this book, an incident is therefore an event that can or does affect the confidentiality, integrity, availability and authenticity of information and communication participants with a focus on IT systems.
	Emergency An emergency is an event in which an organization is threatened with or has already suffered significant damage due to a breach of the protection goals of confidentiality, integrity, availability and authenticity of information and processes. Source: Federal Office for Information Security, Federal Office of Civil Protection and Disaster Assistance; online via kritis.bund.de (retrieved 14 July 2019).
	Crisis A crisis is an "abnormal and unstable situation that threatens an organisation's strategic objectives, reputation or ability to survive" (based on the BS 11200 and BfV/BSI/ASW 2000-3 standards). Not to forget: From the ancient Greek, there are additional meanings of a "turning point" or a decision-making situation.
	Disaster A disaster is an event in which the life or health of a large number of people or the natural basis of life or significant material assets are endangered or damaged to such an unusual extent that the danger can only be averted or the disruption prevented and eliminated if the authorities, organisations and institutions involved in civil protection act under the unified leadership and direction of the civil protection authority to avert the danger. Source: Federal Office for Information Security, Federal Office of Civil Protection and Disaster Assistance; online via kritis.bund.de (retrieved 14 July 2019).
Extended crisis management team	See crisis management team
FOR-DEC	FOR-DEC is a model for decision-making in aviation and a form of $\rightarrow$ crisis management process that is rather rarely used in Germany. The acronym stands for facts (F), options (O), risks and benefits (R), decision (D), execution (E) and control (C).

(continued)

Actor	see stakeholders
GDV	German Insurance Association (Gesamtverband der Deutschen Versicherungswirtschaft e.V.)
GeschGehG	Act on the Protection of Business Secrets (GeschGehG)
GRC	Governance, Risk and Compliance
Gross risk	See risk
Highlander Principle	The Highlander principle is a synonym for the concentration of decision-making authority within the crisis management team with the crisis management team leader. It takes its name from the film "Highlander—There Can Be Only One" starring Christopher Lambert
Incident	See event categories
Indemnity	Organisations may exempt members of their crisis management team from liability or limit liability. Indemnification (or limitation) refers to consequences arising from crisis management decisions and actions. This reduces the pressure on the persons acting.
Information	Alongside processes, one of the two categories of primary assets. Are bundled into information types or categories during the preparation of the protection requirements assessment and assigned to other → resources via the → structure analysis.
Information Risk Management	Risk management approach focusing on information and the supporting resources through which the information is processed; see also Cyber Risk Management.
Information Security Management	ISM is a cyclical management process by which an organization ensures the protection of its critical information and the assets over which it is processed. Essential elements are, on the preventive side, the identification of protection requirements, concrete specifications for various security fields of action (cryptography, access management, protection of network components, etc.) and information risk management, as well as, on the reactive side, the reaction to information security incidents, i.e. cybersecurity incident response.
Integrity	One of the protection goals or basic values in → information security management. Refers to the fact that stored data may not be changed without proof and explicit authorization.
IRBC	IT readiness for business continuity (also referred to as → ITSCM in the ITIL® world) is a term from ISO 27031 and refers to the management system by means of which IT and other (tele)communication systems are made available so that business-critical processes can be maintained at least in emergency operation even in the event of failures. As with other management systems, it is based not only on technical but also on organizational measures. Its most important sub-processes/result objects are the →IRBC gap analysis, → restart plans and → restore concepts as well as → tests to check the effectiveness of the plans and concepts.

(continued)

Actor	see stakeholders
IRBC gap analysis	The IRBC gap analysis checks the extent to which IT services (applications, databases, complete systems, etc.) meet the availability requirements of critical business processes. The results of the gap analysis flow into the risk assessment (IRM, BC Risk Assessment, Cyber Risk Management).
IRM	Information Risk Management
Issue	Topic that moves a stakeholder; can be translated into the expectations that the stakeholder has of his environment with regard to the respective topic.
Issue Management	See stakeholder and issue management
ITC	Information and telecommunication technology
ITSCM	IT Service Continuity Management; one of the classic ITIL processes; other name for → IRBC
ITSiG	The IT Security Act (ITSiG) is a German shell law aimed at operators of critical infrastructures. The BSIG plays a special role within the ITSiG. Section 8a BSIG obliges operators of critical infrastructures to take "appropriate organisational and technical precautions to prevent disruptions to the availability, integrity, authenticity and confidentiality of their information technology systems, components or processes that are essential to the functioning of the critical infrastructures they operate". In this respect, the name "IT Security Act" is misleading, as the measures required by the Act clearly go beyond pure IT security measures.
Leadership process	The command and control process originates from official staff work and is the usual form of → crisis management process in Germany. It is run through cyclically and consists of four steps: • Situation assessment • Options and action planning • Decision and delegation • Situation assessment/control
Malfunction	See Incident
Malware	Generic term for all types of malicious software, e.g. Trojans, viruses or worms.
MaRisk	Minimum requirements for the risk management of banks; issued by BaFin as the competent supervisory authority.
MaSi	Minimum requirements for the Security of Internet Payments; issued by BaFin as the competent supervisory authority. The MaSi represent the national implementation of the PSD II applicable at European level.
MBCO	Minimum business continuity objective; specification of the quantity and/or quality of a process output that must also be achieved in → emergency operation.

(continued)

Actor	see stakeholders
MPSV	Medical Device Safety Plan Ordinance; issued by the → BfArM; regulates, among other things, the term "incident" and reporting obligations for medical devices.
MTO	Maximum tolerable outage; see MTPD
MTPD	Maximum tolerable period of downtime; specifies the period of time for which a resource (usually a process) may be down before serious damage occurs.
NCI	National Critical infrastructures are organisations and facilities of vital importance to the state, the failure or impairment of which could have lasting effects on the state. Supply shortages, major disruptions to public safety or other dramatic consequences would occur. In Germany, the following sectors (and industries) are classified as critical infrastructures: • Transport and traffic (aviation, maritime shipping, inland shipping, rail transport, road transport, logistics) • Energy (electricity, mineral oil, gas) • Information technology and telecommunications (telecommunications, information technology) • Finance and insurance (banks, insurance companies, financial service providers, stock exchanges) • State and administration (government and administration, parliament, judicial institutions, emergency and rescue services including civil protection) • Nutrition (food industry, food trade) • Water (public water supply, public sewage disposal) • Health (medical care, drugs and vaccines, laboratories) • Media and culture (broadcasting (television and radio), printed and electronic press, cultural heritage, emblematic buildings) Source: Federal Office for Information Security, Federal Office of Civil Protection and Disaster Assistance; online via kritis.bund.de (retrieved 14 July 2019).
Net risk	See risk
Normal operations	Form of operation in which all capacities (→ resources) are available.
PNA	See protection needs assessment
Primary assets	See assets
Process	Next to information, one of the two categories of primary resources. Processes bundle individual (sequential or parallel) activities aimed at the same purpose. Processes are part of the process organization of an organization.
PSD II	Payment Services Directive; new version of the directive on payment services; contains, among other things, requirements for the authentication of users.
Ransomware	Special type of malware with which attackers encrypt a victim's data or block IT systems so that they are inaccessible and cannot be used.

(continued)

Actor	see stakeholders
	The encryption is flanked by blackmail: access is released in exchange for a ransom.
Recovery	Describes the repair or recommissioning of resources that were temporarily down or permanently destroyed. Recovery helps us get out of emergency mode and back into normal mode. For IT systems, corresponding documentation (recovery plans) is part of the classic operational documentation. The term recovery is often confused with → restart.
Restart	Procedure for starting emergency operations. The restart helps us to emergency operations while respecting RTO, MBCO and RPO. For IT resources, restart (also) means providing a defined level of services within the shortest possible time by means of redundant systems, hopefully largely automated (e.g. through virtualization or scripted). Documentation (restart plans) is scripted as far as possible. The term restart is often confused with → recovery.
Restart plan	See restart
Restore	Technical recovery of data; described in the restore concept, which in turn should be coordinated with the data backup concept.
Risk	A risk is composed of two factors: Probability of occurrence and expected consequences. It is primarily influenced by the threats that affect an asset and the vulnerabilities that the asset possesses. If a threat can exploit a vulnerability, this results in a risk. The formula $R = S \times W$ is often used as an approximation, according to which the risk (R) is the product of the amount of damage (S; consequences) and the probability of occurrence (W). We can distinguish between gross risk and net risk. The former describes the risk value before risk treatment, the latter the risk value afterwards.
Risk appetite	Risk appetite is the fundamental attitude of an actor towards risks of all kinds. We refer to a risk-seeking attitude as risk-averse, while a more cautious orientation is called risk-averse.
Risk identification	Risk identification is a component of → cyber risk management and serves to allocate • Of threats/dangers, • Countermeasures, • Weaknesses and • FollowTo the individual → supporting resources.
Risk treatment plan	The risk treatment plan is part of → cyber risk management and is required by both ISO 27005 and ISO 27001. The basic idea of the risk treatment plan is to make the status quo of the treatment of each individual risk, including the responsibilities, transparent. It is an important component of risk communication as part of → awareness measures.
RPO	Recovery Point Objective; specifies the maximum time span between two consecutive data backups.

(continued)

Actor	see stakeholders
RTO	Recovery time objective; time span within which a resource must be available again at least in emergency operation or at emergency operation level. Derives from the → MTPD, which is usually greater than the RTO, but at least equal.
Situation Center	The situation centre is the extended arm of the crisis unit. It collects crisis-relevant information and prepares it for the crisis unit. It also supports the crisis unit in monitoring the implementation status of decisions. Depending on the structure, it also coordinates outgoing information.
Training	A training course is a form of continuing education with a predominantly theoretical component. See also Training and Awareness
Protection needs assessment	Sometimes also referred to as protection needs analysis; procedure for determining the protection needs of a specific type/category of information. The need for protection in turn results in a level of protection for which certain asset-specific measures must be taken.
Protection goals	Sometimes also referred to as the core values of information security. In practice, we encounter two (overlapping) sets of protection goals. Set 1: Confidentiality, Integrity, Availability and Authenticity (VIVA). Set 2: Confidentiality, Integrity, Authenticity (CIA) Compromises are necessary in the implementation of both sets, as a simple example shows. Let's imagine that we have a piece of information that we absolutely want to keep secret and which must also not be falsified under any circumstances. How can we make sure of that? Well, we can write it in cipher on a piece of paper and burn it immediately. The problem with this is that if we now run in front of a fast truck with bad brakes at an inopportune time, the information is irretrievably lost. We have done an excellent job of protecting confidentiality, integrity and authenticity—but we have ignored availability.
Single points of failure	Breaking point that determines the functioning of a process, system, organization; head monopolies (individuals with solitary knowledge) are a prominent example.
SPoF	See Single Points of Failure
Stakeholder	Another term for target groups, stakeholders and actors that have some kind of connection to an organization. Also referred to as "interested parties" in the ISO standards. Stakeholder expectations are the linchpin of crisis management. In a professional environment, the subject of a special → stakeholder and issue management.
Stakeholder and issue management	Management system by means of which an organization manages its appearance vis-à-vis relevant stakeholders and their expectations with regard to certain topics (→ issues). Facet of risk management, in particular risk communication.

(continued)

Actor	see stakeholders
Stress	Adaptation reaction of the human organism to changes in its environment, e.g. a cyber attack. The stronger these stressors, the more severe the adaptation reaction, i.e. the stress generated. Systematic (mental and organizational) confrontation with a wide variety of stressors and the practice of coping mechanisms can reduce the stress level and promote expedient decisions.
Structural analysis	Structural analysis is used to determine the interdependencies of primary and supporting → resources so that protection needs and criticalities can be inherited.
Telephone cascade	Telephone-based alerting procedure reminiscent of an avalanche; person 1 calls persons 2–4, person 2 calls persons 5–8, person 3 calls persons 9–12, etc.
TKG	Telecommunications Act; was amended as part of the IT Security Act, which was conceived as a shell law, and with a view to EU GDPR requirements.
Training	A training course is a practical, i.e. action-oriented form of continuing education. See also Training and Awareness
Training and awareness	Generic term for the structured communication of knowledge about a clearly defined subject area to defined target groups. The guiding principle is always a specific target for each target group. A training and awareness programme derives concrete measures from the target and implements them on the basis of comprehensible priorities.
Supporting assets	See assets
VAG	Insurance Supervision Act
VAIT	Insurance supervisory requirements for IT; issued by BaFin as the competent supervisory authority. The VAIT specify the → VAG in more detail.
Trust	Trust is the basis of all relationships, in both private and business contexts. To succeed in the latter is impossible without the trust of key stakeholders. When customers, financiers, regulators, employees and the public lose their trust in our organization, everything is at stake. Maintaining trust is therefore the central concern of Cyber Crisis Management.
VoIP	Voice over IP
VUCA	VUCA stands for volatile, uncertain, complex and ambiguous. The acronym describes the social, political and economic conditions within which people and organisations have to assert themselves.
vzbv	Federation of German Consumer Organisations

Index

© Springer Fachmedien Wiesbaden GmbH, part of Springer Nature 2021
H. Kaschner, *Cyber Crisis Management*,
https://doi.org/10.1007/978-3-658-35489-3

Printed in the United States
by Baker & Taylor Publisher Services